EDUCATION
THE HOPE
FOR A BETTER WORLD

By the Same Author

1. The Teaching of Mathematics
2. School Organization and Administration
3. Methodology of Research in Education
4. Statistics in Education and Psychology
5. New Approaches to Measurement and Evaluation

EDUCATION
THE HOPE FOR A BETTER WORLD

KULBIR SINGH SIDHU
M.A. (Maths, Psy), M.Ed. (Gold Medallist), Ph.D.
Former Principal
M.G.N. College of Education,
Jalandhar City

STERLING PUBLISHERS PRIVATE LIMITED

STERLING PUBLISHERS PRIVATE LIMITED
A-59, Okhla Industrial Area, Phase-II,
New Delhi-110020.
Tel: 26387070, 26386209; Fax: 91-11-26383788
E-mail: mail@sterlingpublishers.com
www.sterlingpublishers.com

Education the Hope for a Better World
© 2010, Kulbir Singh Sidhu
ISBN 978 81 207 4933 7

All rights are reserved. No part of this publication may be reproduced, stored in a retrieval system or transmitted, in any form or by any means, mechanical, photocopying, recording or otherwise, without prior written permission of the original publisher.

Printed and Published by Sterling Publishers Pvt. Ltd., New Delhi-110020.

Preface

Education is so rich in possibilities that we shall never be able to prepare a final list of its outcomes. We may never be able to draw from it, the fullest possible benefits.

It is in the interest of mankind to acknowledge the worth of education and depend on it with unshakable faith even in the most difficult situations.

Mankind is suffering from numerous problems like poverty, ignorance, unemployment, fanaticism, unrest, corruption, injustice, malnutrition, wastage of resources, strife, drug addiction, exploitation, poor governance, etc. Education can definitely help solve these problems and develop a society where such like problems do not occur again.

Education can bless us with such similar possibilities so that we are able to eliminate the hell-like conditions, if any in life and convert them into heaven-like conditions.

Education is a great gift, the value of which goes on increasing with every passing day. It is our obligation to make the best use of this gift and become worthy of its ever-enhancing values.

Education does not end with acquiring a qualification and then getting a suitable job. This stage should be regarded only as a preliminary step in one's lifelong education.

It is binding on educational institutions to impart quality education, which will provide to the society human material competent to convert all failures into successes. By careful planning and data collection, we must eliminate the misnomer of unemployment of the educated. Not a single qualified individual should remain without a job.

It will be progressive, modern, result-oriented and rewarding, if we make education a leading agency among other agencies like family, society, religion, politics and the government. The modernisation of education should remain in the forefront, whereas modernisation in industry, agriculture, trade, health services, communications, economy and governance should be a second priority.

If we could develop ideal individuals in our educational institutions, we would automatically get ideal homes, an ideal society, ideal workforce, ideal economy, ideal government and happiness. Education can provide competent leaders in every field, who will bring about necessary reforms and revolutions.

There are many lofty aims and heights we create in life, which remain confined to our imagination and dreams. We can certainly change those dreams into realities through the pursuit of relevant education.

Education must be empowered, accepted and employed as the hopeful force in every situation of life. It can certainly change the hopeless situations into hopeful ones.

25th November 2009   **Kulbir Singh Sidhu**

Contents

	Preface	v
I.	**EDUCATION**	**1**
1.	Education	2
2.	Aims of Education	11
3.	Education and Values	16
4.	Education and Problems	29
5.	Successes and Failures of Education	37
6.	Educational Reform	43
II.	**EDUCATION AND INDIVIDUAL**	**47**
7.	Education and Individual	48
8.	Educated People	54
9.	Education and Human Nature	59
10.	Education and Mind	65
11.	Interest in Education	71
12.	Education and Character	75
13.	Education and Development of Personality	78
III.	**EDUCATIONAL INSTITUTION**	**85**
14.	Educational Institution	86
15.	Education and Student	92
16.	Education and Teacher	101
17.	Methods of Education	109
18.	Education and Research	112

IV. EDUCATION AND LIFE — 117
19. Education and Life — 118
20. Lifelong Education — 124
21. Education and Health — 128
22. Education and Quality of Life — 132
23. Education and Simple Living — 139

V. EDUCATION AND SOCIETY — 143
24. Education and Society — 144
25. Education and Family — 149
26. Education and Generation Gap — 157
27. Education and Adjustment — 163
28. Education and Media — 169

VI. EDUCATION AS A LEADING POWER — 177
29. Education and Civilisation — 178
30. Education and Culture — 182
31. Education and Religion — 186
32. Education and Politics — 194
33. Education and Government — 203

VII. EDUCATION AND DISCIPLINE — 209
34. Education and Discipline — 210
35. Education and Leadership — 216
36. Education and Justice — 222
37. Education and Sacrifice — 226

VIII. EDUCATION AS A NOBLE FORCE — 231
38. Education and Drug Addiction — 232
39. Education and Suicide — 238
40. Education and Corruption — 243
41. Education and Crime — 247
42. Education and Terrorism — 254

IX. EDUCATION AND SYSTEM — 259
    43. Education and System — 260
    44. Education and Planning — 265
    45. Educational Planning — 269

X. EDUCATION AND WELFARE — 275
    46. Vocationalisation of Education — 276
    47. Education and Work Culture — 281
    48. Education as Investment — 288
    49. Education and Employment — 291
    50. Education and Economic Development — 296

XI. EDUCATION AND THE WORLD — 301
    51. Education and Environment — 302
    52. Education and Environmental Pollution — 309
    53. Population Education — 316
    54. Education and Globalisation — 323
    55. Education and International Understanding — 328
    56. Education and World Peace — 334

XII. EDUCATION AND EXCELLENCE — 341
    57. Education and Development of Human Resources — 342
    58. Education and Modernisation — 347
    59. Education and Social Change — 352
    60. Quality Education — 361
    61. Education and Vision — 365
    62. Education and Creativity — 369
    63. Education and Happiness — 374

XIII. THE HOPE — 379
    64. The Hope — 380

Index — 387

I
EDUCATION

One

Education

Man cannot live without food, clothing, shelter and education. Just as a human being cannot grow without air, water and food, likewise he cannot grow without education. Its unique place in the life of a man can be taken over by nothing else. Even primitive man did have some concern with education.

Informal education cannot serve the needs of the modern citizen. He must receive sufficient formal education for a specified period in order to become a capable individual.

Education is such a gift, which has no other parallel. This gift is one of the birthrights of every individual.

Education today, is vast and rich in its contents. It can satisfy the needs, interests and aspirations of every individual. Its absence amounts to a greater handicap for the modern citizen. The individuals of tomorrow will find it all the more essential.

Even if the contents and programmes of education are not satisfactory, there is no reason for us to deny ourselves its benefit. The improvements in the system of education should be taken up as a separate issue and should be made a continuing process.

Education is the medium for gaining information, knowledge, wisdom, development, health, and also for building good habits and a good character. It also contributes towards progress, prosperity, job-oriented training, employment, a systematic society, effective governance, the art of appreciation, enrichment of a civilisation and culture and much more.

Society has committed a great blunder in giving education an unimportant or inferior position in its set-up. Its leading role must not only be recognised but should also be ensured through necessary efforts. Every generation should strive to enrich education for the next generation/generations to come.

Education should no longer remain helpless against evils like exploitation, discrimination, lawlessness, crime, corruption, drug addiction, antisocial behaviour and unprincipled politics.

Education should become a force to mould the individual and society along praiseworthy lines. It should develop crusaders in very large numbers, who can take up different causes and give them a desirable conclusion. Education should develop leaders in equally large numbers who can provide much needed leadership and guidance in various fields. It should prepare social service workers also in large numbers, who may be able to do selfless service in different fields.

Education should become a force for the much delayed revolutionary measures in society. In spite of various revolutions that have taken place in human history, the problems of inequality, poverty, autocracy in the name of democracy, denial of opportunities to the downtrodden, divisions based on caste, class and religion, fanaticism, and twisting of history and culture continue to prevail. Education has to continuously revolutionise itself and the society in the desired directions, and bring about necessary changes without delay.

There is another great function of education. It leads to openness and curbs rigid closeness. It opens our minds and hearts towards greater horizons. It opens our eyes to observe the vast surroundings and our ears to catch the sounds of various types. It bestows an open outlook and modifies our closed attitudes. With education, we offer our open mind to knowledge, diverse ideas and disciplines. We are in a position to receive humanity with love and open arms. Education thereby, removes the narrow closeness that leads to painful isolation. Therefore, while openness leads to freshness, closeness amounts to staleness. The ideologies, which open and expand our vision, are the medium of global thinking and dealings. Hence, openness ensures broad-mindedness.

Among all the agencies for human development and excellence, education has to be accepted as the master agency or the agency of agencies. When agencies like home, community, organisations, church, media, civilisation and culture fail to show results, education has to come forward to invigorate other agencies and set things right. Education is responsible for the effectiveness of all the agencies. It has to provide short-term and long-term remedies for the ills of the other agencies.

Education is not going to have any authority over other agencies; it will only have a positive and constructive influence over all of them. We must accept education as the backbone of other agencies and for this reason; we should welcome its power and strength.

Other agencies should seek some guidance from education instead of making any attempt to mould education to their choice. Some agencies like the church, community and government have tried from time to time, to run education on their favoured lines. Education should not allow any encroachment into its contents and programmes by any other agency. Education must free itself from wrong dominance and interferences. If any other agency succeeds in making education one of its tools, it will upset the entire structure of society.

We cherish our educational institutions as basic to a civilised and developing society. We have a mistaken notion that schools exist mainly to train students to be integrated with the community. Another error is the view that learning and teaching ought to have immediate results, show gains and lead to success. The real function of education is rather, to develop one's entire personality and lead the individual towards a richer life so that he can appreciate the riches of the past and live creatively in the present and future. Education can best determine the future of an individual, society or country.

Education is regarded as an awakening to the purposes and pleasures of life. It is a journey from learning-to-be to learning-to-become. It is an ascending process involving materialism and morality. Along with the knowledge of science, technology, and vocation, education has to provide the knowledge of life, society, universal love and eternal joy.

Educational institutions largely stress on factors such as hours, points, grades, courses and on passing the examinations. Often, a person completes his education and then discovers that he cannot meet the demands of his later life. Many students also spend their time in educational institutions without ever exercising their minds on the issues that are really momentous. Fundamentally, they remain uneducated. Therefore, the major goal of the entire educational process should be to understand and gain wisdom, rather than hours, grades or credit points.

The lack of common ideals and convictions is more serious than the lack of a common body of knowledge. In many cases, confusion, moral indifference and cynicism have been products of the exposure of young people to the process of education. Real intellectualism does not get a reasonable place in society.

Education as a dynamic force has to help the learner to grow, to mend, to improve, and acquire everything possible to live a happier and fuller life. At the same time, education cannot be made a close-ended process, which stops as soon as adult life begins. It has to be a lifelong process.

"Man is considered as the roof and crown of all creations." According to Shakespeare, "Man is little lower than an angel." Man uses speech to express himself. He can develop sophisticated physical and social skills. He has dexterity of the mind in the form of intelligence, thinking and reasoning. He has dynamism, power of discrimination and creativity. Education is the process of progressively developing man's innate powers–physical, mental, social, moral and cultural. Man sees the meaning of things, comprehends the relations, compares and contrasts, analyses and synthesises, and thus learns through systematic thought processes. Man is reflective and meditative. His mind exercises three functions – cognition (knowing), affection (feeling) and conation (psycho motor). He eagerly enquires and investigates about his natural and cultural environment and its causes and laws. He continues to imagine and formulate new ideas and problems. He can see the shadows cast by the future. He is anxious to acquire knowledge of the self and his environment. He expresses his thoughts, feelings, emotions, ideas, fears and ambitions. That is why man has history, literature, science, and civilisation. His progressivism and versatility contribute to the totality of the experience of the race.

Man has four aspects – biological, psychological, sociological and philosophical. As per the biological aspect, he is concerned with his body: its structure, variation and growth. The organism is preserved and given proper growth through nutritious food and exercise and developed into a sound body. A sound body is a prerequisite for a sound mind.

As regards the psychological aspect, man has to develop his mind towards acquiring his highest possibilities and capacities. He then gradually develops into a personality. Hence, the psychological aspect of a man unfolds the different processes and horizons of the mind, which in turn results in different kinds of behaviours, learning of so many things, understanding, and making efforts towards innovation and creativity.

The sociological aspect of man provides meaning to life. For growth and adjustment, there is need for a sense of belongingness, to the family, to the neighbourhood, to the community, to the nation and to the world. Self-expression and self-realisation is possible only in the context of the society. Man has to integrate himself into the social processes and institutions. His personality is therefore, the result of self-consciousness, intelligent behaviour, characteristic attitudes, sentiments, sociological habits and reactions. Also, there should be no place in the society for an antisocial individual.

The biological, psychological and sociological aspects of a man are mundane aspects. Man must be enabled to transcend all these and probe into his higher reaches by living a life of ideas, experiences and values. This is the philosophical aspect of man. His perpetual quest is to know himself, to understand the world around him, as it is and as it should be. If generations of happiness and more happiness remain one's goal of life, then it is important to understand what constitutes this happines. The answers from philosophy are; make life beautiful and gracious, successful, rewarding and satisfying. How to make such a life possible? Again the answers from philosophy are: through growth, evolution and progress. This growth and evolution relate to the physical organism, mind, sociability and spirituality. Therefore, acquiring a philosophy of life is the most powerful factor in life. For this, man searches for or finds the means to achieve biological perfection, to satisfy his psychological urges, to adapt to the norms and taboos of society and tries to reach the ethical heights. Such a philosophy is to be developed through education.

The impact of education on society is being mercilessly destroyed, and many educated people are behaving in a manner worse than animals.

Almost every individual and every society needs a drastic re-orientation, and it is only through education that this re-orientation can be made possible, if at all.

People concerned with education should no longer remain like helpless onlookers. They must assert their position, restate their duties and fulfil their responsibilities. Education is not, in anyway, at fault for the failures due to its poor impact. The fault lies with us. We have not been able to make full use of the multi-faceted nature of education. Education has been made to fail, just like many other agencies of human welfare.

It is very strange when we hear about the problems of the educated unemployed. It is largely due to the absence of planning in this sector and education should not be blamed for this.

Education as a power must prove to be more than equal to political, social, economic and religious powers. Most of the prevailing powers, consciously or unconsciously, sabotage the power of education. This is the main reason why political, social, economic and religious problems continue to defy any solution. It is wrong to subordinate education to any other agency of human welfare. Rather, it should be given the foremost position and functions in order that it may redirect political power and other such powers. So far, we have reduced education to a very inferior position and debarred it from playing its rightful role. Education must be made to guide all other forces and powers working for the upliftment of mankind.

Education should be entrusted with the task of creating heaven on earth. Most probably, heaven does not exist anywhere else. It has to be created by man himself. So, the concept of heaven on earth will differ from the concept of heaven in the skies. The heaven on earth will not rest only on prayers; but it will necessitate all human activities in their most ideal form. The provisions in this heaven will not come from any heavenly source, but will be created by man through his hard and honest labour.

Life on earth has been dictated by its positive and negative aspects, and it should not be impossible to expect complete eradication of the negative aspects. We should always remember our ultimate goal of creating heaven on earth. Above all, why should there be any sign of hell on earth, when we are so highly educated and so vastly accomplished. Education cannot make any compromise with hell-like circumstances. Creating heaven on earth should not be considered a dream. It is a deemed possibility. The intelligence of man, his sense of aspirations, the known and yet to be known resources that are at his command, and the availability of the highest possible education should assure us that in the hands of man, earth is bound to become a heaven one day. Every human being is duty-bound and capable to create heaven around him. Education has to transform an average individual into a true man. And a true man is in no way less than an angel. And the abode of angels is bound to be heaven.

Education has to be made the power of powers, the strength of strengths and the force of all forces. At the same time, it is the destroyer of wicked powers, evil strengths and inhuman forces. Other agencies and bodies should automatically look towards it for their success.

Education creates learned men. But the percentage of learned men in our society is very low. Let us raise this percentage and we will in return get a far better physical and social environment to live in.

Education has to channelise the energy of the individual into most constructive and creative channels. He must be moulded into the form of a builder and leader of the new world.

Education helps develop the individual in all fields and aspects making him intelligent, learned, courageous and a man of character. An individual's development also contributes to the growth and development of a society, as he becomes a responsible, dynamic, resourceful and enterprising member of the society.

Plato has gifted three things to the world, namely the, (1) theory of a new form of government called republic (2) a new social order and (3) a well-planned system of education. Among these three, he counted education as the first and fairest thing that the best of men can ever have. According to him, the function of education is to prepare the individual for and accelerate his efforts for a good life. He expressed that real knowledge is innate. This knowledge is recalled by stimulating the individual and kindling in him the spirit of enquiry and love for discovery.

Diogenes said, "Education is a controlling grace to the young, consolation to the old, wealth to the poor and ornament to the rich."

According to Howard Gardner, "Education must ultimately justify itself in terms of enhancing human understanding."

Kant said, "Education is the development in the individual of all the perfection of which he is capable."

There is an explosion of knowledge today, due to unprecedented advancements in all areas. Old ideas are gradually giving way to new ones. Beliefs and values are in the process of transformation. This explosion of knowledge should be most welcome in the field of education. In order to update knowledge, the syllabi must be revised as frequently as possible. The textbooks should be updated without delay and teachers should be required to attend refresher courses to enable them to be conversant with the new developments.

The possibilities of education are limitless. We might have acquired only a small fraction of them so far.

*****

Two

Aims of Education

Education is guided by the plurality of aims because of the different types of education, the many faces of human nature, different levels of education, the complex environment, different schools of philosophy and various ideologies.

Education is not a limited venture. It cannot be bound within only a few aims. It can fulfil its responsibility only if it is governed by the ever expanding aims. Its limitless achievements are possible only if it is guided by the broadest possible aims.

After a good deal of thinking, we have evolved a list of aims of education. For example, education should ensure the harmonious, all-round and optimum development of an individual, and should prepare him for life. It should socialise the individual and be able to lead him to a productive, progressive and qualitative life.

In the times to come, there should be greater stress on new realism, humanism and eclecticism. All the aims must agree on recognising the uniqueness and dignity of the individual. They should lead the individual to perfection. For this, an individual must learn through self-activity, social participation and creativeness; his innermost thoughts, desires and ambitions being the chief concerns of education.

The aim of all aims of education should be the development of one's personality, which becomes a high achiever in all spheres of life. These achievements should guide and lead in different activities.

A better life and a still better life should be one of its central aims. And this new life should be characteristic of the physical, mental, academic, social, emotional, productive, economic, political and spiritual growth. Education will remain incomplete if it ignores any of these developments.

Education should prepare our minds to face all challenges whether in the present or in the future. It should strive towards developing the student's observation and exploration and also to promote concern, sensitivity and ability that is necessary for the preservation and development of physical and natural resources. It should infuse in him various environmental concepts. We have many good ideas to implement in education, such as a child-centred education, woman-centred family, human-centred development, wisdom-centred society and a unity-centred world.

Education has to strive for the health, wealth and wisdom of the learner. It has to cleanse human actions, thought, character and personality of all the undesirable elements collected over the years.

The aims of education should no more remain theoretical and philosophical statements. They should be expressed as realities in right earnest. Education should not remain an underachiever with respect to its aims. We should confirm their attainment. Let us proceed with a pledge to achieve the aims, which we have stated after careful thought.

The aims of education do not allow the learner to pick up any weaknesses. Even one weakness may spoil the merit of a number of achievements. For example, a person may be very competent in his job, very efficient, know the rules and regulations, and does not make any mistakes, but suffers from the habit of accepting bribe, then all his merits are reduced to nothing. He is employing his education, but is spoiling its spirit in the process.

The aims of education should be modern, vision-oriented, futuristic, clear cut and realistic. There should be no gap between what we aim for and what we actualise.

Aims of Education

There is need for a balance between immediate and ultimate aims of education.

Education has to set things right in the conditions of an individual, the society, institutions, work places, offices and government. Whenever we find any thing going wrong any of these entities, we will have to review the aims of education. Things cannot be allowed to linger on, making the situation grow from bad to worse. Instead, remedial aims must be worked out promptly.

Education has to concentrate on the phenomena of human nature. There is a need to mould human nature through education. Human nature should not remain oblivious of the impact of education. For example, we should not come across any liars, dishonest people, cheats, shirkers, irresponsible and corrupt people among the educated populace. Education has to purify human nature from these and many other vices.

It is desirable to have high-sounding and lofty aims for education. But they should not be allowed to remain only on paper. The government, society and educators should be made accountable for the attainment of these aims.

The aims should establish a balance between the higher values and materialistic considerations. People should not go crazy for materialistic things. Contentment can be gained only by cultivating higher values. We should be able to conclude the debate between higher values and materialistic values.

Some of the aims of education can be stated as under:

It will develop the individual who can play a significant role in all activities of life and who is reasonably successful in various aspects of life. It develops the individual who is down to earth and at the same time imbibes in him the higher values of life. It develops an individual who makes some memorable contribution to life and society and is a balanced and extraordinary personality. Education will develop the individual as a symbol of work culture. It will remove the prevailing shortcomings of human nature. Through individuals, education seeks to establish an ideal environment, society and government. Education will provide guidelines to all other agencies engaged in the development of an individual. Through knowledge, education will enable the individual to usher into the realm of wisdom. Every educated individual will prove to be a real asset to himself, to family, to society, to the country and to mankind. Education should develop an individual's capacity for clear thinking, scientific attitude, receptivity to new ideas, respect for the dignity and worth of every individual, the ability to live in harmony with fellow men through the cultivation of discipline, cooperation, social sensitiveness and tolerance and a sense of true humanism. Education has also to promote health and vocational efficiency of the individual. It will guide him to increase productivity, accelerate the process of modernisation and cultivate social, moral and spiritual values. In the long run it will lead to the realisation of the self.

In a democratic set-up, some of the prominent aims of education are: optimum development of the individual according to his interests, aptitudes and capabilities, developing his physical and mental capacities, inculcating good habits, lifestyle and character, all-round development of personality, developing social attitudes and democratic values, providing liberal and vocational education and creating a sense of determination for progress, prosperity and modernisation.

The process of attaining the aims of education should remain under strict scrutiny and evaluation. We should stop making compromises with the aims we propose for ourselves. We should have faith in our ability to achieve them. The aims which prove hard to attain should not be diluted for the sake of our convenience. They should be reviewed and discussed from time to time by the best brains among teachers and educationists. They may be restated from time to time in the light of varying demands under changed circumstances.

There are many aims of education that are advocated by different schools of thought like that of knowledge, cultural development, character development, vocational aim, harmonious development, the citizenship aim, aim for complete living, and the self-realisation aim. It is possible to synthesise them and make that synthesis work.

*****

Three

Education and Values

Values are a part of real education and non-values have no place in education. An individual must be gifted with values right from birth and through learning.

Some scholars claim that value is indefinable and that truth, goodness and beauty are direct and immediate experiences. For example, whether something is good or bad in itself is known to us by intuition. Dewitt H Parker says, "Values belong wholly to the inner world, to the world of the mind." For Plato, the world of concepts, universals and values is the real and permanent world. C I Lewis contends that our judgements of value, good and evil, right and wrong, better and worse are a kind of genuine empirical knowledge that is comparable to empirical knowledge in other fields. The supporters of the view that values are objective will point out that beauty and goodness are valued by all.

Numerous classifications of values have been proposed but the most commonly accepted one is the division between intrinsic and extrinsic values. Intrinsic value is the end; this value exists in its own right. Extrinsic value is the means and not the end since it helps in achieving some aim. Examples of intrinsic value are truth, beauty, goodness, etc., which in turn satisfy man's cognitive, affective and conative aspects. Moral values are other examples of intrinsic value.

Money and wealth are accepted as extrinsic values. The ultimate good exists in a chain of values, which affords an appropriate place to each value. Self-realisation is regarded as the highest value that incorporates all types of values. It is wrong to treat values as unreal and fictitious. This attitude goes against the moral, intellectual and educational progress of mankind.

Walter G Everett classifies human values into eight groups: economic values, intellectual values, character values, bodily values, values of association, recreation values, aesthetic values and religious values.

Value means whatever is actually liked, prized, esteemed, desired, approved or enjoyed by anyone at any time. Values should not be crystallised and frozen to the point of rigidity, stopping further growth and renewal. Values are masterminds, which give direction to our strivings. Values represent feelings, desires, interests, attitudes, preferences and opinions about what is right, just, fair or desirable. Creation and preservation of values is an important purpose of man. The greater the consideration and importance of values, the better will be the quality of an individual and his social life. Value has to be regarded as more satisfying than material gains. The age of science has provided us with the values of rationality, utilitarianism, scientific attitude, universalism, individualism, progress and betterment of the world through human effort. Education has to develop individuals who are embodiments of values.

Each individual has some sense of a value system such as love and hate, beauty and ugliness, honesty and dishonesty, kindness and tyranny, etc. These are matters which are of more concern to people than facts and falsehood. Parker lists the following as major values: health, comfort, ambition, place of consideration and power, workmanship, making and using of things, love, knowledge, play, art and religion.

Values that are productive and relatively permanent are to be preferred. The productive and permanent values also tend to be intrinsic values. We ought to select our values on the basis of self-chosen ends or ideals. In our selection, there should be some advancement in the overall values of life. A basic question we face is, whether in our value systems we are encouraging and strengthening the selfish and animal impulses or reinforcing and cultivating the more altruistic and creative aspects of our nature. If there were a single ultimate value for mankind it could be called self-actualisation, self-realisation, integration, psychological health, individuation, autonomy, creativity and productivity. In a nutshell, realising fully the potentialities of the human being.

Life becomes meaningful only through value-orientation. Bertrand Russell has said, "The choice before present humanity is either total annihilation or coexistence through ethical and spiritual values." Values are operational, relevant, dynamic and eulogising. Social values enjoy special importance. Some of these values are: social conformity or observing social norms, discipline, preferably self-discipline; social sensitiveness, altruism, social justice, feelings of brotherhood and togetherness. There is no question as to pick and choose a value. All the values are binding on each one of us.

Values are the guiding principles of life, which are conducive for one's physical and mental health, as well as for social welfare and adjustment. They are the roads to great heights. Values have been created and stated by us for ourselves and are accepted as a necessary condition for a good life. They are meant to glorify life and not for glorifying only our books, history, social sciences, literature or scriptures. Values are the fruits of noble and sincere thinking spread over a long period of time and experiences, and they should not be allowed to go waste. They are a crucial concern for every individual, family, community, institution, and every country or rather, for the entire mankind.

It is not easy to give a conclusive list of values. However, some values worthy of mention are – truth, beauty, goodness, sincerity, humility, respect, simplicity, acceptance of one's fault, universal love, broad-mindedness, service to others and respect for all religions. Moral values can be described as honesty, good character and conduct, and moral stability. Cultural values comprise of tolerance, peaceful coexistence, courtesy and dignity of manual work.

However, the erosion of values can be seen everywhere and at all levels. In spite of marvellous scientific and technological progress and prosperity, man is unhappy and frustrated, not at peace with himself, and not in harmony with others. There is a crisis of character in our age owing to the deterioration of values. The question of erosion of values demands contemplation and pondering. Only a revolutionary type of change would be able to set things right.

There are quite a number of factors which are responsible for the erosion of values, such as marital frustration, corrupt practices, social fragmentation, lack of justice, lack of system and discipline, materialism and selfishness, social exploitation, poverty, lack of effective education, etc.

The politicians have set the worst example by trampling over established values. Politics of one form or the other has entered in the sacred profession of teaching also, which may harm the value system.

The situation at home is devoid of values like love, brotherhood, the feeling of togetherness, interdependence, sacrifice and sincerity.

Social groups are suffering from jealousy, hatred, ill-feeling, non-cooperation, self-centredness and individualised style of living. Society is full of ill-values like crookedness, egotism, deception, hypocrisy, etc. Religious institutions have deteriorated in terms of moral standards and social values. Wrong values have also crept into the fabric of education and there is a need to enlist them and replace them with positive values.

In some cases, quality education is measured in terms of its cost. As a result, quality education becomes the monopoly of the wealthy and is beyond the reach of the common population. This is an exploitation of the desire of the people who want quality education but cannot afford it.

Sometimes, quality education is judged in terms of examination results alone. It introduces a mad race among educational institutions at the cost of genuine education. Education remains confined to textbooks and information. It narrows down study habits and learning. Learning remains divorced from actual life and its problems.

There is a tendency of educational institutions to also impress the society through means which are not of primary importance. For example, in some cases, achievements in games or inter-institute competitions are allowed to overshadow everything else.

In addition, imparting the same kind of education for all up to the school stage is another limitation. We have not been able to individualise education.

Teachers and some others with vested interests remain inimical to necessary changes in the structure and process of education. Thus, the pace of progress becomes slow and delayed and education cannot be updated earnestly.

Sometimes, there is too much emphasis on false publicity. Especially in the case of job-oriented courses, professional courses and new type of courses, there is an attempt to trap the maximum number of students. Disproportionate expansion of job-oriented and professional courses is a wrong and wasteful emphasis.

Most of the learners consider education as the medium of enhancement of opportunities for the self and glorification of the self. They have forgotten that the cause of humanity should be taken as more important than limited personal interests. Learners should be able to pass on the benefits of their education to the society instead of retaining everything for themselves. Their overriding aim in life should be to serve others.

There are also no checks on group formation among the students on the basis of religious affinity, sectarian and status considerations. This further leads to the division of society on misguided lines.

Some educational institutions are sponsored by religious groups. These groups try to pass on the dogmas of their own religion to all the students. As such, they indulge in religious education of a restricted type. The students belonging to other religious groups are forced to accept the religious teachings of the group that controls the institution. This is a sort of religious enforcement. Some institutions are also set-up by certain sects and castes. They also preach narrow religious loyalties instead of giving broad religious education.

Some philanthropists set-up educational institutions for their personal glorification and for immortalising their names. They consider the institution their private property and the students as well as the teachers their humble subjects. They interfere with the day to day functioning of the institution to an undesirable extent. They want to take credit for all the achievements of the institution and want to gain publicity through it.

The management of some of the institutions consists of persons who have the least concern with education. Their motives behind acquiring these positions are more social and political in nature rather than educational.

Some institutions are more after show-business and extravaganza. They try to gain recognition by arranging colourful celebrations and glorifying functions, which have the least educational value for the participating students.

Some business houses have opened educational institutions with ulterior motives. The step enables them to save on income tax, to use their black money to earn goodwill of the society, to create employment opportunities for the people of their choice, to earn gratitude of the government lobby, to get favours from the powers that be, and to earn honours, awards and political positions from the government. In the long-run, these educational institutions become additional sources of income for the sponsors. The educational objectives become secondary and business considerations remain primary.

For an individual the programme of education ends with the final examination, degree or diploma. These should not be taken as destinations. There is no limit when we dedicate ourselves to enhance our mastery.

Moral standards in many educational institutions are hardly up to the mark. These institutions have many unscrupulous elements in them. Immoral and amoral activities go on unchecked there.

The central purpose of education is to develop a man into an ideal human being. This value should not get ignored. Many other schools of thought have tried to overshadow idealism, which should be of pivotal importance to any educational philosophy. If idealism has not served our purpose well, let us try to evolve super idealism.

Our educational endeavours remain pre-occupied with the stages of information and knowledge. There should be greater effort towards acquiring wisdom.

The many ills that our society is suffering from today are mainly due to the crisis of values. Modern man has become so materialistic, bewildered, frustrated and confused that he has forgotten the place of values in his life. The all-round erosion of values is below the dignity of man. We must not forget that values are the priceless assets of a human being.

Education has to play a major and leading role in the revival of human values. It has to develop individuals into personalities, that are value-oriented and value attached and that are gifted with a strong conviction to stick to their values in spite of unfavourable conditions. We should start developing values when the intellectual life of the child begins to take shape, that is, at the age of adolescence. Values are inculcated from the environment also, which must be exceptionally good. Values should be identified and defined. Human excellence in values needs to be stressed and appreciated. Learners should develop the ability to choose the right values. Some of the methods of inculcating values can be: setting an example, discussion, dramatisation, value classification, and exposure to incidents full of values. Education has been miraculous. It can be miraculous enough to be able to revive values too. The research workers in education should also concentrate on the area of crisis and revival of values. Thoughts, ideologies, discoveries, codes of conduct, sets of values, psychological basis of behaviour and many other tools can be employed with advantage. Value education develops a person into a man of words, a man of fulfilment, a man of vision, a man of honour and a role model for others. The worth of a value remains dynamic and ever enlarging.

With the help of families, the community, media, religion and state, the programmes of education have to re-establish higher values in the mind and heart of the learner. These values are essential for everybody and not for pious people alone.

When we want education to be value-based, it implies that the same values will become the basis of the behaviour of the learners. The human material of educational institutions will believe in those values and reflect them in their behaviour. An educational institution can never allow wrong and negative values to exist on the campus. Rather, it has to pass on its values to the parents, society and all other agencies looking after various services in the society. It cannot allow the crisis of values to affect its value based functioning. It has to protect the values, reinforce them and pass them on to the new generation. If necessary, education has to purify the values and ensure that they are imbibed deep into the minds and hearts of learners.

Sometimes, it is said that it is better to rule in hell than to serve in heaven. There should be no justification about giving any respect to hell.

There was a need for methods to understand and interpret moral conduct. These methods may be named as the evolutionary method, the historical method or the genetic method. These methods could provide insight into what was to be preserved and strengthened and what was to be modified and changed. Today, there is a need to rescue ethical teaching from formal verbalised moralising. It is a wrong assumption that character can be built only by the inculcation of moral rules.

The emphasis on moral training should come through positive participation rather than through teachings alone. The chief and most important moral habit to be cultivated in the child should be that of an interest in community welfare, an intellectual, practical, emotional interest in perceiving the behaviours that make for social order and progress within the activities of the school first and then, within the activities of the much larger society.

One of the external motivations for moral values is to win the affection of the teacher. Another external motivation is fear, not necessarily fear of punishment, but the fear of losing that affection and approval.

People should strive to deal better with evils and should be able to prevent themselves from sliding along the wrong path. The average individual faces great difficulty in battling with inferior temptations. Evil should not be regarded as transcendental which can never be annihilated. Every individual must live like a crusader against evil and be wise enough to live an evil-free life.

To treat values as unreal and fictitious is a sign of defeatism and pessimism, and to give the lie to all human achievements and progress. This attitude discourages us in our duty and possibility to achieve the highest values. The contemporary philosophy treats these values as a part of reality.

If everything is God's creation, then some people may attribute God to be the creator of evils along with virtues. If God is truth, then He is not a creator of evils but is a destroyer of evils. We can quote innumerable instances from human history when God came in some form or the other to destroy evil. It is a different matter that evil continues to survive and grow in spite of God's might. If we believe in God, we must understand our obligation towards the destruction of evil. Even if we are non-believers of God, we have still greater a responsibility towards the destruction of evil, as we consider ourselves capable enough to shape and determine our destiny. And even with minimum common sense, an individual must understand his natural duty of never making a compromise with evil.

There is a widespread agreement about various groups of values: religious, moral, aesthetic, intellectual, scientific, economic and the like. Of course, there is no agreement about their rank and the principles to be used in selecting them. Some of the major values are enlisted as: self-preservation, comfort, and ambition like securing a place of consideration and power in the social order, workmanship in the matter of efficiency in making and using things, love in its various forms, parental love, friendship, generic love, community love, ideal love, knowledge, recreation, art, religion, etc.

Many thinkers have stressed three values as superior to all others – goodness, beauty and truth. These three values are considered self-sufficient. Some would add happiness as the fourth value.

The long period of human experience shows that the social, intellectual, aesthetic and religious values tend to give more permanent satisfaction than the material values do.

Self-discipline based on a well thought out scale of values is the mark of a mature man. We must always act in a way that there is some gain or advance in the total values of life.

Some values are relative in the sense that they are determined by questions of age, sex, intelligence, culture, technology and other conditions. Still, there are a large number of things that all men in their right minds would want to value.

The great task before man today is to discover anew, the genuine values of life and to impart them to the new generation. Man must learn to unify and harmonise the world of facts with the world of values. Facts and means may serve as tools towards the awareness and realisation of values and the ends of human existence.

Nel Noddings has said, "Interest in preserving the lives of our children and fostering their individual growth provides a compelling interest in moral life and moral education."

The quality of moral life is a sign of the quality of social life. The trinity of factors involved in a moral act – feeling, thinking and muscular response is part of a coordinated function. The good man, in short, is his whole self in each of his acts. We have to call attention to the moral trinity of the school which demands social intelligence, social power and social interests.

Mere academic review of the ethical theories of various philosophers is not enough. The students should get an opportunity to discuss about the varied theories and the analysis of actual motives and behaviour. Various theories of ethics agree that conduct is immoral, while its motive maybe pure.

It is difficult to improve character and behaviour by the inculcation of rules. Our goal should be to help students to develop insights into how ethical choices resulted in certain positive consequences in actual human relations.

We cannot overlook the fact that evil exists at the material, biological and intellectual levels. In the clash between good and evil, man continues to progress and retreat because this route is full of conflict. This conflict ends only when the individual transcends the intellectual and arrives at the spiritual. Even if we cannot agree to believe in spirituality, we cannot ignore that it has a significant role in saving us from the evil.

Value becomes the aim of one's life; one attempts to live for it and is prepared to make the greatest sacrifices for it as well.

Values change with the level of development. The difference in human reactions occurs because we regard different things as valuable according to our interest, opportunities, moral levels and levels of development. It is therefore, possible to transform the values of an individual by taking him to a sufficiently higher level of development through education.

Violence, frustration, immorality, crime, self-centredness and egoism are rampant in the social set-up. There are small and big scams in the political and bureaucratic circles. In the present developing situation of our society, it is important for us to give value to our system of education. Value has its worth. Only a person with values is able to see and recognise what is right and good. Values aim at perfection, self-realisation, satisfaction, integrity, cohesion, etc.

Kant believed in universal moral values, Spencer believed that an action is right which is conducive to self-preservation and Dewey believed in pragmatic values, i.e., all that works well is valuable. The conflicting viewpoints of great thinkers should not lead to any confusion for us. In the field of education, we have to reach an agreement or consensus on values.

Objective values are universal values, which have nothing to do with the liking or disliking of an individual. They are intrinsic, inherent or self-contained. They are generally ideals, which need to be achieved, but are not achievable, as it is generally believed that truth has no boundaries.

Then there are subjective, relative, extrinsic or instrumental values, which are judged because they are good for some reason. Such values change with time, man, society and the country. They are subjective in character and relative to people and situations.

Absolute values are true for all times, at all places and in all societies. They are also called sovereign values.

Educational values are accepted by students, to develop their character and personality. At times, such values are common to economic, social or cultural values. Idealists place spiritual values above material values. They are considered as the source of achieving union with God, which is the ultimate value in life. Materialists emphasise upon those values, which deal with worldly affairs and the environment. The existentialists believe in the development of human personality as the top of all values.

Educational values can be enlisted as materialistic, social, moral, intellectual, aesthetic, religious and cultural values. These values will ensure physical, vocational, intellectual, moral, social, cultural and harmonious development of the learner. He will be able to inculcate in himself democratic qualities, a cooperative spirit, a humanitarian outlook, the complete sublimation of his instincts, broader perspectives and an abiding faith in values.

*****

Four

Education and Problems

There are no instant solutions and readymade answers to our problems. Patience and perseverance will be our golden rules to face and tackle them. Education is a means of uprooting age-old problems and to anticipate and prevent new ones.

To begin with, education should sort out and eliminate its own problems. Only then will it become a more dependable tool for handling problems existing all around. It cannot escape its responsibility towards them by attributing the problems to some other factors. Education, with the help of all concerned has to establish a problem-free society. May be most of the problems come under the purview of the government and society for their solution. Education has to create a climate and a workforce for their removal. The government and other agencies should no more be allowed to sleep over these problems.

The complicated and old problems should be handled through well-planned, far-reaching and consistent programmes of education.

An individual should not become a source of problems for others. People should understand that they have not to create problems for one another. Some people enjoy creating problems for others. Instead, everybody should be educated enough to provide a helping hand in solving the problems of others.

Many unforeseen problems seem to appear suddenly before us. They maybe in the form of floods, drought, earthquakes, epidemics, riots, terrorism, external aggression, rising prices, communal tension or economic crisis. Education has to prepare individuals to rise to the occasion and not to show helplessness. The educational institutions have to gear up their students to play a leading role in these critical times. Such crises have to be faced with a spirit of social service. Even in normal circumstances, teachers and students should participate in the social reconstruction of the society.

Educated people must be able to fulfil their duties towards problems with credit, irrespective of whether they work as students, teachers, parents, clerks, officers, workers or employers. They should realise that individual failures in such crises causes backwardness for all.

We have seen a number of movements and revolutions in human history from time to time, but none has been able to provide any permanent solution to the problems faced by man. Human society is dynamic in nature; therefore, we cannot imagine any permanent solution to its problems. Only education can be given the responsibility of any lasting solution through step by step changes and reforms. The interim solutions, if any, should not be allowed to fade away.

New problems will continue to arise, and education will anticipate them and propose more scientific solutions well in time. In this race of endless problems and their solutions, education will devise new ways and means to play its never-failing role of wiping away all problems.

Every individual has his own long list of problems. Similarly, we can seldom find a family which is free from problems. Every social group and every institution has a host of problems on its agenda. The regions, countries and sub-continents have also quite a large number of them. The world as a whole suffers from very serious problems.

Every individual, every group and every institution is trying to solve the problems within their domains. The list of problems in every case goes on expanding. The progress of mankind is no guarantee to the solving of its problems.

Perhaps, we have to agree under compulsion that problems are an integral part of life. In spite of the efforts made by a number of agencies, problems continue to grow. It is again the agency of education which should come out with a consistent programme of reducing the intensity and number of problems.

Every individual, every social group and every nation has the tendency to create problems for its counterparts. Our education and upbringing can certainly convince us to desist from creating problems for others. Most of the problems faced by human beings are man-made. Creating problems for others and inviting others to create problems for us in return is a very bad and wasteful game. If everybody is made to take a pledge that he will not create problems for others, there will certainly be some relief from problems.

Rather, everybody should develop a habit of providing help to every friend, neighbour, relative or even stranger in solving his or her problems. If all of us decide to help others in their problems, we can certainly reduce the number of human problems to a great extent. Instead of taking delight in creating problems for others, we should take delight in helping others in solving their problems. The joint efforts will create a congenial atmosphere and effective strategies for solving problems. General cooperation in solving problems will generate a sympathy wave, which will reduce the sting of problems.

Every group should collectively help a member in trouble. It should be the spirit within every family, every institution, every social group and every national group.

We should avail the services of the power of education to ensure that problem creating individuals and groups are pacified. The entire governing machinery, social groups, and human welfare agencies should join their hands to see that problems no longer spoil the normal life of a common man.

There should be a regular system to enlist the problems of a common man, an average family, the village as a unit, big and small city. Then there is the possibility of peculiar problems of different categories of groups, professional groups, vocational groups, commercial groups and social groups. No problem should be left unattended. If any problem proves to be hard and persistent, it should be dealt with and eradicated through reinforced strategy and resolve.

The existence of problems which defy solution is an insult to the genius and possibilities of human elements. The problems continue to be there because we have not made determined and sustained efforts to remove them.

There are numerous problems before us which should not go unattended and allowed to become more complicated. Some notable ones are – student unrest, teachers' dissatisfaction with their service conditions, poor infrastructure in educational institutions, lack of supervision for these institutions, students' lack of interest and commitment towards education, absence of job opportunity after education, poor examination results, parents' apathy towards the education of their children, financial handicaps of some of the students, poor influence of social environment on the development of children, lack of system in the society and government, attitude of shirking work and responsibility, corruption of various types, unnecessary tension in the family, social environment and establishments; lack of recognition for merit, absence of arrangement for measuring student's capabilities and weaknesses, thefts, crimes, murders, absence of love and concern within families, anxieties, worries, depression, lawlessness, injustice, mad race for money and material goods, drug addiction, suicides, capitalism, hoarding, adulteration, black marketing, black money, absence of work culture in public offices, unjustified litigation, poor nutrition, poor health facilities, exploitation, bad character, abnormalities, spread of vices, abuse of authority and power, etc. The list of problems seems to be endless. This long list is not meant to frighten anybody or to advocate helplessness and pessimism.

Various agencies like the government, social organisations, religious institutions, reformers, and welfare bodies are trying to do their bit to ameliorate the sufferings of the common man as caused by these and many other problems. But the intensity of these problems is not getting any better. If you happen to invoke any individual to narrate his problems, you are likely to get a disheartening story in each case.

How to remove or reduce the problems being faced by each individual is a formidable question. Education can certainly make a remarkable contribution in this matter. While we prepare a young man to live life, we have to ensure that he is a staunch optimist with a strong confidence to meet and overcome every problematic situation. In no case, he has to admit defeat. He will continue to engage in the struggle against problems and will be an example for others. He will never think of creating problems for others or enjoy while others are getting thrashed by their problems. Having faith in his learning and experience, he will move in his life with the hope that he will be ultimately victorious over his problems. He will try to help others up to his optimum capacity in order to remove their problems. He will join hands with groups that work for people who are suffering from various problems.

Professionals like teachers, doctors, lawyers, counsellors, psychiatrists, social workers, political workers, religious leaders and public representatives can play a significant role in this crusade against problems.

The individual has become dangerously individualistic. He has made life problematic for himself. Society has made itself problematic. Government has made governance problematic.

Individuals should be educated to come together to face and solve these innumerable problems. There will be no end to our problems, if we consciously or unconsciously continue to behave as sources of new problems. Members may organise themselves into various groups, each group being allotted one of the problems. Through the medium of education we have to develop every individual to act as a competent and sincere volunteer to attack these problems and never to accept these problems as beyond him. If some people think that problems were always there and will always remain a part of life, they are sadly mistaken.

We must understand that most of our problems are man-made. The responsibility of solving them lies with us. We should never expect that some miracle, magic wand, external force or congenial occurences will one day come to our help and solve the problems for us. We should have no doubt that our problems have to be solved by us ourselves.

There is no justification for helplessness towards our problems. We have been gifted with enough intellect, enough of energy and confidence to overcome our problems. It is a wrong attitude to ignore our problems and wrong to suppose that one alone has no responsibility to solve them. There is no sense in shifting the responsibility of our collective problems to others. Even if others do not come forward to join us, we should not hesitate to proceed single-handedly in the campaign against these problems.

In an era of multi-faceted development and affluence, hunger is still the most common problem that has afflicted a majority of the human race. There are some factors which are responsible for the lack of satisfaction of this first among the basic needs of a human being: increasing population, unemployment, lack of awareness about nutrition, drawbacks of education, wrong priorities in life, poor planning in agriculture, forestry and industry, wastage of food and other resources and above all, poor governance. Most of these factors demand the relevant impact of education.

In societies where the distribution of wealth is imbalanced, dissident groups attempt to capitalise on social, economic and political unrest. The result is the adoption of desperate means leading to civil strife, social disintegration, political instability, anarchy, civil war, militancy and terrorism. Through education we have to develop peace-loving individuals. Surrounded even by the most severe provocations, the individual will not lose his calm or cross his limits.

We live in an age when problems are becoming increasingly worldwide, such as the problems of world peace, world population, world environmental crisis, world drug problem, food problem, problem of terrorism, threat of inflation, etc.

These problems can be solved only through global cooperation. For example, the ecosystem of the earth will remain capable to support human life only if all the countries cooperate to control the discharge of waste materials. Education has to help mankind to evolve a new social ethic which emphasises economic, industrial and demographic stability and the recycling of material. Such an ethic replaces international competition with global cooperation and brings harmony between Nature and man.

Arresting the deterioration of the environment does not seem possible within the existing framework of independent nationstates. It can be better secured within the framework of an educated and unified global society. Among the most striking forms of interdependence evolving as the world economy modernises is energy interdependence. Modern man is an enormous consumer of energy, depending on it for mobility, for manufacturing goods of all kinds, for producing food, for light, for heat, for cooling and even for thinking and education. Education has to promote the idea of simple living and economical use of all types of energy.

There are a large number of obvious problems in the field of education. We are required to correlate education with life, its needs and problems. We have to make our educational research, educational courses, training activities and cultural activities futuristic in every way.

Education has to be made more efficient than all other agencies around so that it can convey a message and an example of efficiency. In this age of modernism, it is very sad on the part of the people to fall behind the requirements of time.

In the age of scientific and technological advancement, education has to prepare the individual for occasional re-adjustments. Along with liberal education, he should be given vocational education for ensuring economic development and independence. The individual must be given a wide range of opportunities both of formal and informal education, so that he comes out victorious against all problems.

*****

Five

Successes and Failures of Education

Education takes the credit for many things but there are many failures associated with it too. If we start enlisting its successes, we can say that education is the main agency which has brought about so much progress and enlightenment for us.

Education has produced scholars, philosophers, writers, scientists, technicians, sociologists and research workers who have enriched human life in their own way. Some discoveries have revolutionised human existence. Some ideas have given a new boost to human thinking. Certain theories have given new dimensions to the social system, economic system, political system, quality of life and values.

Education has brought about a process of all-round awareness and awakening. It has defined and explained mysteries of the past. It has brought about the expansion of knowledge, so much so that we cannot keep count of the number of disciplines and their offshoots today. It has opened the human mind to vast and useful information, knowledge and experience. The vast literary contributions are also a result of education. Education can also help aspiring people to attain great heights through self-study and self-education. In fact, education has enabled us to understand Nature, explore it and use it to our advantage and achievements. It has supplied to society a host of qualified and trained personnel who can take care of varied responsibilities.

Basically, education has removed ignorance and illiteracy. It has opened the eyes of common man to his tremendous capabilities and possibilities. It has provided scientific methods to measure the capabilities of the individual.

It has introduced manners and etiquettes in the behaviour of a common man. An educated person for instance is not expected to engage in indecent behaviour.

Education has enabled us to measure many measurable things and brought exactitude in our quantification. An individual's personal and social life in the present and the future can also be planned in a better way through education.

Education has enhanced the power of expression of the individual in an unlimited number of forms. It is likely that it will develop many new forms with the passage of time.

Through education, languages have become rich and meaningful. And with the help of languages our cultures and traditions are preserved and enriched.

Education has contributed towards mental and emotional development of individuals. An educated person is now equipped to adapt himself to different situations in life.

Other agencies like home, society, media, etc., give us many benefits directly or indirectly, which are a result of education. In other words, education prompts other agencies to transfer educational benefits to young minds.

Education is a success when it provides a medium to the learners to demonstrate their excellence. It promotes creativity and enables learners to find better alternatives for self-expression and self-realisation.

Success being a gift of education, it is right to assume that results to any examination should be excellent. Even in special cases, that of physically challenged people or slow learners the results should not be disappointing. Every personality developed through education should be attractive and impressive in every way. Everybody's adult life should be satisfying. Educational institutions should churn out capable individuals in sufficient numbers so that they can perform leadership roles in various fields. Ideally, no educated individual should be a problem to others, a misfit in his environment, incapable, a nuisance, ill-mannered, having poor habits or any type of shortcomings.

Education seeks high standards of living, quality of life, a tension free society, and a disciplined population, qualitative performance of every type, improvement of the environment, a people friendly government and the enrichment of traditions. These standards will not remain fixed; they will be continuously made to rise. There will be no limit to these standards. There should be no cause for the criticism of the results of education. Education should be made result-oriented and successful in every way.

There is no doubt that the list of successes of education can be stressed upon. However, now we will look at its failures.

So far, education has failed to clarify and finalise its own aims. Its institutions have not been able to incorporate in them many essential values.

It has not been able to free man from his numerous vices. It has provided a tool to clever people to exploit others.

It has failed to remove unrest, frustration, anxieties, fears and negative tendencies from the life of an individual.

It has failed to create a crime-free, drug-free, terror-free and corruption-free society. It has still not enabled society to tackle problems like population explosion, shortages, poverty, inequalities, injustice, and ecological imbalance.

As an agency of agencies, it has not been able to inspire and prepare agencies like home, society, religion, media and politics to play their desired roles. It has failed to create international understanding and unshakable hope of world peace. The ideals of education have failed to influence social organisations, political organisations, governance and judicial system. It has not succeeded in providing competent and effective leadership for various walks of life. Educational institutions have not been able to establish a link with the community and other agencies working for the welfare of the society.

It has not been able to integrate knowledge with practical life and the learner remains doubtful about the utility of most of what he learns. Education again, has not succeeded in planning its job-oriented and professional courses as per the demands and placement possibilities of trained personnel.

Education has not been able to become in the real sense, child-centred and life-centred. It has failed to build good habits, character and personality. It has failed to bridge the gap between the educated and the uneducated, rich and poor, rural and urban, privileged and underprivileged, developed and the underdeveloped, new generation and the older generations.

It has failed to clarify numerous notions about religion, spiritualism, mythology and God. It has not been able to create an understanding between different sub-cultures, conflicting political ideologies and varying social norms. Education has not succeeded in understanding, controlling and predicting many natural phenomena and natural calamities. There is absence of futuristic policies, plans and programmes in education, which may convince and assure people concerned with it.

It is very difficult to admit that education has failed. In fact, it is not education that has failed, it is we who have failed to realise its values. We have reduced this all-round hope into a failure.

Learning the many possible lessons of education still remains incomplete in spite of our best efforts. Even if we judge in terms of the scores in tests, we seldom feel satisfied with the performance of most of the students. The teacher has failed to maintain his status. He does not become an effective source of inspiration and guidance. He has failed to become a role model for the students. He has lost confidence and hope that he can shape the personalities of children as demanded. He has been unable to become a symbol of character. He suffers from many shortcomings and transfers these shortcomings to the young minds.

Our educational institutions are often found to be the arenas of jealousy, hypocrisy, groupism, bullying, unhealthy competition and shallow scholarship.

Our philosophy of education has not kept pace with the times. We have not been able to formulate the resultant philosophy out of the many available. Overemphasis on bookish knowledge and examinations has also taken away the real achievements of an individual. Such education is restricted to information and does not come anywhere close to knowledge, wisdom, enlightenment, vision or creativity.

Education has produced scholars, thinkers, research specialists and authorities on various disciplines but not in sufficiently large numbers. Education has not been given due importance by society and the governments. They have failed to provide modern facilities, effective supervision, up-datedness and quality to education. Most of our educational institutions are ill-equipped. In the case of libraries for example, our stocks of books lie unused. We have failed to motivate the students towards reading these books.

Everybody is after a job through education and very few people are serious about realising its noble goals. Our job-oriented courses have also failed to ensure jobs for all. Our system of examination remains confined to periodical tests. We have not been able to introduce evaluation as the real index of learner's achievements. Most of our institutions have not been able to introduce report-card system. The report cards being prepared by various institutions cannot be called sources of complete information. There is no arrangement for collecting and entering data about the child. This data should include creativity index, intelligence quotient, aptitude, interest, level of aspiration, special qualities, difficulties in learning, home conditions, participation in co-curricular activities, etc. It should provide comprehensive data about the personality of the child.

We have yet to reach the goal of providing education to the entire population. Education has not become a lifelong passion for every individual. It has restricted itself only to paper qualifications for a job. After getting jobs of their choice, most of the educated individuals just forget about education.

The most disturbing failures of all is the non-availability of committed teachers. If a teacher does not possess a very strong commitment and involvement in his job, he cannot become a nation-builder in the real sense.

The textbooks proposed for the students are not attractive enough as well. The students seldom engage in supplementary and extra reading. They rather restrict their studies to guide books and help books.

Education has failed in showing its worth and in claiming its rightful place in the overall process of development. It has failed to become an effective instrument of social change. It remains helpless when changes for the worse happen around. It has not been able to establish an ideal society, an effective work culture, a praiseworthy law and order system, a people-friendly system of justice and governance. In a nutshell, it has failed in giving satisfaction to its recipients.

The knowledge of a qualified person is a social asset and not his personal property. He must be able to influence the less qualified people. Otherwise, he fails to become leader of a qualitative life. He should look after others and others should look towards him for guidance.

All these failures and many more should not make us pessimistic about education. Instead, we should be optimistic and full of hope. It actually rests upon us, to successfully realise those hopes and possibilities.

*****

Six

Educational Reform

Educational reform is a never-ending process. Different aspects of education need reform from time to time. We should ensure that every incorporated reform brings the desired results. Reforms cannot be taken as a formality, a routine affair and a ritual. We should be clear about the purpose of a reform and should see that it is realised.

Reforms are regularly needed in the aims and objectives of education, in the curricular and co-curricular activities, for the institutional climate, for the methods and techniques of teaching, for teaching materials and for the evaluation of different aspects.

Some educational institutions should be known as torchbearers of reforms and should be the places to be visited by others for guidance and direction.

There should be no delay in reforms which are urgently needed. Rather there is need for reforms in anticipation of the appearance of reform demanding situations. There should be a permanent agency to think and plan reforms well in time. Everybody associated with education must welcome reforms and carry them out with enthusiasm and commitment.

Every new generation must be provided with the latest system of education required by the circumstances of the future. If possible, there should be a formulation of a year-wise reform programme. We have been experiencing maladies like copying in the examinations, lack of basic amenities in educational institutions, teachers with poor standards of commitment, outdated textbooks, the distance between education and life, the lack of confidence among qualified students for self-employment, poor quality of education, absence of all-round development, and the unpreparedness of the learners for the emerging society. The process of reform should be extra vigilant and prompt about the existing maladies and the likely maladies of the future. There should be no delay in the reorientation and reinforcement of reforms.

Education should spearhead all types of reforms, social, religious, economic and political. It will happen only if education reforms itself without delay.

The focus of education has differed from age to age and there are new aims waiting to take their turn. We should be prepared for these changes in right earnest. Education will continue to enlighten its own path from destination to destination. The seeker will move from enlightenment to more enlightenment, will have no excuse to get slow and will have no fear of losing the way. One has to develop a taste for lifelong learning and should never think that he does not need more of education. Demand for a better tomorrow will need expansion of one's education from day to day.

Since reform in education brings many times more returns, we should be eager for it. Reform in education introduces reform in many allied areas like: placement, productivity, efficiency, adjustment, environment, family atmosphere, social set-up and governance.

We should assess from time to time the areas which are not up to the mark, and the educational system should be geared accordingly to bring the required reform in the area concerned. For example, if we find that people do not care for social norms, we should provide better lessons to the new generation to achieve the desired effect.

Quality education is the victim of insufficient fund allocation, expansion and blatant commercialisation. Reforms should provide related remedies. Although there are many factors responsible for the poor quality of individual and social life, the people responsible for education can have no excuse to escape from this blame.

The best among planners and visionaries will have to sit together and deliberate over evolving a perfect system of education. Perfection in educational system is not a vague idea; it will have to be translated into reality. Education, which is entrusted with the task of solving our problems, cannot be allowed to remain a problem in itself. The system does not satisfactorily tackle some of the basic requirements of the learning process, such as developing ability of conceptualisation and problem-solving. These are the requirements of the present-day competitive life. The textbook culture should no longer dominate in the classroom. Teachers should encourage probing questions by the inquisitive students. The information should be disseminated to them in an innovative manner. The student should be associated with the group mind for the development of his personality and enhancing his dignity.

An urgent reform is needed in respect of half-hearted approach towards education. The government, society, educational planners, educational administrators, teachers, parents and students have to be awakened to take education more seriously and to do sufficient justice to its programmes. All should get determined to make it an effective agency and should make a resolve to draw maximum benefits from it. The claims of education must get translated into reality. It should not be accepted as one of the numerous failures being witnessed by us. Quite helplessly, we accept the failures of the political, economic and social system, governance, and law and order. We have to ensure success of education which will in turn eliminate the above mentioned failures. Success in the system of education will guarantee all-round success.

We have developed clear-cut ideas about the form of campuses of educational institutions, the latest aims of education, the curricula in vogue in some of the leading institutions, the methods and techniques of teaching as advocated by different educational thinkers, the strategies to ensure self-effort on the part of the student in learning, about scientific assessment of the child's capacities and his accomplishments in learning, the new approach towards discipline, and the real developments desired in a personality.

These and many other requirements of modern education have yet to be faithfully implemented and maintained.

We have to make education so effective that not a single educated individual disappoints us in any way. The reform in education is urgently needed, to bring about a significant reform in the student, in respect of his individual and social life.

*****

II

EDUCATION AND INDIVIDUAL

Seven

Education and Individual

The use of the pronoun "I" means the dawn of selfhood and its wide range of possibilities. The individual is capable of retaining memories of the past to extend himself into the future and to live in a world of new meanings. He exhibits the vast range and depth of appreciation and creation of beauty. His creativity involves the search for truth, beauty and goodness. He has been able to express it in many ways like art, science, philosophy and religion.

Human beings can be classified into many categories, some of which are: mineral men, vegetable men, animal men, human men and God's men. Mineral men are self-centred, lethargic, selfish and ever dissatisfied. Vegetable men are concerned about the well-being of their immediate family. Animal men are sectarian and identify themselves with a particular caste, creed or community. They cause more pain to other sects than the happiness they can give to their own sect. Human men identify themselves with the whole mankind. They are extremely sweet and sacrificing towards all fellow beings. But God's men are the most evolved individuals who have completely annihilated their selfishness.

As for their emotional temperament, the self-centred man remains very restless and is always disturbed because of unfulfilled demands. There is no equilibrium in him. Perfect equilibrium characterises the most evolved group, which is not only free from every tension and fear but stays in harmony with the world. The fundamental goal for the individual is evolution towards this higher state of living. Education has to shape the unfinished human beings into complete human beings. Perfection must be taken as an overriding goal for every individual. The facilities for him should be so upgraded to fulfil the desired perfections. What is actually lacking is the will to invest in children. It is time that the government and non-governmental agencies realised that healthy and capable children alone can achieve a healthy economy and a healthy mankind.

Education should make endeavours to distinguish the uniqueness of every individual, develop it and describe it in his testimony. We should be able to discover quite early in the case of children, as to who is a born poet, artist, scientist or craftsman, etc. It is now agreed that every individual is gifted with multiple intelligences. There is need to study every child thoroughly and measure the different intelligences possessed by him.

The first five years are very crucial in the life of an individual. Studies have shown that 90% of the brain growth takes place during this period. If children in this age group are not given nutritious food, they will not be able to grow to their full potential. A large number of children are born so poor that they do not get balanced food, and are therefore unable to attain what they maybe capable of. Though not quantified, the worldwide loss on this count is gigantic. Educational institutions have to come forward to supplement the diet of such children after allocating them into different classes. They may persuade the state and other welfare organisations to come to their help in this regard. Again, these initial years are very important for the mental and physical growth of an individual. Most of the knowledge and experiences should be imparted through light, enjoyable and refreshing activities. These activities should be planned by psychological and educational experts for different age groups of pre-primary classes. Their small books should be pictorial, colourful and play-oriented. The games associated with the child should be thrilling and thought-provoking. It should be a medium of auto education. Latent powers of the child are fully discovered and developed in this way.

Dewey has suggested four basic impulses on which the foundation of a child should be built: (1) the social impulse rooted in the need to communicate something about a social situation (2) the constructive (3) the investigative and (4) the expressive. Under the stimulus of the desire to communicate, he searches for and welcomes all means of letting others know what he has done, felt and experienced.

The human organism has to be seen as the fundamental actor, not the mind or the body but the organism in its total range of interaction with its environment. Processes of learning and thinking are advanced modes of adaptation and are related with evolutionary development.

Dewey and Aristotle agree on the point that the goodness of a man shines through his deeds. The self reveals its nature in what it chooses. The theory of morality is recognised by the study of the self and its actions.

The individual's natural desire is to share, to do, and to serve and when this desire is not fulfilled, work becomes a burden. The growth of an individual depends upon a developing society which in turn is constantly changed by the contributions of the individuals who constitute it.

Every individual has his own individuality and also a sacred constitution of his own. Education has to lead to the exaltation of his personality. The central function of education can be the making of the full Man. Education will naturally be based on the scientific knowledge of the man as an integral being.

Every individual is unique. Let us strive towards finding this uniqueness, make the individual aware of it, focus our educational efforts on that uniqueness, enable him to excel in it and become a role model for others to follow.

Investments made towards the development of that uniqueness will bear distinctive fruits. The consciousness of this uniqueness provides a clear-cut direction to the individual, his parents and his educators. Due to the lack of awareness of this uniqueness, the individual may continue to wander in life without a goal.

Man is considered a creature of unlimited possibilities either for the good or for the evil. Education has to sharpen his possibilities for the good and blunt his possibilities for evil.

According to T P Nunn, "Education is the complete development of the individuality of the child so that he can make an original contribution to human life according to the best of his capacity."

Every individual should be educated to play some meaningful role in problems like pollution, water and food shortage, unemployment, chaos in society, poor governance, and threats made to world peace. An individual should realise the value of life, and should not squander it on petty pursuits. He is duty-bound to grow as an asset for himself, for the community, country and mankind.

Education has to provide great lessons to the individual. The lives of great achievers provide to the learners ever-inspiring lessons. For example, Thomas Edison, the inventor of the electric bulb had to make hundreds of unsuccessful attempts till his final invention.

The individual has to learn his rights and duties and stick to them as best as he can. He must understand that he does not have to live a life confined completely to himself. He should know and perform his responsibilities towards the family, friends, relatives, acquaintances, the needy, society, nation and mankind. He should endeavour to make some memorable contributions in these areas and will never become a target of criticism but will be a recipient of appreciation from different quarters. He will employ his education, abilities, experiences and resources for the general welfare of the society and thereby will earn a distinguishable individuality, not only through his individualistic excellence but also due to the services he has offered to mankind.

Piaget has proposed for the universal child to look at the world through nine universal cognitive contents, which are: action, objects, spaces, time, causality, play, imitation, self and language. Learning based on these aspects is going to be an exciting venture and real education for the individual.

According to Rousseau, children should be educated first for manhood and then for citizenship. Natural man is greater than the citizen.

Montessori called children forgotten citizens and felt that they deserved much better consideration. The child, she held, is gifted at birth to become something. She wanted the child to be educated individually. Individual development was best directed by means of a graded series of educational apparatus, which she improvised in abundance. She formulated four principles for the education of a child: (1) education must be an individual business (2) individual development was best directed by graded series of apparatus (3) all education should be self education (4) for self education, children should have the necessary freedom and impersonal directress instead of ordinary teacher.

Dewey agreed with the aim of education as self-realisation of the individual.

A S Neill was strongly committed to the freedom of the child. He was of the opinion that in order to do this, we had to renounce all discipline, all direction, all suggestion, all moral training, and all religious instruction. If a child is allowed to develop naturally, he will not need any promptings and sanctions.

Rugg suggested a child-centred and society-centred education and advocated a profound commitment to individual creativity.

To understand the process of development of the individual, we must have a clear understanding of various stages of development. Both heredity and environment should be made to work together in a complementary and supplementary way for smooth and balanced development of the child.

According to John Dewey, "The function of education is to help the growing of a helpless young animal into a happy, moral and efficient human being."

As the individual is the prime beneficiary of education, the process of education is full of influences for the learner. It imparts lessons to the child to adapt to his environment, as lack of adaptation creates maladjustment, which leads to decay and destruction of the individual. It develops the capacities of the individual to mould and modify the environment according to the ever-changing situations and circumstances. It enlightens him so that he can behave as a cultured and civilised human being. It develops the capacities and shows the way to satisfy one's needs and solve one's problems. It helps the individual to achieve necessary vocational efficiency and professional competence. It enables the individual to attain material prosperity and welfare. It makes the individual self-reliant, self-sufficient and progressive enough. It develops his character so that he is devoted to high ideals of life. It develops his personality by inculcating moral qualities, spirit of service and sacrifice and a sense of responsibility and duty. It prepares him for the present as well as for the future. Education inculcates the continued re-construction and re-organisation of experiences that leads an individual to higher and still higher levels of progress. It creates citizens who are dynamic, enterprising and resourceful. It promotes efficiency in work and prepares individuals for leadership roles in various walks of life.

*****

Eight

Educated People

There is bound to be a clear, observable and vast difference between an uneducated and an educated person. The nature, structure and quantum of present day education have been evolved through long and painstaking efforts of exceptional human beings and experts. These efforts must guarantee a marked impact on every recipient of education. The people who are privileged to receive education are bound by duty to show results. Their achievements, behaviour and contribution should testify that education by itself is a great quality and a gift. An educated person should be different from an uneducated person in a way that he should not spite him, but instead should be able to show him the way, to encourage him, to carry him along and to assure him that he is also capable of similar possibilities. An educated person by virtue of his development carries greater responsibilities on his shoulders. He is responsible to himself, to his family, to his neighbourhood, to his community and to the entire humanity. Almost all these agencies have helped him to avail a special opportunity for growth and development. It is not a mere question of repaying the debt. This debt is, perhaps, not repayable. He, who thinks only in terms of repaying the debt, insults the very education he happened to receive. He should try to repay many times more than what he received.

Education is not a commodity purchasable by investment, time, effort, intelligence or traits. It is a value,

Educated People

which cannot be measured by any yardstick. Every educated person should try to honour the respect which education stands for.

The difference between educated and uneducated should not be treated as a matter of superiority and inferiority. It is the duty of the educated to bring the less educated and uneducated people at par with them. It is a great crime, when educated people employ their education to exploit the uneducated.

It is wrong on the part of educated people to maintain a distance from the uneducated or to hate them in any manner. It is not befitting on their part to take pride in their educational qualifications in the presence of less educated people. Higher the educational qualifications, greater should be the humility in one's behaviour. The educated people should be able to accept the uneducated persons as their friends, relatives, companions and co-workers.

It is not very rare to find an educated person committing follies. The person intentionally or unintentionally, forgets everything that education conveyed to him. He disowns education and in return gets disowned by education. His innermost mind may still dissuade him from that folly but he refuses to listen. He may refuse to return a small amount borrowed from a friend and may pose that he had already returned it. In the bargain, he will lose a dependable friend and earn a bad reputation.

The educated people, in return for their education demand privileges, rewards, positions, comforts and superiority, by which they not only belittle education but disgrace it. Education must prepare people for giving primarily and becoming as much selfless as possible.

The educated person must know at least one field with adequate thoroughness. By virtue of that, he should be able to enter a vocation with a reasonable degree of confidence and success.

He should be able to communicate with the local people and even with foreigners. He should be able to adjust in this ever-changing world and should be able to entertain new ideas. He should be able to live cooperatively with others. This principle applies to groups as well as nations.

He must have developed a rich inner life and a wide range of appreciations and inner controls. He should feel as though he is in good company even when alone and live by some coherent personal philosophy of life. If he acts merely because of custom, law, fear or some other external pressure, he is not genuinely mature. Self-control or inner discipline is a prerequisite of significant achievement in any field. He is sensitive enough to the vast order of which he is a part. He is a creature involved in and acted upon by the flux of Nature, yet his detached consciousness of his involvement enables him to achieve some control over this flux.

Throughout the history of mankind, only a handful of individuals have been able to prove themselves as really educated. The entire mankind has been enjoying the fruits of their labour and claiming to be highly modernised. These few individuals, by their educated existence, noble ideas, and selfless conduct have been able to revolutionise the entire humanity. They have proved to be the torchbearers of progress and are the real role models of education.

It is not difficult to imagine, what will be the glorious position of our culture and civilisation, if all the individuals had become educated in the real sense. If all the educated persons play their reasonable role, society will attain the heights of prosperity in a short span of time. During such times, the educated will provide leadership, but will never think of maintaining a distance from the less educated. The latter should like to accept them as their dependable companions, friends and helpers.

An educated person, by virtue of his being a greater beneficiary, should consider himself as more dutiful to repay. He will never hesitate or withdraw from leading roles expected of him. Without taking any pride in his education, he will become a more humble servant of the people. He will not try to stay aloof in order to monopolise on his time and resources for selfish motives. He should regard his education as a universal property.

There are many demands on his personal conduct. He ought to have a scientific and healthy posture, an extra attractive style of walking, a comfortable style of sitting in a chair, a saintly style of sitting on the ground, a healthy and nourishing manner of eating, a rare cleanliness visible from body and dress, a simple but impressive dress leading to enhancement in personality, mannerism personifying gentlemanliness, use of sober, polished and rich language, a sense of humour, signs of courtesy and respectfulness in every gesture and behaviour, a liking for likeable things, a dislike for things worthy of it, an aura of maturity drawn from education and other experiences, an absorbent attitude in studies and work, and so on. He should be exemplary in all the possible descriptions of an educated person.

Educated people have to strive for an orderly, balanced, harmonious, organised, prosperous and humanistic society. They have to provide services to a vast majority as compared to what narrow-minded selfish people actually don't do.

But it is so difficult to find individuals praiseworthy in all respects from amongst the vast population of the educated people. It is not the degrees, diplomas or qualifications which will create educated people for society. Learners must be enabled to imbibe the true spirit of education and put their education at the disposal of society.

They have a special responsibility towards the problems and issues that bother mankind. They should focus their attention and energies on something significant in this direction. They may select a mission in life to make some memorable contribution. They should raise their voice against antisocial elements and social evils. They should make themselves improvement-oriented. They may work in any capacity but they should be keen to solve the problems of education, society, economy, development and politics. They should be able to positively influence their family life, social life and vocational life. They should try to contribute towards research, literature, technologies and culture. It is their duty to keep growing through education.

*****

Nine

Education and Human Nature

The great issues of education, psychology, philosophy and practical life involve the question of human nature. There is evidence of an inner element of some sort, which may be called human nature, self, ego, agent, mind, knower, soul or spirit. The self has, so far, defied adequate description and definition. The difficulty lies in the very concept of self which defies analysis in behaviouristic terms.

The human being may live his life totally at a biological level, where he seeks to satisfy his appetites and desires. Unless he consciously seeks to live on the higher level and tries to maintain deep- rooted ideals of personal honour and responsibility, he is likely to revert to the level of animals.

Rousseau and some other thinkers have postulated that man is basically good, and that he only becomes bad with the influence of society. Others such as Spencer believed the opposite; that man's supposed innate selfishness, aggressiveness and other such characteristics are curbed only through the controls exercised by society.

Man is a rational being and reason is his highest quality that guides his conduct. The ideal person is the wise man who suppresses his emotions and governs his world by controlling himself and his behaviour.

The classical view of man is optimistic. He is a creature of great value or worth. He is a creature of almost unlimited possibilities. From the scientific angle, man is viewed with regard to his physical and chemical aspects. He has many characteristics in common with other animals and is said to be part of the age-old process of evolution. Many physical characteristics at the same time set him apart from other animals. His upright posture frees the arms and hands for exploration and manipulation. His fingers and thumb enable him to grasp objects. Because of flexibility, he is a manipulator, a toolmaker and an inventor. His large head and brain and the highly organised and intricate nervous system permit varied and subtle behaviour.

Articulate speech, oral and written language and the use of symbols enabled human being to evolve from barbarism to civilisation. Scientific and other inventions enabled man to live a fuller life.

Human progress depends on the ability of man to cooperate and work in groups. Social cooperation is a condition for a good life in an interdependent society.

A physiochemical or a biological view of man is not sufficient by itself. It is not possible to reduce the rich qualities of human personality to the mere functioning of biological organism. The sciences with their emphasis on objectivity are likely to neglect what is distinctly human about man.

Man can live on different levels. For instance, he can merely vegetate or he can live as a responsible person with broad interests and aspirations and with great growth and intellectual possibilities.

While animals are conscious, man is self-conscious. This quality makes possible imagination, foresight and creativity. His reflective thinking enables him to carry on the trial and error process mentally, and to distinguish between true and false. It enables him to retain memories of the past, to extend himself into the future and to live in a world of new meanings. Due to ethical discrimination and the power of choice; in the life of what is, he can say, what ought to be. Man can not only appreciate beauty but can create it. His creativity finds expression in art, science, philosophy and religion. It incorporates the quest for truth, beauty and goodness.

Education has to safeguard and develop the angelic human nature at birth from being disfigured by the not so supportive environment. Every child can be developed into a possessor and protector of nobility. Let us believe in the possibility of eradicating, rather than re-shaping the poor specimens of human nature. Their eradication and re-shaping should be ensured at the level of education through development and re-orientation rather than at the level of society through the laws, police, courts and punishments. Showing and living the true form of human nature is the obligation of every human being. A blotless human nature is gifted to every human being and this has to be preserved as a lifelong gift. Let us stick to the belief that there is no other description of human nature except that of Godliness. It has not to make any compromises to tarnish its image. Education has to re-establish human nature in its true Godly form. Different individuals may develop different characteristics of Godliness.

It is somewhat disappointing to admit that human nature is not found to be like that which it ought to be. As per religion, human nature usually suffers from five vices. The lesson taught by religion to human beings is to free oneself from these five and other vices. A person who rises above these vices can be called a saint. But a common man feels that it is almost impossible to free himself from the most powerful vices known as lust for sex, anger, greed, attachment and haughtiness. He also thinks that it is difficult for him to become a saint. Moreover, a saintly person can hardly adjust to this wretched world. It is thus wasteful to try to become a saint as it is too high a position for an ordinary human being. Without making a serious and sincere effort to free himself from these vices, man has already admitted defeat.

Shall we fail forever against these vices? Can't human beings understand that remaining a slave to these vices is below the dignity of human nature? They have to make up their minds that they will no longer remain subservient to them? These vices may have a strong hold over human beings, but an individual must ponder over the fact that he can, with his determination, prove to be stronger. It is only a question of making a resolve or pledge to fight these vices.

Human beings have conquered Nature in many ways. They can certainly conquer the faults of their own nature also, if they try with some confidence. If some saints have shown that it is possible to conquer the vices, then individuals can also make it possible in their own case. Life will become a golden experience if all people succeed in conquering the vices.

Conquering one's mind and thoughts becomes the core issue in this struggle. Education cannot remain a helpless spectator in this great and noble venture. Human nature should not be allowed to remain pitiable. Its strength should be awakened to achieve a gradual control over the vices. The partial success of a human being will motivate him towards decisive victory.

Human nature should no more remain a puzzle or an enigma before us. If we intelligently try, we can certainly understand our mind and its functioning. A controlled mind provides great peace, which has its own taste to relish.

Education does refer to the lives of saints and their attainments. It will have to lay stress on every individual to exercise control over his mind to make his life sublime. Education therefore, provides peace of mind and should be given a fair deal of importance.

It is a well known fact that many saints also suffer from many vices. It is the responsibility of the saints and ordinary men alike, to realise and achieve true human nature.

Human nature becomes a target of many more shortcomings like lying, stealing, deceiving, jealousy, intolerance, antisocial behaviour, being mean, etc. Education should so manipulate the working of the human mind that it develps an aversion for any kind of evil or immoral behaviour.

It should be an endeavour through education to seek the purification of human nature from its negative and unhealthy aspects, if any. The overbearing form of these aspects is one of the signs of abnormality. An individual's mind should be strengthened enough to be able to resist the negative and unhealthy aspects of human nature.

It is again the responsibility of education to insulate the innocent child from the undesirable effects of physical and social environments. None of the agencies should be allowed to spoil the child and his nature. The innocence and pure nature of the child should be kept intact and developed on the lines which don't adversely affect his fundamental nature. All other agencies like home, society, religion and state have to cooperate in that direction.

It was once claimed by a great educationist that he may be entrusted with the development of any child and he would make him into whatever you want him to be. The question is not of making a claim, but of making a determination to develop human nature, as we want it to be.

It is also felt that we cannot do much to change the inborn and innate tendencies of a human being. We cannot leave the matter at that. We want every individual to do his best in education and life. Therefore, we must educate and mould the inborn and innate tendencies in favour of the individual. We should face this task with confidence in a way that we are able to shape human nature to become more compassionate.

Education needs to be empowered to mould the human nature. It should not allow any conflict to grow between human nature and human welfare. Education should be able to develop unshakable sincerity in the learner's mind. He should always be sincere towards himself, towards his family, towards society, towards the country and towards mankind.

According to Rousseau, education must be in harmony with the original and unspoiled human nature. The function of education is to preserve the child's goodness and purity without being stained by the world.

We can proceed in a systematic way to remove certain beliefs and attitudes altogether, to change an anti-attitude into a pro-attitude, to prevent the development of certain beliefs and attitudes, to encourage the development of healthy beliefs and attitudes, and to change the content and specificity of a belief or attitude. It is essential to diagnose the nature of the belief or attitude that is to be changed, developed or prevented from developing.

If beliefs and attitudes are to be controlled, all their characteristics must be worked upon. We should try to control the perception, needs and emotions involved in beliefs and attitudes. A major part of any control programme is that of controlling the perceptions involved.

Our programme should be a multi-dimensional one. There should be change in the environmental support lying behind percepts, there can be coordinated change in the environmental supports lying behind needs and emotions, and both of these can be influenced by a change in the nature of social support that beliefs and attitudes receive.

Effective measures must seek to create new group identifications for people so that the social support for the new beliefs and attitudes will be forthcoming. In order to seek social support, we should try to educate the individual as part of a group and we can do that by taking advantage of the diversification existing within the cultural pattern of the group.

*****

Ten

Education and Mind

Psychology is regarded as the science of the mind. In order to make education effective, we have to understand the functioning of the mind. The mind is a combination of mental processes and stands for personal and internal experiences of a man, such as his pleasures and pains, hopes and wishes, dreams and desires.

Mind has continuity with a constant flow of mental processes in quick succession. It never stops and continues to receive formal or informal educative experiences and give its responses. It is a unity, although we may analyse its processes for purposes of study. It is continuously active. It is better to keep it engaged in meaningful education. Since we cannot perceive it with our senses, its functioning is its proof. Education has to be the mind's main function.

Scientific study of the mind is very important for the purpose of individualising education, harnessing its receptivity in education, making its thinking and reasoning the main approaches in learning, broadening its vision and awakening its creativity.

Greater understanding of learning and dependence on the mind will prompt us towards insightful learning. Insight is like an invention; a sort of creative consciousness. It draws upon the mind as if to illuminate it, thereby promoting the intellectual level of the learner.

The mind thinks, feels and acts. Psychologists consider the mind the sum total of all mental processes, experiences, ideas, desires and sensations. Some regard it as intelligent behaviour. Psychologists feel that remembering and forgetting are two activities that have helped build and define the mind. As the brain and the nervous system develop, the powers of the mind also increase.

Leibnitz believed that the universe had been made with such skill that the mind and matter were always meant to operate in harmony. Both Spinoza and Kant regarded the mind and body as two aspects of one reality. Certain processes taking place in the brain and nervous system produce sensations, feelings, emotions, imagery, thought or other types of consciousness. All behaviours associated with a person with which he can communicate have consciousness. Modern psychology is studying the various degrees of consciousness, expression of which is possible by bodily behaviour or in the form of emotional experiences.

Freud divided the mind in two parts: (1) topological aspects of the mind (2) dynamic aspects of the mind. He further divided the topological aspects in three parts: (1) conscious (2) subconscious and (3) unconscious. The dynamic aspect also has three parts: id, ego and superego.

The clear and distinct present knowledge of the stimulus is the consciousness. It is a means of attaining knowledge. Consciousness can also be described as emotion, memory, thinking, logic and mental processes.

Mind does not work as a number of faculties, such as thinking, reasoning and imagining. It is one and the same mind which thinks, reasons and imagines.

Mind is immaterial. It is not made of flesh or other matters like the brain. It is extremely personal. No one else can observe anyone's thoughts and wishes except himself. Mind is a distinct level of reality.

There are three kinds of mental activities: cognitive or knowing, like thinking, reasoning and imagining; conative or doing, like walking, swimming and dancing; affective or feeling like feeling happy, sad and angry. Thinking, feeling, appreciation and sense of values are central to the individuality or personality. They are the very things that give sense and meaning to the human venture and to the universe itself, yet they are not things that can be counted, measured, touched and seen. When memory, imagination and self-consciousness developed, greater steps were taken ahead. Men could see and hear what was not present.

According to John Dewey, there are four basic impulses on which the education of the child should be built: (1) the social impulse rooted in the need to communicate something about a social situation (2) the constructive (3) the investigative and (4) the expressive. He held that the child has a basic need to express himself in activity and to share and tell the results of his activity.

Science, art, philosophy, religion and moral distinctions have been realised through the mind. The self is the being who does or who experiences the things. The self is the living individual with his needs, and interests and his capacities for feeling, thinking and creative imagination. The self is the living being that carries on these mental processes.

Mind is our most valuable asset, and we have not to allow even a fraction of it to go waste. Rather, we should try to draw from it the maximum possible returns.

Let us believe that no mind is perverted by birth. It is for education to block the entry of any perversion into it.

Only the mentally deficient are the unlucky ones, who, because of lack of proper mental development are unable to profit from education. Mental deficiency originates since birth.

There should be no cause for the mind to go astray, to think negatively or to behave destructively. Mind is responsible for all our learning and activities. Since it is the controller of a human being, its controls should never allow the human being to go astray. It must be developed into an unfailing judge of what is right and what is wrong. Its positive judgement must remain binding on the behaviour of an individual. Mind will not allow the body to misbehave.

Educational research should be focused on the capabilities, possibilities, functioning and acquirements of the human mind. When we understand it better, we shall be able to achieve higher goals and intellectual heights through it. Mind should be enabled to become strong enough, not to be misguided by external influences. Education has to acquire new techniques to train the mind to rise above the limited world of senses.

There are a number of mental disorders and abnormalities which obstruct the functioning of the mind. Some of these are: psychoneurosis, schizophrenia, and manic-depressive psychosis. These disorders create serious problems in learning and adjustment. A number of methods are available for their treatment. Hypnotherapy is one of the methods, which involves reprogramming of the subconscious mind as required by the condition of a person. It uses the mostly unused power of our mind. It solves most of the physical and mental health problems of a human being by finding the solutions which actually lie within his own mind. This therapy applies to emotional and personal issues, personality problems, study related difficulties, habits, fears and phobias.

Education has to provide some lessons for the peace of mind. A person may have plenty of money, but no peace of mind; a person may have a big job with power, but has no peace of mind or a person luckily gets all his needs fulfilled, but still enjoys no peace of mind.

Peace of mind is definitely more important than plenty of money, a big job with power, fulfilment of all our needs and blessings in the form of many other fortunes.

We must seriously think about the problem when we cannot enjoy peace of mind in spite of being blessed with everything else.

Religions suggest the ways of meditation and prayer for achieving peace of mind. Education has to provide some other alternatives too. The individual must be educated to achieve peace of mind under all types of good and bad circumstances. A person should develop such self-control that he does not lose his peace of mind even in the worst of situations.

One of the approaches can be to cultivate an outlook of confirmed optimism. A failure at present should not be taken as a failure forever. A person should try to do his best, accept the results whatever they are, and have faith in a better future.

Each member of a family has to conduct himself in such a manner which does not disturb his own peace of mind and that of others. Same is true for the members of an institution or community.

We must try to set-up a system or a society where every member enjoys a sense of security and peace of mind. An individual should not be left alone to suffer under adverse circumstances. He should have an assurance that all the individuals and agencies will come forward to help restore his peace of mind.

In educational institutions, the administrators and teachers should be the persons who are examples of those who can provide peace of mind. They should be able to create a peaceful atmosphere in the institution. If someone is found gloomy, he should become a cause of concern for the rest.

Peace of mind should not be regarded as a supernatural state of mind. It should be considered necessary, real and feasible. Some yoga exercises can certainly help us in promoting our peace of mind. These exercises may be introduced into everybody's daily routine. Playing games and enjoying some entertainment programme can also act as an aid towards peace of mind.

So far, education has not played any distinctive role towards cultivating peace of mind among learners. Peace of mind of the learner is very important for his educational and other kinds of achievements. Educational experts and research workers should also pay attention towards exploring new educational devices for help in achieving this state of mind.

Young students should be made aware of the meaning, importance and methods of promoting peace of mind. We take pleasure in creating trouble for others. In due course of time, this disturbs the peace of mind of both sides.

If we help a person in distress, if we can save somebody from a difficulty, if we can do some selfless social service, if we can enable a person to achieve his goal, if we can fight for justice for the victims, if we are generous in giving financial help to the needy, if we can contribute in some way towards the upliftment of others, these and many other actions of this type bring peace of mind to us and others.

If we provide peace of mind to others, we shall get the same in return. We should learn to enjoy the satisfaction which is gained from giving peace to others.

Even when a difficulty gets prolonged, we should not lose our heart and our presence or peace of mind. We should remember the examples of those who had to bear lifelong difficulties with unshakable faith in a better future.

We should draw joy and peace of mind from our successes, but it does not mean that we should lose our peace of mind in the case of failure.

*****

Eleven

Interest in Education

There is a general complaint against education that it is not interesting for the individual. He should be attracted towards education just as a hungry child is driven towards food. Food is regarded as a biological necessity, and a human being cannot live for long without food. Education is no less than a biological necessity because without it the human mind cannot grow. The development of human mind is equally important as the development of the human body. It is the human mind which makes the existence of human beings worthwhile in many ways.

A child has to be prepared to take a stronger interest in mental development and education. Taking interest only in biological food and neglecting one's interest for mental food is like deciding to live life like an animal.

The interests of the human body may be confined to nutritious food and good physical health but the interests of the mind are limitless. It is probable that the mind will evolve and develop such interests in the future which we cannot imagine today. Fruits of the mind are more tasteful, nourishing and healthy as compared to the fruits of the body.

A human mind should not stand in need of artificial devices to help create in it an interest for education. Human interest in education should be natural, spontaneous, voluntary and self-willed. Let us convince human beings that an interest for education should be an interest by birth. As education unveils its secrets before him, his interest in it should grow with every step. There are unlimited mysteries, delights, charms and enlightenments which education will reveal to him. As education unfolds itself before the human mind, interest in it should expand and not shrink. A mind which has learnt to take interest in education will eventually develop an interest for the various activities in life.

Motivation is considered an art of inculcating and stimulating interest in studies and other such activities. It is a process in which the learner's internal energies or needs are directed towards various goals. It arouses eagerness and readiness for the task. It increases the attention and concentration of an individual. It ensures persistence in work and effort.

Physiological needs, psychological needs, drive, incentives and motives are major sources of motivation. Motivated behaviour shows eagerness, concentrated attention, persistence, mobilised energy, achievement of the goal and finally, reduced levels of tension.

Apart from developing the interest for education among students, motivation helps in the prompt acquisition of knowledge, in the development of the sense of discipline and in progress according to individual differences. A committed interest may result in motivating a person to enjoy the process of learning and thereby create a deep desire to excel.

Interest has been called a feeling which accompanies special attention to something. It is a behaviour that is directed towards certain objects, activities or experiences. It is an expression of our likes and dislikes or our attractions and aversions. The objects, activities or experiences which command our interests are stimulating, enjoyable and pleasurable.

The phenomena of interests involve choosing the most acceptable alternative, going after preferred objects, etc. and consequently deriving satisfaction, success and happiness out of one's own interests.

Interest is important in its own right and represents a trait distinctively different from other traits. Its role in the performance and achievement of any kind is no less significant than that of any other relevant traits. Interest suggests to a person as to which direction he can take to be happy in his life. Interest influences the efficiency, both in education and vocation.

Without interest, one's ability may go waste. The interests of the learner should be duly considered in determining both the content and the methods of instruction. Education must be based on the interests of the child, always starting from his existing interests and seeking to develop new interests on the foundation of these. Learning cannot take place without a feeling of interest and its aim is to induce many sided interests.

The study of interests has probably received its strongest impetus from educational and vocational counselling. At the stage of diversification, the learner must be guided to choose the subject areas in accordance with his interests. Similarly, at the stage of vocationlisation, the learner must be helped to choose the right type of pre-vocational and vocational courses keeping in mind his interests. The selection of the right person for the right work is very important to society in view of utilizing his optimum capacity. Such a selection is important in order to save the likely misfits who lead a frustrated, disappointed and unhappy vocational life.

We should focus special efforts on the beginner to develop his interest in education in general. He should be provided with colourful material, toys and equipments with which he can play without getting tired and without losing interest. He should get well illustrated books to read, and play captivating outdoor games. His interests should be watched and recorded for the purpose of giving guidance in the future.

The principle of interest is often abused by being reduced to the concept of amusement. Complete interest in education is realised only when the child puts his entire self into the activity. Work is regarded as incompatible with play. When the child becomes conscious that he is not working but only playing, he ceases to play, because his interest dies out.

Genuine interest is involved when the self is in the process of realising itself. Learning is marked by spontaneity and personal commitment.

Education should help the individual to acquire healthy interests for food, dress, games, enjoyment, family life, vocational life, social life, self-study, lifelong education and creativity.

*****

Twelve

Education and Character

Character building is one of the important aims of education. Men of character are very rare in our vast population. The world always needed men of character in large numbers. A man of character will possess various qualities expected of a true human being. He is generally a man of word, action, conviction, clean image, a true citizen and a respectable person.

John Dewey says, "The establishment of character is a comprehensive aim of school instruction and discipline."

Raymont says, "The teacher's ultimate concern is to cultivate, not wealth or muscle, nor fullness of knowledge, nor refinement of feeling, but strength and purity of character."

Education has to play a positive role in shaping the character of individuals. The formation of character should not be left to the influence of only the home, society and environment. Most of the individuals around us exhibit a weak character. Weakness of character on the part of a person creates difficulties for the individual as well as for the society. The soundness of character enhances the quality of life.

There is no justification to understand character as the private affair of a person. The boundaries of liberties are definitely earmarked for him. If he chooses to take unguarded liberties in the matter of his character, his behaviour will be objectionable and unlawful.

Take the case of the desire for sex. There are only one or two socially permissible ways of soliciting sex, and no one can be allowed to cross those limits. When we find widespread abuse of sex, we have to seek the intervention of education to safeguard the situation. Learners have to be convinced to exercise self-control in this matter and should not require external inhibitions for this control. The boys and girls should be free to mix with one another. They should learn to respect the dignity owned by each, and should learn to enjoy each other's company in a civilized manner. However, there is more need to cultivate respect for women. Some societies have become unduly permissive in the matter of sexual behaviour. It is against the norms of character. Abuse of sex often leads to tragedy.

The teachers and administrators working in educational institutions should be living examples of good character. Their influence will have a positive impact on the character of young learners. The weaknesses of their character, if any, impart bad lessons to the students. The teachers, who are weak in character, may be asked to improve or leave the profession.

Teachers should recommend character building books to their students. Such good books should be available in plenty in the institutional library. Biographies of great men can also provide good material for character training.

Moral education may be made a part of the curriculum for young children. The textbooks of languages, history and social sciences can also carry suitable lessons for character formation. The celebration of religious and cultural festivals also imparts lessons on good character. Teachers, who are well known as men of character, may be invited by other schools to speak to the students of other schools about nurturing a good character. Similarly, some prominent persons of the community who are examples of good character may be invited to talk to the students on the importance and cultivation of character.

The concept of character may be made clear by displaying mottoes, charts and pictures in the classrooms. A list of contents of good character may be prepared and incorporated in the diary to be kept by every student. An institutional prize may be introduced to be given to the student who tops in character traits. Small habits like depositing in the 'lost and found' box, any article belonging to someone else but found by another child, may be appreciated and rewarded. Such cases of honesty may be mentioned in the morning assembly.

Some projects like the student's cooperative store, collecting money and keeping accounts of students' educational tour, and keeping accounts of a celebration may be entrusted to students as a training in honesty.

Some news about the cases of poor character may be shared with the students and they may be invited to express their reactions. Let there be debates among the students on the need of good character. They may be invited to write articles on good character for a competition.

Everybody is bound to his duty to improve the quality of the self and one's social life. Personal character is the minimum which everybody should work towards. A person of bad character is a misfit in his family, in a town, community, religious group, institution, office, administration, political field and in every other walk of life.

Elements of good behaviour are very rare to find. The behaviour which should be automatically acquired through observation, now requires classroom teaching and text book lessons. Even the systematic teaching of good behaviour seldom makes the desired impact.

Good character automatically earns respect and bad character gathers only disrespect. Good character makes its own contribution in the success of a person in any walk of life and this is what education can impart to every learner.

*****

Thirteen

Education and Development of Personality

The development of a learner into an ordinary individual can no longer remain the target of education. Seeking quality through education is a reasonable demand. The development of a desired personality for achieving the desired goals will remain one of the chief functions of education. We must be very clear about the characteristics we want everybody to acquire. We should not show any laxity about their acquirement.

We should gather reliable data about the possibilities, competencies, difficulties, boundaries and impossibilities of every personality and then evolve the programme for optimum development in every case.

In his most formative years, the child has to remain in school for a period of ten or twelve years. It is the period of life in the making. After such a long stay, the learner must grow into an ideal individual in every way. This stay should ensure a full-fledged development of the personality. The contents and activities of this compulsory period of education should be so rich and effective that the developed personality carries no weak points.

In spite of good opportunity for education, a large number of individuals today suffer from numerous abnormalities. Education should not fail like this. After completing education, every personality must be reasonably balanced and mature. If education continues to leave behind drawbacks in personalities, we should become extra cautious.

A good book on etiquettes will help improve personality as will close observation of those people who are admired because they are successful, wise or self-assured. Young people who develop social skills early have a great advantage over those who delay or refuse to acquire accomplishments valued by their associates. People who can do things are more likely to be accepted or admired than those who cannot or who offer excuses.

Personality is all that you are and all that you hope to be. Try to penetrate through and understand your real motives, be ready to appraise them and revise those when new conditions so demand. Personality is to be understood as the organisation of traits, modes of adjustment, the ways of behaviour that characterise the individual and his relation with others. It is a patterned body of habits, attitudes and ideas of an individual as they are organised externally into roles and status and as they relate internally to motivation, goals and various aspects of selfhood. It has two aspects, role and status with regard to internal motivation, and the ways of viewing one's own and other's behaviour. Some thinkers emphasise the conformity aspects of personality, others, the unique aspects.

Personality has biological as well as cultural boundaries. Heredity supplies the raw material and the general design of personality comes from the individual's culture, which sometimes limits the number of fields of personality expression.

The environment plays its own role in the development of a personality. The question of adjustment and maladjustment is closely linked with the personality and its environment. The geographical position of the place where a person lives has a good deal to do in the shaping of his personality. Our environment is full of various objects and materials. Different articles provide different foundations for the behaviour of the individual and his personality. The individual has to grow up either in healthy or unhealthy, clean or unclean, beautiful or ugly, peaceful or noisy, lawless or lawful surroundings and so on. These surroundings gradually make desirable or undesirable influences on the growing personality. Rural vs. urban areas make marked impressions in their own way. Different environmental pollutions create their own problems for the developing personality. There are numerous types of confusions in our environment which make adverse influences in shaping one's personality. Education has to supplement positive influences and to neutralise negative influences of the environment.

The individual's view of the world and society is largely dependent on the information provided to him by the people and education. They provide the normative information about right and wrong conduct, desirable and undesirable behaviour. The individual has to seek and develop positive personality traits through influences of various sources. One should be quite sure and sincere about his motives. He should hold fast to and defend what he believes to be right and reject what he believes to be wrong. The acquirement of scientific attitude is a step in the right direction.

Stratification in a society is another characteristic feature to mould the personality. Each stratum has free interactions with the members of that stratum and restrained interactions with the members belonging to the other strata. This is because there are different styles of life in different stratas of society with respect to education, manners, occupations, recreations, etc. Education has to be made effective and similar to ensure healthy development of the personality under all the variations created by different stratas.

In caste ridden society, the status is associated with the caste, while in the class based society, the status is achieved.

Our system of education must sufficiently convey the need for earning status not by birth but by achievement. This system will provide an open society by ensuring equal opportunities of education irrespective of caste or status.

Social stratification creates differences in the styles of living of the people. In an open society, due to equality of opportunity for all, it should be made possible for each individual to achieve the highest possible standard of living through his knowledge, skill, abilities and qualities. Education has to compensate for any deprivations suffered by a child due to any aspect of his background. The impact of education should be so strengthened that any wrong influences are decisively neutralised and positively replaced.

If education can focus strictly on the child, then this man of the future will come up to our expectations and will rise to the occasion in every way. One day this man will be at the helm of affairs in different capacities. But how far are we satisfied with the role of the man of the future? How is he making a mess of everything? How is he in need of so many dos and don'ts? How is he in need of so many laws and courts? How is he in need of a strong and massive police force to behave as a good citizen? And how is he in need of strict rules and regulations to keep his whims in check?

An educated man also sometimes gives a poor example of a law-abiding citizen. Why should he not become a master of his own behaviour and why should he need outside agencies to control his behaviour? He should be such a good judge of his behaviour that every action of his draws voluntary approval and commendation from society.

The development of human behaviour and personality is a collective responsibility of many agencies like home, society, education, religion, media, etc. It is not wrong to say that all these agencies make less or more contributions in spoiling human behaviour. It is wrong to assume a compromising and helpless attitude towards sub-standard human behaviour. Let us again turn to education and demand from it the development of a flawless human behaviour and personality. Education should provide a lifelong guarantee in the matters of human behaviour.

Doing wrong is a trend with many people. A big stock of human energy goes waste in the clash between those who do wrong and others who want to set them right. The people who try to defend society from wrong doers could do a lot of constructive work if they are spared from this wasteful clash. Most of the wrong doers can distinguish between right and wrong, but still they cannot get rid of the wrong done by them. Perhaps, they are accustomed to enjoy it. Many people may claim that it is a habit. But it is an insult to the calibre of a man if he is a helpless slave to his bad habits. An average man is duty-bound and competent to remain on the right side of habits. There is no dearth of good habits. One's lifetime is too short a period to imbibe all of them. Inculcating good habits has become a big challenge in the development of an individual and his personality.

It is sad when we find a large number of learned people, philosophers, littérateurs and wise men displaying bad habits. Some of these bad habits are smoking, drinking, gambling, maintaining illicit relations, losing one's temper, nurturing jealousy, and following unhealthy daily routines.

Psychology has found the causes of bad habits and suggested suitable remedies. But human beings continue to suffer from bad habits. It is wrong to believe that habits die hard. The human being is himself the originator of all habits – good or bad. It should be his privilege to select habits for himself. It is the duty of education to help him acquire good habits and reject or get rid of bad habits.

Education has to convince everybody to become an attractive personality in which socially desirable traits predominate. The traits being developed should be a matter of pride throughout one's life. Some of the desirable personality traits are: health, cheerfulness, courage, self-confidence, calmness, enthusiasm, self-assertion, sense of humour, sympathy, unselfishness, etc. Rather, we can categorise them as physical traits, intellectual traits, emotional traits, social traits, volitional traits and moral traits.

Personality is the sum total of physical, mental, emotional, social and temperamental make-up of the individual. It is the essence of the person's instincts, feelings, emotions, sentiments, thoughts, ideals, attitudes, aptitudes, intelligence, experiences, habits, perception, memory, imagination, etc. Some of its characteristics can be listed as self-consciousness, uniqueness, sociality, adjustability, goal-directedness, unity and integrability, consistency, persistence, dynamic, flexible, etc. According to another classification, there are three types of personalities; i.e., men of feeling, men of action and men of thought. The process of education has to be so rich and varied that it covers all the aspects of personality development.

Education has to harness both the hereditary and environmental factors to play their part in the development of a personality. The hereditary factors are physique, intelligence, sex, nervous system, chemical organisation, etc. Environmental factors are: geographical environment, family, early childhood, neighourhood, friends, educational institution, media, religious places, etc.

A healthy personality exhibits acceptance of feelings, self-esteem, living fully in the present, continuity in learning, openness to new ideas, ability to make independent decisions, creativity, realistic goals, consistency with age and abilities, acceptance of responsibility, expression of appropriate emotions, ability to have good relations with others, etc.

Self-actualisation is a central theme. It stands for the human being's tendency to fulfil his potential, particularly with regard to higher and positive needs and motives. While describing the hierarchy of human needs we can arrange a range such as physiological needs, safety needs, belongingness and the need for love, esteem needs, and the needs for self-actualisation. The individual is destined to deal with higher needs and his life cannot be dominated by hunger or thirst alone. If all the needs have been adequately satisfied, the person can aspire to become one of the rarest people who ultimately get self-actualised.

Self-actualising people are gifted with qualities like truth, goodness, beauty, justice and perfection. They demonstrate an acceptance of themselves, of others and of nature in general. They derive great inspiration and ecstasy from the basic experiences of everyday life. They tend to identify themselves with the entire mankind. They get wise enough to free themselves from any negative characteristics associated with men.

Exemplary personalities are very rare to find. There is need to carry out thorough psychological and educational research to formulate an unfailing procedure for the development of personality. There can be a specific programme focussing on this as a part of overall activities in an educational institution. In the case of every child, there should be a progress report based on personality assessment from time to time. Educational institutions should not continue to turn out poor and sub-standard personalities. It is their duty to provide to society, individuals rich in requisite qualities. There should be no laxity in providing necessary resources to educational institutions needed for the development of a personality. This development should not be sacrificed or ignored in view of greater attention to academic work. A qualified person must also be a meritorious personality.

*****

III
EDUCATIONAL INSTITUTION

Fourteen

Educational Institution

An educational institution will be a specimen of care which we reserve for our new generation. Maybe, it is not as majestic in its neighbourhood, but it should look magnificent. Its layout should represent all the factors outlined in educational literature. Its campus should make maximum possible contribution towards the healthy growth of the students. It should present an attractive, invigourating and inspiring atmosphere. There should not be any ugly or depressing spot in any corner. We have advocated many high sounding principles for the campuses of educational institutions. They should be strictly observed in letter and spirit.

Educational institutions are regarded by some as temples of learning. It is a temple of thought, reason, knowledge, wisdom and faith. The educational institution offers a bright face, a well planned set-up, a dedicated work culture, an inspiring philosophy, a recordable history, a sound discipline and an ideal society.

The look of such institutions should invoke attraction and admiration among its students. Its neatness, beauty and upkeep could be cited as an example in the area. Its design and layout should be such that it is never noisy even if all the classes are out during recess.

Let us find out the colour/shade which is pleasant to the eyes and minds of the young students and paint our institutions accordingly. The students should be given the

Educational Institution

chance of growing plants and displaying decorations for their institution.

Some educational institutions try to impress people by the hugeness of their structures. The elegance matters more than the hugeness. The concept of big institutions should be replaced by the concept of great institutions. The spirit or soul is more important than the size. An educational institution should be a symbol of plenty, as well as austerity. Its set-up should be simple but rich and complete.

Every educational institution must shape its marvellous history with every passing year. It must develop many special things about itself. Institutions have got only the examination results as the one thing to boast about and display on its honour boards. Let us find out and frame some more yardsticks for publicising our worth. Every institution should have something new and different to mention about itself, such as games, other co-curricular activities, local and inter-school competitions, social service, mentionable incidents, and professional growth of teachers. The institution should have not only one but many honour boards.

An educational institution adopts a motto, which should be made a meaningful and valuable emblem for everybody connected with it. It also decorates its walls with many mottoes. Every member of the institution should be enabled to grasp and imbibe the spirit behind the motto or mottoes.

Sometimes, an institution attaches a great name with its own name. It should rightly prove to be a worthy monument to that great memory. A great name and poor achievements do not go together.

An educational institution has to function as an agency of agencies. It has to perform many functions like imparting knowledge and skills, looking after health and hygiene, mental and emotional training, character formation, personality development, community life, value education, vocational education, and preparation for a quality life. It has to continually reform and modernise society in view of the advances in knowledge, and scientific and technological development.

It is the duty of every educational institution to develop into a modern, progressive and futuristic agency. The distinctive features of a modern educational institution can be framed and revised in the light of new experiences. Some of the mandatory features can be the importance of the learner's personality, the individualisation of education, activity-centred education, role of the institution as a centre for community life, and emphasis on constructive and creative activities.

An effective educational institution is to be judged in terms of its professional leadership, shared vision and goals, positive reinforcements, monitoring results and progress. There are many innovations which are needed in it, such as special stress on mathematics and science teaching, programmed learning, personalised system of instruction, subject laboratories, micro teaching and interaction analysis, mastery learning, co-related teaching, brain storming and special interest clubs.

As life becomes complex, the functions of an educational institution also multiply. It maintains the continuity of social life by transmitting the customs, traditions, values and experiences of the society to every new generation. It imparts knowledge about civilisation and culture and plays its own role in enriching the two. It promotes nationalism and internationalism among its students. It prepares them to play an effective role against problems like pollution, antisocial elements, crime, drug addiction, social and political tensions, corruption and injustice. It develops the qualities of leadership among its students so that they can provide better directions and goals to society. Through its curriculum and other activities, the educational institution emphasises the need for social change and activates the new generation for this change.

By its magazine, the educational institution will disseminate its suggestions and programmes for the betterment of individual and social life. The parents will be invited to the functions of the institution. The institution will also join community functions and carry out necessary social service programmes. The sports meet of the institution will also be an opportunity for the institution and the community to come closer. The institution will provide guidance and counselling in maladjusted cases and will also seek the cooperation of parents and community for the purpose. Through educational seminars and seminars on social issues, the institution will establish a relationship of mutual benefit with the community. The visiting teacher will visit the homes of students who need special attention, care and advice for their development.

The governing bodies and advisory bodies of the educational institutions will share their views with the teachers and administrators to ensure better and more effective services from them for the society. With the cooperation of the society, they will equip the institutions with the best of facilities.

When some people talk of de-schooling, there is no need to feel alarmed. For the education and development of the future generations, there can be no substitute for the educational institution. We cannot think of any better alternative and we are not likely to devise any better alternative in the times to come.

According to UNESCO, "Schools may, and generally do represent the best elements in the surrounding culture. They should be and they generally are, above the average level of the community in their regard for truth, honesty and fair dealing. They contrive to raise appreciably the standards and values of people."

An educational institution has also to study the community around. It has to try to become a centre for the community. It will devise some such programmes for itself so that it becomes worthwhile as a centre. Its programmes for the community should be indirectly educable to the adults, giving them some better techniques in the vocations, suggesting to them some avenues for their economic development, giving them some hints to make their family and community life more pleasant, presenting to them some images of their history and culture, giving some guidance for all-round social uplift, showing to them some glimpses of an ideal community life, preparing them for a better role in social, religious and political fields and inspiring them for better work habits, progress, modernisation and qualitative existence.

The school takes the central position to get the cooperation of other agencies like family, community, state and the media.

Harold Rugg says, "There is no royal road into the new epoch, at the crossroads before which we now stand, there is only the hard way of education... In this process the school can and must provide leadership. Through the study of society and its problems the school must devote itself to the development of sensitive, clear-headed, fearless and confident young men and women ... ."

John Dewey has said, "The controlling aim of the school was not the aim of present progressive education. It was to discover and apply the principles that govern all human development that is truly educative, to utilize the methods by which mankind has collectively and progressively advanced in skill, understanding and associated life."

The chief objective of the school is to secure a free and informal community life in which each child will feel that he has a share and has his own duties to perform.

The educational institutions have to satisfy the rules for the safety of the student population. Their buildings and structures must be safe from floods, fire, lightning and earthquakes, as far as possible. Their campuses should have a healthy atmosphere in the form of flowers, plants and trees.

The educational institution is intermediate between the family and other larger social organisations. It must therefore, grow out of one and lead up to the other. It has to be active and progressive in all the required aspects and dimensions.

Neil Postman has said, " My faith is that school will endure since no one has invented a better way to introduce the young to the world of learning, that public school will endure since no one has invented a better way to create a public."

The equipment of an educational institution should not be judged in terms of physical facilities alone, but more so in terms of mental, moral and emotional facilities. Mental facilities are to be provided in the form of periodical testing, a well-stocked library, testing of intelligence and aptitudes, honour board, prizes for outstanding academic performances, creative and constructive activities and academic competitions. Moral facilities can be provided in the form of debates and other competitions on moral issues, recognitions and record of moral behaviour, celebration of occasions providing moral lessons and display of mottoes and other sayings. Emotional facilities can be given in the form of playgrounds, outdoor and indoor games and cultural programmes.

The educational institution has to fulfil many functions towards the education and development of its students such as development of mental faculties, cultivation of a dynamic and adaptable mind, preservation, transmission of culture, vocational and technical education, organisation and re-construction of experiences, development of citizenship, development of character, all-round development of personality, development of aesthetic and creative faculties, discovering and sharpening capabilities thereby inculcating some exceptional goals in life, preparation and guidance for some rare contributions, provision and guidance for job-oriented courses, and preparation for a balanced and fruitful existence.

*****

Fifteen

Education and Student

Education is both a birthright and responsibility of a student. He is the representative of education and all its possibilities. Education has to inspire him to struggle for perfection. He is to be made to understand that education is his top priority. He will be the centre of all educational efforts in the true sense. Today education revolves around him and he has to be well prepared for tomorrow when life will revolve around him. He is the hope of the future and he has to be so educated that he does not belie our hopes. He has to be taken care of and developed as the most valuable asset. By his excellence, intellectual contribution and service to society, he must be able to prove that education is a supreme force.

Every student must get our special attention during his education. Not a single child should get neglected in the matter of development and education. We have to look towards every student as a promising individual for the future. We must notice the items of appreciation about him and express this appreciation through our eyes, words, gestures and reactions. Every student must be made to feel that teachers are deeply concerned about him.

The student must be convinced that he is duty-bound to learn for himself and for humanity. For a good number of years, learning is his main activity. He must devote himself to do full justice to his learning programmes. There is no possibility of running away from learning.

To be tender is a young student's privilege, which must be recognised and protected, but it cannot be taken as an excuse from shouldering small and big responsibilities. The young student is dependant today, but he has to learn to be self-dependant as early as possible and dependable for others. The innocence of the child should not be ignored, but it should be channelised with sweet procedures towards maturity.

Hard work is a blessing and there is no justification in postponing this blessing for the child. His small attempts should be appreciated for prompting him to do more. We should, as often as possible, give him words of encouragement. We should never look down upon him for his innocent mistakes. Rather, we should give him a chance to correct his mistakes on his own.

Even if a young student is loaded with a heavy bag, he must be made to feel that every item of his load is indispensable in the programme of his education. He is not less capable to carry it, handle it and avail it. His school bag is an ordinary challenge for him. He is to prepare himself for heavier challenges. Our reactions to his performances should always be positive to convince him that he can perform better and should do it still better next time. When he solves problems step by step, we should watch and ensure that he makes the best use of self effort. If necessary, he should be indirectly guided to overcome his difficulties. His difficulties should not be allowed to accumulate. His self-confidence is very important, and it should always be strengthened.

The physical, mental and emotional health of a learner should be an important concern of the teachers and educational institutions. A child's health has to be watched, assessed and improved throughout his stay in the institution. He should get sufficient opportunities for the sublimation of his instincts and development of his abilities to adjust even in the most difficult situations. He will be given physical and mental exercise through various sports and other co-curricular activities. There should be no loopholes in the development of his habit and in his character building. It should be ensured that during his stay at the educational institution, he is able to gain health, interest, intellect, creativity, qualities of personality and vocational and social competence. His personality must have gained sufficient plus points to remain admirable in different aspects of life. He must have obtained all the possible benefits from education.

Special attention should be paid towards the learning of fundamentals. The basic concepts should be made clear and should settle firmly in his mind. He should go through a variety of experiences and practices about the basic items of learning.

The student should be helped to develop a love for learning. He should try to become an untiring and visionary learner. He should regard learning as his foremost engagement. He should be able to learn with the best of energy, intellect, dedication and commitment at his command. He should be able to face the challenges of learning with determination, and should be able to seek help for removing his difficulties from all the availabele resources and should not shirk away from his goals. He should never exhibit half-heartedness in learning. He should be able to thoroughly understand whatever he learns. He will set his eyes on the optimum heights in scholarship and excellence. He will strive for wisdom through knowledge.

He will be a strict disciplinarian for himself for maintaining high traditions in learning. He will understand that he learns for his own benefit, for the betterment of environment, for the growth of society and for the welfare of humanity. He will pick up virtues and discard vices by his discriminating capabilities while learning his lessons. He will try to grow into a unique, ideal and admirable individual.

It is understood that education will prepare its students for simple living and high thinking and will protect them from wasteful luxuries and dirty ideas.

There is need to discover and record the capabilities of every student. We must start and work with the belief that every child is capable of doing something great in life. If his special capability remains unknown, it is our fault. We should watch and study him carefully and arrive at a scientific prediction about him. Then he has to be guided and encouraged to make that prediction a reality. It is possible for a grown up student to discover himself and strive for achievement in his favourite direction.

Some of the students are by nature serious in their studies. Their possibilities for special achievements should be noticed and harnessed. Their seriousness should not be allowed to go waste. They have to be guided towards excellence. They should be reminded again and again that they have to work for higher goals in education and life.

There are some students who show exceptional interest in one or two subjects and are only average in other subjects. They should not be distracted from their exceptional interest for the sake of equal achievement in the remaining subjects. Their exceptional talent deserves special attention. There is nothing wrong in one's exceptional achievement in a subject or two and remaining average in other subjects.

Some students are found to be less careful by nature. They must clearly be told that they are in no way less competent than others. Their carelessness should not be magnified and blamed. Perhaps, they do not appreciate the real worth of carefulness as yet, so the teacher will have to handle them tactfully. He will affectionately tell them that they are no less competent. They are destined to make their life worthwhile and for that they have to be careful in right earnest.

Some of the students do not get a congenial atmosphere at home for their studies. The teachers should not ignore this situation and should get it improved by holding meetings with the parents.

There may still be some students who do not show progress in spite of all efforts on our part. There is no justification in getting disgusted with them. They should be shown extra concern and care so that they do not turn out to be hopeless cases. The teachers must handle their students with the determination that there will be no failures.

The student should not be regarded only as the learner of a few subjects and a candidate for an examination. His subjects and syllabi are only a medium towards an all-round development. He has to equip himself for life to such an extent that he does not fail to tackle any situation or complication. He should be provided with a broader view of life and its aspects and educated as a student of life.

There are some children who are physically crippled and mentally handicapped. If the government, society and family pay adequate attention towards the health of children, the number of such physically challenged cases will be very small. It will not be difficult to provide special care, upbringing and education to them so that they are able to stand on their own feet and do not remain a lifelong burden on the family, society or government. It is the duty of the family, education, society and government that every child howsoever physically or mentally challenged is developed and enabled to take care of himself or herself. We should be left with only a negligible number which can be taken care of in special homes.

There is nothing wrong in making young students aware of the social and economic problems of life. They should get determined to make their life better in every way from that of their predecessors. They should be made to start life with a resolve that they would control the vices in society and lay foundations for new hopes. When the previous generations have made them prosperous in many ways, they should take over with higher motives and expectations in mind. They should make the best use of their inheritance and make it more bountiful. They should be made to decide that they have to make some new beginnings in order to remove the dark spots.

The events in society which pinch every right thinking person have no reason to persist. Vices have to be uprooted so decisively that they do not reappear. Crime is one obnoxious black spot which must be taken as a challenge and be eliminated once and for all. Let us ask ourselves these questions. Why should crime persist in spite of numerous law-enforcing agencies? Why can't the concept of crime be removed completely from the human mind? Students should be enabled to become responsible, to develop clarity in the mind and necessary willpower to pursue that clarity, to become confident problem-solvers and motivated risk-takers to meet the various challenges of life.

As the student grows physically, intellectually and emotionally, he should be enabled to develop self-knowledge, self-control and self-realisation. By his maturity, he should be able to exercise intelligent control over the situations around him.

Unrest among various segments of society has become a very common phenomenon. Student unrest is an offshoot of this general unrest. Some of the causes of student unrest are: unrest in society, in the labour class, among unemployed people, improper socialisation, family problems, inequalities, uninspiring educational system, corrupt and discredited authority, misuse of student force by the politicians, administrative lethargy in meeting the needs of the students well in time, communication gap, conflict of values, lack of opportunities for development, gap between aspirations and achievement, lack of determination to succeed in education and life, atmosphere of irresponsibility, negative influence of movies and media, etc.

Students should be enabled to develop self-discipline. They should be convinced to use their maximum time and effort for their main activity of learning. They should be made wise enough not to indulge in student agitations to escape from their main activity. There may be many justifications for student unrest. But there is a very strong justification for creating and maintaining a peaceful and constructive atmosphere in educational institutions. For the students, this period of life is meant primarily for education and they should not allow anything to interfere in their quest for knowledge. The wrong notion that the two generations of young and old are in any way in conflict with each other should be uprooted from the minds of the young students. There should always be a cordial relationship and communication between the students and teachers. The student community should not allow itself to be exploited by the often not so sincere politicians. Even when many wings of society are victims of unrest, educational institutions should be visible exceptions.

When an educational institution has convincingly transformed, uplifted and educated him, an ex-student may feel tempted to revisit it as a pilgrimage site. He should often be able to recall many happy, sweet and enlightening memories of his stay in that institution.

Every student is duty-bound to secure for himself an all-round development. He should by his educational record be able to get an encouraging placement in a vocation and life. He must have understood that learning is a lifelong mission for him. He should be determined to gain enough credits in education and in life. He must become a firm believer in mentionable successes in his life. He must always remember that he has to make some outstanding contribution to the welfare of humanity. For significant and creditable performance, he should continue his pursuit for learning and excellence throughout life.

He should always remember that he has been recognised as the most valuable asset and provided development and education for maturing as that asset, therefore, he has to prove himself as an asset in every way. He should know that he has to repay the debt by giving many times more to the society than what he received.

He should not be allowed to leave his education halfway. He must get the highest possible education in accordance to his capabilities. His teachers, the educational institutions, his family and he himself should feel satisfied with his level and type of education. He must have discovered the area/areas for his lifelong education.

He must be given quality education of every type and prepared for a qualitative life. He has to uphold this quality in his individual and social life. Even if his education remains below the criteria of quality, he should try to make up for the deficiency by his hard labour and self-study. Hard labour should become a trait in him in learning and in relevant activities of life.

The measurement of a student's abilities is a precondition for good education. The educational institution should maintain a complete record of his physical and mental growth. A complete knowledge of him is helpful in his learning, adjustment, achievement, guidance and choice of academic and vocational courses. None of his potentialities, possibilities and difficulties should go unnoticed. The record of his behaviour provides a guideline for the development of his personality. As we want him to make the best use of his educational opportunities, we must measure the level of his intelligence, his aptitudes, his interests and attitudes.

The student of today suffers from unrest. He revolts against his uncertain future, the system of education, strict control, poor facilities and infrastructure, hard system of examination, rising cost of education, poor quality of teaching, and teachers with low calibre of leadership. The media have also added many factors to student unrest. Educational administrators should be able to show foresight and psychological ability to handle such unrest among students.

Quite a large number of students come from families which indulge in antisocial activities like corruption, bribery and adulteration. Such children are likely to take part in acts of indiscipline. They have to be understood and shown sympathy for self-improvement.

Quite often, the student body feels agitated. Their grievances are often exaggerated by political forces and vested interests. The youth have to be convinced not to waste their time and energies on less important issues but to devote themselves to their main task of learning.

*****

Sixteen

Education and Teacher

Teachers will always occupy the central position in any programme of education. They must deserve and match this position. A teacher is morally responsible to see that education attains its aims and objectives.

Only extraordinary workaholics, affectionate, studious, seekers of knowledge, and persons with all-round personalities should come forward to become teachers. A teacher is required to be an embodiment of wisdom, health, stability, qualities, inspiration, dedication and creativity.

The teacher should be creative enough to explore new avenues of his work, approach his subject from fresh angles and discover hidden layers in its meaning. His creativity should have no bounds and no terminus. He should be able to generate new currents of thought among his learners. He reflects and recycles the old knowledge with a new magic. New ideas will fill him with new competence, direct him to explore new directions and enrich his confidence.

In fact, a teacher must be a mental hygienist, a philosopher, a moralist, a guide and much more for his students. He will be expected to perform the role of an organiser of curricula, innovator of educational ideas and practices, writer of radio and television lessons, a resource person in the transmission of ever expanding knowledge, expert in the preparation of programmed tests and motivator of learners in creative and unconventional ways.

He would be lucky if he can notice sparks in the eyes of his students.

He should be a leader who is willingly followed and obeyed by the students. He should not assume leadership just by virtue of his position. Under his control, discipline among students should be spontaneous. There should be no need on his part to use harsh language, warnings and threats. He should be a forceful speaker with his soft spoken style.

There will never be an opportunity of clash or conflict between him and his students. He will wield all powers but without giving any indication of doing so. The students will enjoy their submissiveness towards him. There will be no place for misbehaviour among students under his charge. He will never be required to scold a student. He will look to them as flowers with different colours and fragrances. He will be extremely happy in their company and they will automatically be happy. He will deal with them with the confidence that each one of them will develop into a unique personality one day and he will be proud of them all.

There should be a perfect equation and understanding between a teacher and his students. They will be truly faithful to one another. There is no cause for them to turn away in different directions.

The teacher will adopt a sound philosophy of life. He will be known as a man of principles. His exemplary conduct will be reflected in his ideas and actions. He can be a fountainhead only if he possesses inexhaustible qualities. He should be a symbol of qualitative life, thinking, conduct and contribution to society. He will earn respect among his students and society by virtue of his qualities of head, heart and hand. He will not demand respect as a matter of right.

There are no shortcuts to good teaching and similarly, there cannot be a conclusive list of qualities of a good teacher. It is generally said that a mediocre teacher talks, a good teacher explains, a superior teacher demonstrates and a great teacher inspires. The teacher has to be a hard task master for himself while performing his duties. He should not think that his job ends within the four walls of the school. He should exercise an influence on the social environment through his conduct. He should keep a watch on the society which is now constituted by a good number of his old students. If his old students do not carry out their duties towards life and society, he should now rethink as to how he can better mould his present students so that they come up to the mark when their turn comes.

The success of the educational process is ultimately the responsibility of the teacher. If he finds any bottlenecks, it is for him to work out the remedies. He should not feel satisfied by blaming any other agencies for the failure of education. He has to take his job as a mission and with full responsibility.

A teacher should not be at fault in any way in the discharge of his duties. There should not be any complaint against him from any quarter. His reputation and dedication should be well known to everybody. He must be gifted with fundamental qualities like truth, honesty, kindness, compassion, fairness and nobility. He is to constantly improve his image. He will not think or do anything which brings disgrace to him or to his profession. He will try to serve the cause of education to the utmost of his ability and capacity.

Being a person of high calibre the teacher will engage in hobbies which are creative in nature. He should be in a position to write for general welfare, progress and peaceful atmosphere. He should be able to fearlessly condemn evil.

As the teacher is responsible for the development of the personalities of students, he will be in a better position to fulfil this responsibility, if he continues to develop his own personality.

In addition to his regular teaching duties, the teacher of higher and professional classes has the responsibility towards research and experimentation. He should centre his attention on problems of education, learning, development and adjustment. He must take it as a duty to focus on a problem and try to find some solution. The solution thus arrived at may be put into application and revised or improved in the light of new findings. The problems of this most important field should not be allowed to linger on.

The qualified and trained teacher is not qualified and trained for all times to come. The curriculum, textbooks and techniques of teaching are undergoing frequent changes and the teacher must get himself acquainted with them to update his competence. In order to become a better and a still better teacher, he must remain a student of in service education for all times. There are a number of facilities which are available for his professional growth such as seminars, refresher courses, workshops, conferences, study groups, professional literature, visits organised to experimental and outstanding institutions, correspondence courses, educational tours, extension lectures, radio broadcast, TV programmes, film shows, exhibitions, open university, distance education and exchange programmes for teachers.

There should be re-orientation of one's knowledge and methodology from time to time. The teacher's misconceptions and doubts must be urgently removed. Whenever a new concept is introduced, its learning by the existing teachers may be made mandatory. The teachers of in service institutions should also be made to attend refresher courses for their professional upkeep and growth.

There is need for a vast network and coordinated programme of in service education for teachers, which should be organised by universities, colleges of education, in service training institutions and teacher's organisations.

Teachers should love their work, love their students, acquire and continue to update immense knowledge. The teacher has to present himself as a symbol of virtues and should be able to place before the students lofty ideals. His duty for professional growth demands action research on his part. He should be able to pinpoint his own pedagogic problems, and carry out studies to find out their scientific solutions. He should welcome such an opportunity for constructive imagination and ingenuity. By remaining a student, the teacher will continue to grow throughout his life. He should be able to give some new ideas to his co-workers by virtue of his study and research findings.

A teacher cannot claim and enjoy privacy in his personal life. He must not be a man of bad habits and bad character. It is below his professional status if he smokes, drinks or gets addicted to any drug. He must not have converted his home into a broken home. He must not be partial and corrupt. He must be a good friend and should be able to keep good relations with his acquaintances and near and dear ones.

His students must often remember him with a sense of reverence and gratitude. It may be a delight for them to quote their teacher/teachers. Their students, parents of their students, the community and the country should be proud of them. They may be given opportunities, incentives and recognition for their research, innovations and creative work. The society and the government should initiate different types of teacher welfare schemes. The would-be-teachers, before their selection, should be made to realise that their profession involves more sacrifices than rewards.

Any system of education cannot rise above the level of its teachers. Teachers should engage themselves in the pursuit of excellence and they should start enjoying their professional work.

A teacher's indifference to the problems of schools is self-defeating. Teachers must realise that the very nature of the task of transmitting knowledge and thinking skills requires continuous search for better techniques. They should try to become teachers cum scholars. Their profession requires them to be continuing scholars of their subjects and of the processes of education.

A good teacher must develop a love for books. Reading something new must be a regular habit for him. A huge volume of literature is available on every item of interest. It will not be difficult for him to make a right choice. The study of relevant literature can certainly make him a great teacher, if he makes it a lifelong habit.

It is equally important for him to participate in co-curricular activities side by side with his teaching duties. He should also take part in the social functions of the society around him. It will help him to develop good relations with the community and will bring the community and educational institution closer.

The primary purpose of a teacher's organisation is to help teachers and watch their service interests. But these organisations must broaden their activities for the welfare of the society also. They should make people aware for creating a better society for themselves by creating good socio-economic conditions, and by fighting against exploitation, injustice, antisocial elements, corruption, crime and wastage of resources.

Parent teacher association is another important forum for his activities. This association develops between educators and the general public such united efforts as will secure for every child the highest advantages in physical, mental, social and moral education. It can undertake a number of projects: (a) inviting educational and vocational guidance experts (b) arranging expert talks on current issues of importance (c) inviting artists to perform in the institutions (d) providing encouragement and financial help to talented and needy students and (e) organising book banks and book fairs.

The teacher by his learning, experience and wisdom becomes a dependable source of guidance and advice not only for his students but also for the members of his community. He must also carry out self-evaluation. He should not feel satisfied only by the good results of his students. He should judge his success from the way his students are conducting themselves in life and the way they are enriching their life. He should be able to count some of his students who are now shining like jewels in society.

The headmaster or principal is a teacher first, and then an administrator. He should be able to claim expertise in both the duties. His subordinates should like to emulate his example as a teacher. He should be able to give good suggestions during staff meetings for the improvement of day to day classroom teaching. The teachers should willingly come to him for pedagogic advice.

Students are now being encouraged to be curious, explorative, critical and innovative instead of being mere passive receivers of knowledge. To make learning more effective, meaningful and efficient for students, it is important for the teacher to incorporate the use of self-learning as part of his teaching methodology. The self-learning method can take various forms, e.g., project work assignment, programmed learning, personalised student instruction, computer-assisted instruction, and laboratory techniques.

The research functions of the faculty are its distinguishing characteristic. The knowledge explosion of our times has added greatly to the significance of this function. Research and teaching sustain each other.

Extension activity is one more function of the teacher. Thus, programmes like the national service scheme, national adult education programme, programmes for flood relief, afforestation, celebration of important festivals, etc., provide opportunities to teachers and students to render useful service to the community. An important aspect of extension work relates to the linkage between institutions of higher education and schools. Extension work includes extramural lectures as well as popular writings. Consultancy may also be considered as a form of extension work. Every teacher should make it a habit to assess his own performance in terms of all the functions at the end of each year.

*****

Seventeenth

Methods of Education

There are a number of methods available for imparting education to young learners. We should make a choice suitable for the age of children and nature of the subject matter. The child of the future has to be developed into a self-educating lifelong learner. The methods which involve over dependence on the teacher need to be discarded or used sparingly. Some of these methods are lectures, deductive and synthesis. The teacher should prefer the use of methods like inductive, analysis, heuristic, project and laboratory depending upon his situation. He should minimise the use of lecturing in his day to day work.

For the nursery child or the child of primary classes, greater dependence needs to be placed on playground activities. The children may be enabled to sing, enact and recite the subject matter. The books meant for them should present the subject matter in the form of songs, poems, plays, anecdotes, games and activities. The knowledge should be imparted and presented in an attractive, colourful and enjoyable way. They may be given the maximum possible opportunity of observation and self-expression. There may be ample use of toys, models and pictures, which may combine play, observation and knowledge.

The grown up children may be given sufficient opportunity for practical work, discussion and expression.

By and by, we have to prepare the young learners for self-study. Cramming should be discarded by both processes of learning and examination. Children should be given maximum possible opportunities of finding, discovering, exploring or experimenting things for themselves. The teacher's main job should be to put activating questions to the children. They should provide answers to these questions with self-effort. The learner should no more remain a listener; he should be encouraged to become an active participant and discoverer in the process. The child should be given such assignments which necessitate vast and deep self-study. He must be motivated to depend on books other than the text book.

Practicals in sciences, craft work, project work, hobbies, fine arts and creative expression should be incorporated with greater frequency in our teaching.

There are a large number of devices which are suggested for making teaching interesting and effective, but the actual use of these devices is almost negligible. Their use must be made mandatory for the teachers. We talk of devices like learning through games, learning by doing, learning through observation, insightful learning, learning by experimentation, learning by thinking, and learning by discussion, but we have not been so far able to give them a practical shape.

Co-curricular activities of the children should be expanded beyond the limits of their school, area or state. There should be provision for their participation in the radio and television programmes relevant to education and culture. They should be given the opportunity for inter-school, inter-state and inter-country cultural programmes and competitions. Inter-state educational tours are quite common. We should expand this facility to introduce inter-country trips. There is much for them to see in the archaeological sites, museums, exhibitions, science cities, industrial fairs, big cities, countryside, historical and religious places.

It will be worthwhile for the experts of methodology to meet quite often and discuss the use of available methods, as well as to evolve better and more effective alternatives. There is an urgent need of modernisation of our methods of teaching. We should not remain satisfied with the traditional methods. We should continue our search for the methods which can capture the interest and attention of students, which can motivate them for new learning, make them active participants in the process of learning, improve the style of the teacher, eliminate the problem of classroom indiscipline and ensure understanding of the subject matter by students.

As the industrial age gradually evolves into the knowledge age, there has to be a corresponding change in our methodology. From survival learning, we need to move to creative learning and from cognitive skills to an exploration of the multiple intelligences that a human is endowed with.

There is news that some schools have introduced the use of laptops as the main source of learning mathematics. It is considered comfortable by the students. They think that with it they learn better. Learning is like playing a game, reducing the need for textbooks, notepads, and paper, and in some cases reducing the need of the school and teacher. If the teacher is there, he will not deliver lessons but will move around and pay individual attention. Let us wait and see when online teaching of subjects becomes more common.

Michael Oakeshott says that teaching can be achieved in countless ways including hinting, suggesting, urging, coaxing, encouraging, guiding, pointing out, conversing, instructing, informing, narrating, lecturing, demonstrating, exercising, testing, examining, criticising, correcting, tutoring, drilling, and so on.

*****

Eighteen

Education and Research

For the purpose of relating theory to practice, Dewey proposed a triadic relation of professional workers. Those working on the side of pure research have to clarify the nature of basic concepts like motivation and cognitive learning. Secondly, middle level educational theorists should be able to make the classroom itself a centre of inquiry for testing hypotheses. Thirdly, some classroom teachers, trained in observation and research skills should be partners in verifying and generating hypotheses.

Researchers trained in behavioural and social sciences should analyse the curricular, the administrative, economic and political problems in education. Those with psychological training would investigate the nature of motivation and learning and school activities. Those engaged in historical and philosophical enquiries would provide their own perspective and the design of the content of the school curriculum would be evolved jointly by academic scholars and educators. Again, there is a need to base the preparation of teachers on a well-grounded research.

The main distinguishing characteristics of productive research are: it contains an element of thinking ahead, it becomes effective by changing the problem, it enables the new problem to be solved by restating it in the light of established knowledge or explanation, and it appears when a new problem situation arises. The situation may be material, social or personal.

The research in education must focus its attention on fundamental issues which are still to be resolved. The most important questions are: Why has education not been effective enough in shaping and moulding human behaviour? Why is there a wide gap between the aims and accomplishments of education? How should education be re-planned and reshaped so that it can shape young men of desired capabilities and character? What type of education should be given in order to achieve a praiseworthy type of behaviour in the case of every individual? What should be the form of education to create dedication and work culture in the learner? What should be the stress in education to create a crime-free society? What type of new courses should be introduced to remove unemployment?

What are the different causes of certain failures in education and what should be the remedies? How should we eliminate the wastage of education? Why does an educated person not give a clear proof of his learning? How can education become a formidable force to structure the society and political set-up on right lines? In what way has education failed to produce ideal individuals for an ideal society and how it can be made successful in this respect? How should we upgrade aims and objectives, curricula, methods of teaching and various programmes in education?

How can education secure a bright future in every way for the next generation? How can we remove distractions in the way of quality education?

Which are the values and ideals paramount in education, which of them have been lost by us in our educational institutions and practices, and how can they be revived? Let us trace the parallels between the degeneration of education and society and how both should be re-oriented for better results.

What are the significant differences between a truly educated person and an everyday educated person? Why are individuals lagging far behind their goals and possibilities even after receiving exceptional qualifications?

What should be the inherent characteristics of quality education? How can we relate education to the needs, interests, aptitudes and aspirations of the individual?

Let us work out an ethic, as well as a code of conduct for every field and then have a regular follow-up of qualified people to know their status in this respect.

Let us see why our pious slogans written in every text and painted on the walls of every school fail to make any impact on the youth. Let us examine, to what extent the learner blatantly abuses these slogans in his future life? We have to go deep into the problem when we find a reasonably educated person turning out to be the opposite of what he should have cherished, that is, values, goals and qualities of life.

Is it possible to work simultaneously at the levels of education and society to develop a better generation? How can schools remain unaffected by the shortcomings of the society? How can we narrow the gap between educational institutions and the society in respect of qualitative behaviour? How can the society and educational institutions work in cooperation to develop good citizens?

There is need to investigate the formation and reform of human nature and to develop educational strategies to mould it as per the demands of the future. Ways and means should be evolved by which human nature can attain the heights expected. Let us investigate the causes of disinterest, indiscipline, unrest and maladjustment among students and then find out the possible remedies. The problem of aversion of students to education is very common. We have to discover and implement the ways and means to convert an indifferent learner into a devoted learner. Attempts can also be made to find some special techniques for creating interest in various topics.

The educational needs of the future are likely to become more vast and complex. The research worker has to anticipate those needs and provide requisites for the same well in time. There will always be a need for future-oriented and vision-oriented education.

Educational research has to focus its attention on practical solutions for the long standing problems. It should be relevant to our needs and circumstances. It should obtain feedback regularly. If the proposed solutions do not work as desired, the research should engage in the quest for better solutions. Research should be adopted as a constantly uplifting medium. It should be focused on the outcomes of education in respect of development of personality, solving the problems of life, establishing values in society, serving futuristic needs, improving the standards and quality of life, and contributing towards the progress of civilisation.

An educational research worker should develop a multi-dimensional competency to cover different aspects of life in relation to education. He may enlist the philosophical, social, sociological, economic and political issues before the society and then search for the role education can play to resolve those issues.

Education should be made research-based in every possible way. Its programmes should be planned, carried out and evaluated by scientific approach. There should be greater stress on action research so that education is better related with the existing and anticipated problems. Scientific investigations should be regularly employed to discover the weak points and the remedial programmes.

There is need for setting up educational institutions meant exclusively for research. They will be staffed by research guides and research scholars. They will focus their attention on the educational problems of their areas. They will provide workable and effective solutions to these problems so that after some time the number and magnitude of the problems becomes insignificant.

There is a demand for further research on the relation of studies to the mind in its various stages of development. The ultimate problem is to understand the processes in the evolution of mind and experience and to coordinate the psychological factors with socialisation and self-actualisation.

The revolution of knowledge is a critical factor for the survival and progress of modern societies. It is customary to confine research techniques to the sciences, humanities, agriculture, government and industry and to bypass the generative institution, education, on which others depended.

There is need to fix the accountability of teachers, administrators and supervisors. Through an investigation, we should evolve a comprehensive criterion to judge their proficiency. Mere examination results are not a fair index for evaluating this.

Apart from academic examinations, we should prepare some valid tools to measure the progress of the students. We should be able to give a comprehensive and reliable report in the school leaving certificate of a student.

Further investigations must be carried out with special cases also in the interest of their education. The slow learners, backward students and problematic cases are separate categories. The causes of their failure or incompetence may be found to adopt suitable remedies. Then there is the category of bright, gifted and creative students. Their most favourite areas may be discovered to give them the richest possible education in those directions.

It is wrong to accept the prevailing situation and agree to live with problems in education and in society. Our research must constantly work on the lines to create a problem-free system of education and a problem-free society.

It is wasteful to carry out research merely for the sake of research. Its findings should not be such that they remain buried in the pages of dissertations. Research is undertaken to solve problems and so it should live up to its claim.

*****

IV

EDUCATION AND LIFE

Nineteen

Education and Life

Education and life are complementary. Education is the highest purpose of life and life is a great source of experience and education. We often advocate life-centred education and education as a preparation for life. There may be many purposes of education, but the fullest possible life is the central purpose. Again, there may be many purposes of life, but getting the highest possible education is the most rewarding purpose of life. We have to bring the two so close to one another that each becomes the image of the other.

When we dedicate a part of our life to education, the remaining part of life draws immense dividends from it. Education enhances the worth and status of our life to a great extent. As we decide to pursue education alongside our work, our achievements, successes and contentments multiply.

Let us be very clear and honest to find out where we disused, misused or abused education in life. Education has taught us many good things which we have failed to apply. Education tries to bring freedom from vices, whereas in actual life we allow these vices to prevail. Even when we are acquainted with some notorious aspect of history, we are left with a moral or a lesson to learn from. Then why should notorious parts of history be allowed to repeat themselves?

Education warns us and cautions us against vices and tries to convince us to embrace virtues. Vices should have no place, at least in the lives of people claiming to be educated. Education will never betray us. On the other hand, if we bypass education we get betrayed. When we find an educated person committing a crime, it amounts to wastage of both, his education and life. Education has enabled every learner to distinguish between right and wrong and to pursue only the right path.

Through education we wish to promote life which should be worth living in every way. Not a single individual should ever get disgusted with life. It is wrong to describe life as a painful tragedy and a bed of thorns. We have to wish for a life that can be a happy experience and a bed of roses for everybody. Life cannot be completely free from its sorrows. But it should be so filled with pleasures that an occasional sorrow gets drowned in them. It should be so plentiful that an occasional shortage may seem only a passing phase. Though short-lived, the pleasures and joys of life can be widely available only if they are fairly distributed among all. In addition, there can be abundant happiness in life when people live for the happiness of others.

Education has to turn life into a blessing, which it rightly is. Let us accept education as the hope, and then it will steadily infiltrate into all other agencies and revive the hopes inherent in them.

Life is defined by some as a pilgrimage and as a rare opportunity towards salvation. Every step in life has numerous possibilities. Life is a reality with a vast scope for accomplishments. Every moment of life is priceless. Life has its own lessons to teach and its own experiences, which put a person on the path of wisdom and enlightenment. Every moment in life is therefore; to be lived with an open mind and awakened conscience that education rightly gives us.

Let us first analyse the pleasures of life which are available free of cost, and train the young minds to gather and share these pleasures. Then we may enlist the pleasures which demand some investment. Let us procure those pleasures for ourselves and share with others as much as we can spare. Most people are found to be sad for one reason or the other. Let it be everybody's mission to share and remove the sadness of others.

We should be prepared to earn the pleasures of life with hard labour. Let us think of every small achievement as a pleasure. Thus, we shall be able to enjoy countless pleasures. A single sadness should not be allowed to overwhelm this long list of small pleasures. We should rather avail the reverse of it as training. A single pleasure should be remembered and enjoyed even in the midst of many sad occasions. A single moment of sadness, howsoever severe, should not be allowed to become the remaining theme of one's life.

Education should be made so comprehensive that it provides training for all aspects of life: viz. personal life, family life, social life, vocational life, economic life, aesthetic life, missionary life, exemplary life and a successful life.

It is ultimately the quality of life, which is the concern of a quality education. Life should be developed as a pleasant journey. Individuals should learn to derive consolations even from its not-so-happy situations.

There should be a joint effort towards the establishment of grandeur in life. Resources should be pooled in a way for everybody to enjoy this grandeur. Life should not be allowed to become a luxury for a few and a burden for the rest. The possessive nature of human beings should be moulded towards common good. The few who happen to be fortunate should voluntarily share their fortune with the less fortunate ones. People should be convinced to follow simple living as a creed. Even if a few people can afford luxuries, they have no right towards them alone. People should observe a self-imposed ban on luxuries. We must understand that the luxury of a few is at the cost of the necessities for many and leads to a deprivation of those basic necessities for them.

Many people live aimless lives or they pursue some narrow aims in life. Education has to prepare people to adopt and follow some higher aims in life.

We should be in a position to draw a blueprint for art of living and be able to give it a practical shape. This art should specify our behaviour in all activities of life. The individual should continuously try to become a master of this art and reduce his digressions from it. This art of life provides many lessons, such as, conquering the angry man by love, the ill-natured by goodness, the miser with generosity, the liar with truth, etc. Mastering the mind, enhancing self-esteem, creating inner happiness, using the healing power of silence, and finding balance in a busy life will move a man towards living a happy and beautiful life.

Our education should be reflected in our standard and style of living. Our style of living should be simple, straightforward, and humanitarian. The art of living a righteous life is the most important and most difficult art to be learnt from education and life. An educated individual should not be faced with disgraceful situations and should live with dignity. It should be a pleasure and a thrilling experience for everybody who happens to meet him. His personality should appear down to earth, mature and respectable from every angle. He should be a stalwart who radiates innumerable positive influences to the persons who come in contact with him. As a near perfect individual, he should be a source of inspiration for many. Some people may raise a doubt about the possibility of every educated person to be a near perfect individual, but the near perfection stage should be a goal for everyone to achieve in the present advanced stage of education and civilisation. One should succeed in this aim to rise as an individual and in one's social life.

We may not include in our curriculum specific lessons for the art of living. Every verbal and practical experience in education should focus on the quality of life. There should be no leniency in respect of the art of living as demonstrated by schools or colleges.

It is a great wastage of education if any educated person turns out to be a disgraceful creature. It is wrong to say that an educated person cannot remain oblivious of the wretched aspects of the society to which he has to belong. We should not agree with the argument that an individual cannot remain good in a bad society. If the individuals decide to uphold their principles within the unprincipled society, they can definitely mould the society to their point of view. It is wrong to merge helplessly in the existing society and become part of the deterioration. Educated people must sit together and resolve not to accept the drawbacks of society as they are, but to make determined efforts to reform the situation. Every generation of educated people has a duty towards enhancing the quality of society they inherit.

Learning to live is the primary need of the learner. If this learning is not up to the mark, his many-sided learning does not ensure quality of life. There is need to reinstate the art and science of living. The material comforts of life are multiplying and thus creating a false impression about the rising standards of living. We should be able to distinguish between the standards of living and quality of life, which should be our ultimate aspiration. The quality of life should not be sacrificed for the sake of our standards of living.

Life is a great opportunity, great experiment, great challenge, very noble, grand and a royal journey. It is great not only for great men alone; it is great for every human being. Men become great when they do not miss the opportunities of life. Others miss this greatness as they miss the chances. Life is neither a bed of thorns, nor a bed of roses; it should be regarded as a stage for adventures, an arena for marvels, and a saga of continuous achievements. Education inspires us to live dynamically, productively, competently, morally and creatively. It imparts many aspects to the quality of life, some of which are: self-respect, self-expression, openness to one's feelings, self-exploration, responsibility for oneself, care for one's body, sympathetic understanding of other people, listening to other people, attentive, warm and active relationship with others.

It is not convincing enough when some people call this whole world and life an illusion. There are innumerable realities in the world and life which cannot be brushed aside. We should learn to understand and realise these realities. Whatever is taught and learnt should have relevance to the world and life. Even the basic or fundamental researches should be related to life and its needs. An educational thinker, philosopher, psychologist or research worker should always keep life as the point in focus. It is our duty to make life worth living for all and make it a story of satisfaction and happiness.

Excellence in education and later in life should be a natural criterion of a human being. Let us not try to make education very convenient for the child, as life itself is seldom convenient. Life is very tough and hence, education cannot be too soft.

We have yet to learn and understand a lot about the secrets, mysteries and purposes of life. Education is a dependable instrument to solve these riddles.

*****

Twenty

Lifelong Education

We are ever growing human beings in this ever changing world. Many fundamental questions will continue to bother us throughout our lives, calling for more complete answers. One is seldom satisfied with old explanations and the quest is bound to go on. The desire to achieve excellence in various areas of life continues to push us on. Life is an invitation to creativity, to do something new, to give a new idea, to find a new path and technique, to create a better society and to evolve a more effective system.

After a lifelong journey everybody tries to leave behind such memories, so that when anybody remembers him, his words pay tribute and homage to the departed soul. One's lifelong learning is a good testimony to make him a learned and respectable man.

An educated man is he, who by the age of twenty-five years has acquired a clear theory formed in the light of human experience down the ages of what constitutes a satisfying and significant life, and who by the age of thirty has a moral philosophy consonant with experience. In this way, he will continue to grow intellectually from one age to a higher age. Education has to be taken as a continuing, flowing and never-ending stream of thought and learning.

The individuals who are directly or indirectly concerned with knowledge should be more serious about the never-ending continuity of learning. Relevant literature should become their permanent companion. For example, professionals like doctors, engineers, lawyers, teachers, research workers, scientists and technicians cannot do justice to their professions in the absence of lifelong learning.

In many other fields, updating one's knowledge enhances one's efficiency and job satisfaction. Even a less educated farmer today will make his occupation more productive and remunerative, if he remains in touch with the latest developments in the field and takes the trouble to implement them.

Even an ordinary housewife can improve her cooking by acquainting herself with new recipes and new techniques. Similarly, a tailor has to keep himself abreast of the trends in fashion. Also, a concern can be managed more efficiently with the help of new theories and practices in line.

People must spare a part of their leisure time for gathering new information, for studying books and for broadening their vision. It will keep one's mental make up fresh, active and progressive.

There should be no retirement in life as far as learning is concerned. A retired person should continue to learn as a happy pastime, for promoting a hobby, for satisfying the thirst for knowledge, for being of use to society in some way and for breaking the loneliness and idleness of this part of life. There is no limit to the channels of new learning. One can adopt more than one channel at a time and can shift channels at his own pleasure. Everyone should always be in search of fresh air, as far as lifelong learning is concerned.

It will be a source of great satisfaction, if people come to an old person for professional and personal advice and guidance. One should try to become the source of information, advice and inspiration for others, as long as possible. It will keep him profitably busy and will provide escape from drudgery.

One cannot allow life to run on its traditional lines. Education should enable every learner to find an alternative to traditions not approved by him. One should never close one's mind to new ideas. One should renew and enhance his taste for newspapers and books. Without new learning one will become unaware of his surroundings. A person with renewed knowledge enjoys self-confidence, competency and respect.

As food, air and the like remain our lifelong requirements; education should be accepted as a similar lifelong necessity. After all, mental growth and expansion of knowledge do not have any age limits.

A lifelong education does not ensure mastery over even a very small area of knowledge. This is because knowledge is vast and the total life span of a man is too short to do some justice to even a specialised area.

There is no limit to acquiring qualifications for improving chances of promotion in our job when facilities of distance education are available from many sources. Distance education and in-service education should be readily available in every region and for every stream. It should be made efficient and universal through guidance, contact programmes and with the help of media and bridge courses. In fact, distance education can take the facility of lifelong education to the remotest of areas. It can be egalitarian, can be free from repressive actions, can even cater to the masses, and can be the most accessible and flexible form of teaching and learning. It is an offshoot of industrial civilisation and may raise mankind to higher levels of civilisation.

Lifelong education may become a basis for directing and expanding one's creativity. One can choose an area in which one would like to express oneself. This expression will become more satisfying and useful if one continues to expand his command in the area. It becomes a means of sharing one's learning with others. It enriches the area and provides an inspiration to others to continue to study and learn.

A man should be clear about his main purpose in life, so that he can focus his lifelong education on that purpose. An individual can plan numerous short-term and long-term purposes in life. These purposes make continuous education a necessity and a virtue.

Every single item of learning must turn out to be of immediate utility and a lifelong utility.

In order to provide part-time education to in-service or self-employed people, there should be widespread arrangement of correspondence courses, distance education, open schools, colleges and universities. All types of higher education, no less in quality as compared to regular courses should be made available to adhoc employees, contract employees, under employed people and people who are not financially in a position to pursue regular courses. Every type of distance education may be made available at international levels also. A deserving and keen learner may get opportunities of education for improving his contribution towards the quality and production at his job. The degrees and diplomas awarded through these correspondence courses should be treated at par with the regular ones.

R S Peters has said, "Education, then, can have no ends beyond itself. Its value derives from principles and standards implicit in it. To be educated is not to have arrived at a destination. It is to travel with a different view."

Life is an invitation to individual growth and achievement and to the creation of a society in which people have an optimum opportunity for fulfilment. These conditions demand a continuing programme of education. We are always confronted with problems that require a lot of intellectual power. The important and immediate task is the continuous development of this power.

*****

Twenty one

Education and Health

Education and health are two basic ingredients of the development of human personality. Healthy habits should be firmly fixed in the human behaviour. One should believe in self-imposed discipline and strictness in matters of health. Everybody should become a follower of a healthy routine in their daily life.

Education should play a major role in developing the physical, mental and emotional health of the individual. Educational institutions should satisfy themselves about the health and growth of students by holding check-ups periodically. They have a duty towards providing games, exercise and drill sessions for the students. Their target should be to improve the health of the people from generation to generation. The health department should be come to their help on it's own.

The first lessons for health have to be learnt from home in an informal way. The school has to impart systematic health education to young children. They should be initiated into healthy habits of day to day life, healthy diet and healthy food habits. They are already being taught subjects like Health and Hygiene, but the impact of this learning is far from satisfactory. Take the case of simple and routine activity of breathing. Its theoretical principles are seldom translated into reality. Most of us do not understand the benefits and secrets of healthy breathing.

Developing good habits for health must be taken as one of its prime responsibilities by the school. Everybody must be tempted to adopt activities like walking, exercise and yoga as a routine in life. We should aspire to develop such a healthy lifestyle so that every individual acquires immunity against diseases. Through the medium of education we should try to create a disease-free world.

In this age of advanced awareness related to healthy habits, people should not take delight in breaking the rules and guidelines. Good health must be understood as a basic need and responsibility and as a source of well-being and happiness. One should understand that maintaining one's health is one's own responsibility towards self, family, vocation and society. Due to sound health, the individual is able to enjoy agility, cheerfulness and longevity. An unhealthy individual becomes a liability and burden to others. Therefore, poor health is similar to a handicap.

George Bernard Shaw said, "All sorts of bodily diseases are produced by half-used minds." For good health, the development of a sound mind can play a significant role. The school should introduce activities to tone the body and the mind. It should provide a healthy environment in every way for the child to learn and grow. The individual has to be taught to look clean, tidy, smart and alert. He should be able to fully concentrate on any work in hand. He should not look inactive and be exhausted too often. Juvenile delinquency and drug addiction are very serious health issues for students. The school should be careful about these problems and in dealing with them. An abnormal behaviour from a psychological angle may also be caused due to a health problem. Any maladjustment on the part of the child should not go unnoticed and uncared for by the school authorities and teachers.

The student should not exhibit a sleepy behaviour. He should not feel weak after a short interval of work or study. He should be able to show interest and enthusiasm in the activities of life. The functions of his physical organs should be normal as per medical standards. He should be able to enjoy recreational activities and take active part in them. He must be made aware of all the signs of good health. The formulae of good health should be enlisted, imparted and confirmed in his mind. The child's mental health also, is to be watched regularly, and necessary guidance and remedies have to be provided without delay.

The school has to ensure clean and fresh air, safe water, proper sunlight and safety in classrooms and the playground for its students. There may be a regular check-up conducted for their cleanliness as well as diet. Any deficiency in their diet should be compensated through arrangements in the school. There should also be regular arrangement of providing, the facilities of disinfection, inoculation and vaccination to the students in school.

From time to time, the school may hold competitions among students in respect of their growth and strength. The studious among them should be especially watched to see that they do not harm their health by overworking themselves.

Health is one of the conditions for happiness. Physiology, hygiene, first aid and safety education contribute in their own way towards maintenance of health. A comprehensive knowledge of healthy habits and healthy attitudes is necessary for every child. If everyone follows the principles of health education, people can be happy, strong and energetic.

Health education consists of three phases; health instruction, health services and health supervision. Health instruction in school may include an elementary knowledge of diseases, the causes of diseases, the preventive methods and treatment, personal cleanliness, community hygiene, care of important organs of the body, diet and evil effects of intoxicants. Teachers must be able to recognise the signs and symptoms of childhood ailments so that necessary steps are taken in time. The health service programme consists of medical examination of the pupils, protection from communicable diseases, first aid services, and correction of postural defects and regular follow-ups. The physical education teacher should be able to detect cases which are to be referred to the doctor. Health supervision ensures the cleanliness and hygienic conditions of the school and playgrounds. This supervision includes food and eating, elimination of body wastes, exercise and play, sleep, rest and recreation, needs of the important organs, posture, diseases, accidents and injuries, emotional adjustments and sex education.

Safety education is also important in an educational institution. All the areas inside the school, sports material, and electric fittings should be safe. Fire extinguishers may be fixed at proper places. Laboratories and all equipments should be inspected periodically for the safety of students. First aid facilities and services of a physician should be available without delay.

*****

Twenty two

Education and Quality of Life

There are many factors which are a hindrance to the promotion of quality of life such as poverty, hunger, malnutrition, disease, disparities, exploitations, inadequate infrastructure, misdistribution of resources, ignorance, poor educational system, population explosion, environmental pollution, unemployment, crime, terrorism, global conflicts and tensions.

Take the case of education. Almost every national government has adopted the goal of compulsory education, but many countries have yet to reach this goal. It may be due to the lack of financial and other resources and indifference of the people.

The technological advancement, the growth in productivity and the accumulation of wealth in global terms have now evolved to the point where it becomes obligatory and possible to provide a reasonable standard of living for all people.

A minimum nutritional objective should ensure optimum physical and mental development. The next necessity is the provision of all the required health services to everyone. The objectives in terms of economic growth have not worked well. They often permit further concentration of wealth among the elite groups. We can no longer argue that there are not enough resources to provide a universal and reasonable standard of living.

There is a need to mobilise scientific knowledge and resources and more efficient technologies to attain a higher level of living at a much lower cost. Attaining a higher level of living with a low investment may be possible with the adoption of a development model discovered through scientific research.

When we count the many forms of global interdependence, we can certainly realise that quality of life depends on sharing of resources and cooperation among nations. As technology becomes progressively sophisticated, it becomes virtually impossible for any single country to conduct research in all areas. As the global economic activity is laying stress on the ecosystem, a new dimension of international cooperation to preserve the functioning of the ecosystem is called for. Even the security of our food supply is becoming dependent on international cooperation. Serious social evils are emerging which cannot be solved by individual countries acting unilaterally. For the rich countries also, growing addiction to hard drugs and the associated rise in crime greatly diminishes the quality of life.

In some situations, social disintegration is adversely affecting the quality of life. A socio-political factor which is very much influencing the quality of life in the world is political and racial repression.

There is need to change social ethics through education and other agencies. The new ethic encompasses a new naturalism which places greater emphasis on man's harmony with Nature and less on his dominance over it. The emerging global society needs to formulate a new child bearing ethic to neutralise population explosion.

The new ethic must seek to eliminate territorial discrimination in matters of development and prosperity. Super affluence in a part of the world with continuing abject poverty in another part is going to be considered as immoral. Governments, individuals, institutions and corporates are excessively growth-oriented but the attitudes, economic tools and policies for achieving a stable economy do not yet exist. The new ethic must broaden the scope of decision-making. Traditional loyalties to the nation must be expanded to include all of mankind.

The cost of maintaining the existing system of independent nation states is extremely high. If we want to save ourselves from this international wastage, we must create a global system of rules and laws binding on all the countries. More important is the control of huge wastages for the security of our borders.

A unified global society must now be regarded not as a fiction, but as the inevitable reality towards which we must move. Even a modest shift in resources from military budget to education, agriculture, health, industry and family planning could make a great difference in the efforts to improve living conditions.

Quality of life is only partly determined by the satisfaction of economic needs. Education of a high standard, good means of communication, social welfare organisations for different groups and facilities, free and expert health services, civic sense and civic amenities, a helpful and sympathetic social atmosphere, a system of justice and security, absence of crime, an effective political system and government, absence of irrational divisions and conflicts in the society, well managed units in the form of family, village, institutions, municipality and state are also necessary. Religion may also play its part by broadening the loyalties of the people.

In this advanced age, we want to achieve super quality in every item we produce. There is no doubt that these items of quality have been evolved by human thinking and practices, then why should we come across human beings of inferior quality at every step. Just as there is no finality in the matter of quality of human beings, a human being is capable of developing in himself innumerable qualities. Quite often, individuals want to live by and seek all the possible privileges by virtue of even one single quality possessed by them. He wants maximum credit for a minimum number of qualities. Possession of one or a few qualities does not release him from his duty to possess and master a large number of qualities. Larger the number of qualities possessed by him, higher will be the level of quality of his life.

There is no limit to the variety of good people – they can be players, singers, painters, carpenters, farmers, doctors, engineers, lawyers, teachers and intellectuals. Again there is no limit to the variety of bad people – they can be thieves, cheats, exploiters, gangsters, drug peddlers, rapists, murderers, war mongers, etc. The world and the society need the services of the individuals and not their disservices. A man can easily decide for himself, whether he would like to fall within the wanted category or unwanted category. The people of wanted category are examples of those who lead a quality life. We cannot expect a qualitative life among people in the other category.

For any society aspiring for high standards in the quality of life, it is imperative to believe in the following directions and put them to practice: there should be no politics without principles, no wealth without work, no commerce without morality, no education without wisdom, no pleasures at the cost of other's misery and no great achievements without sacrifice.

Education has become a tool to achieve a good lifestyle and not a bad lifestyle. It is sad that we have so much knowledge but so less implementation. Other agencies will also cooperate with education in its efforts towards enhancing the quality of life.

The nature of a qualitative life from vocation to vocation and from region to region will have to be described to highlight variations. There will be some uniformity for all but diversities have also to be made clear. It will not be out of place, if the educational institutions convey the lists of dos and don'ts to the outgoing student groups who are going to start life after that. For example, the quality of life of a doctor will incorporate things like: his ability to win the faith of his patients, his expertise in diagnosis, his keenness to develop his expertise through self-study and experience, to deal with every patient with patience, never to keep the patient in the dark about the nature of his illness, never to employ trial and error approach in the treatment of a patient, giving advice to the patient without delay to approach a more advanced centre of treatment if necessary, never to unnecessarily prolong the treatment of a patient, sparing some time for his family, never have making money as his sole concern, trying to give free treatment to the very poor people, etc. Similarly some of the signs of the quality of a farmer can be: keeping in touch with the latest innovations and techniques in agriculture, developing relations with more progressive farmers, bringing diversity in his profession for better returns, to keep funds in reserve to meet the crises like floods or drought, supporting his children for quality education, sparing time for relaxation and social gatherings, to avoid the use of harmful fertilizers and insecticides, accepting better alternatives for his techniques without delay, etc.

There should be absence of disgruntled elements in life. Everybody should get his due and there should be enough opportunities for everybody to rise and make progress. There should be no dearth of facilities and possibilities.

Qualitative life need not be measured only in terms of riches, etc. Life should remain simple in spite of the riches. Quality should be based more on sound values. Men should be free from wretched thoughts and actions. They should be noble in every way.

Nobody should have any complaint about his fate, circumstances and destiny. There should be peace, progress and prosperity for everybody.

Everybody should receive education up to his optimum level so that he understands the secrets, the charms, the possibilities and the limitations of life.

Life should become worth living not only because of its comforts but also because of its sweet challenges and day to day achievements. Everybody should be able to feel proud of his journey of life and should have something worth mentioning about his life. Everybody could be rated as a high achiever in education as well as in his vocation. It is not necessary that a large number of people remain low achievers or mediocre. Only a small fraction of our population should fall into this category.

Struggle will not be missing but every struggle will receive its well deserved rewards. Miseries will not completely disappear from life, but the sufferer will not be left alone to suffer. He will receive help and sympathy from so many quarters that this bounty of consolation will soon enable him to overcome his grief.

Families, colonies and townships, should enjoy internal and external harmony. Differences and disputes should not be allowed to persist. If still we find that some people continue to exhibit discordant behaviour, they should not be isolated. The sober majority in the society will reform them by persistent influence. In the long run, we have to create a society in which the misfits are in a very small minority.

People should not practice artificial and superficial relations with one another. They should believe in heartfelt relations. One should always seek opportunities when he can be of some use to others. One should devote oneself to some noble cause and should see that he makes some significant contribution towards that.

There shouldn't be too much need for the police, judiciary and jails to maintain law and order. Self-discipline should become a doctrine for life.

*****

Twenty three

Education and Simple Living

We often speak of the dictum, simple living and high thinking. But we seldom practice this in actual life. This preaching can be further extended to say that living in luxury and high thinking cannot go together. The dictum of simple living is not meant only for the deprived people.

Living in luxury is a sign of ignorance and is a sign of the poor impact of education. It is the duty of even the rich people to learn to lead a simple life. The resources overspent by them on wasteful things can be put to more productive use. It is in the interest of greater development and progress if affluent people decide to forego luxuries.

Luxurious living is the sign of lopsided thinking. It may be due to some inferiority complex, demonstration of ego, inherent hatred for the poor, denial of some demand in the early stages of life, diversion from some mental complexes, pride, undue self-assertion or some other maladjustment.

If a person can afford luxuries, he must remember that simple living will make him more respectable. Simple living is a social and moral duty of everyone. A life of luxury makes a person lazy, careless, selfish, haughty and shallow. A person's luxurious life is full of dangers and will spoil his next generation. One should try to select better means of exhibiting his status.

Luxury is not the privilege of anyone, howsoever rich he may be. It is a sign of absence of feelings for others. While indulging in luxury, one must remember that there are millions of people around who cannot satisfy even their basic needs. He must also understand that he is humiliating the less privileged by the exhibition of his wealth. Living a luxurious life is caused by an attitude of selfishness which should be smoothed out by the powerful impact of education. Simple living is the sign of enlightened personalities.

It is wrong to judge the socio-economic status of a person by counting the items of luxury possessed by him. We should try to evolve better yardsticks for determining the socio-economic status of individuals, families, communities or nations. Lust for luxuries is a poor demonstration of the spending capacity of individuals or groups.

Simple living and high thinking is a great lesson provided by our education, literature, history, religion and culture. With the expansion of knowledge, experience and wisdom we should make this lesson more meaningful and practical. Luxurious living of a few can cause inequalities, classes, clashes and conflicts in the society.

All around us we find people living a luxurious life in the form of five star hotels, luxury trains, luxury buses, luxury cars, palatial houses and shops, big government bungalows, costly decorations, costly furniture, costly domestic equipments, jewellery, diamonds, costly rings, costly watches, costly dresses, too many costly celebrations, wasteful expenditure on marriage ceremonies, and having a useless variety of costly food articles on our dining tables. We should learn to apply a self-imposed ban on luxuries.

Wealthy people are blessed to have inexcess wealth of what they need. Sometimes, they adopt a way of life and squander their wealth on a variety of pleasures some of which are objectionable. Some of them are misers. That is also a wrong attitude. They are the custodians of wealth and they must learn how to make the best use of it. They need not distribute it among the poor. But they should know how to invest it so that it generates jobs for the needy, raises the standard of production and results in an all-round progress and welfare of the society.

Luxury goods and facilities can be easily identified. They should be made unpopular through education and media. At the same time, the state should be convinced to exercise a control over their manufacturing and marketing.

The politicians should prove to be real and humble servants of the people. They should not indulge in luxuries at the cost of the state exchequer. They overexploit their positions of authority to show off through luxuries to the common man who is the real paymaster. Indulging in luxuries at the cost of public money should be treated as a crime.

The public servants who indulge in luxuries are committing a double crime. They waste the resources, not created by their own labour. They present a poor picture of their educational qualifications, their sense of duty, their spirit of dedication and their profession of social service.

In the field of education itself, we are introducing luxuries in the form of expensive public schools, palatial buildings, air-conditioned classrooms, three star hotel type hostels and costly co-curricular activities. It is indirectly creating an elite or privileged class in the society. This trend needs to be checked.

Our games, sports and entertainments also have an inclination towards a luxurious lifestyle. Let us not make them so expensive that they become the privilege of a few selected people. They should remain within the reach of every common man.

There is need to evolve some better status symbols like educational qualifications, services rendered to the family, locality, society and nation, innovative and creative work, sacrifices made, inspiration given to others, contribution made towards production and economy and leadership provided in any walk of life. These status symbols should overshadow the luxuries of life.

Simple living can be easily explained to constitute simple but nourishing food, simple but clean dress, simple but full-fledged house, simplest possible mode of transport including cycle, straightforward dealings, aversion for very costly goods when cheaper and equally useful alternatives are available, simple decorations, simple celebrations and simple but efficient style of life for bureaucrats and politicians and others in the public eye.

*****

V
EDUCATION AND SOCIETY

Twenty four

Education and Society

Thinkers give first position to education as the source of prosperity both to the individual and to the society. Whenever a serious problem arises in society, whether it is of personal, domestic, social, economic or political type, we are almost certain to insist that education is the cure.

From society, we receive the gift of our individuality and in it we express our personality. The same society which limits the activities of the individual also liberates his energies and talents.

A society which is both democratic and progressive must impart a type of education which gives to individuals a personal interest in social relationships and control, and dictates habits which secure social advancement without introducing disorder. The verbal commitments to democracy, freedom and equality become hollow in the absence of supporting social realities.

A school should be able to balance the various elements in the social environment, and should see to it that the unlucky individual gets an opportunity to save himself from the unhealthy social group in which he was born and is able to live in a healthier environment.

Society is a social organism. Individuals are the limbs of the society. Limbs separated from the body become lifeless, and similarly individuals separated from society have no life.

Education and society should not pull an individual in different directions. There is need to understand and emphasise the commonness of the goals of the two.

Society is the laboratory for conducting educational experiments. Both society and education have to continue to evolve towards greater perfection.

The learner must not only adjust with his social environment, but should constantly improve upon it and upon his own adjustment with it.

Education is an agency to define and establish social norms. Society should accept education as its reformer and cooperate with it in every possible way. When the society needs reforms, it should strengthen the role of education for the purpose.

The positions of reform in education and society should remain parallel to one another. Any retardation of one will get reflected in the other. When the society neglects education, it neglects itself. It should make higher demands on education and must deserve them. It should ensure its sustained progress and purification by its own efforts in that direction and ensure the role of education in the same. It must take good care of itself first and then take equally good care of the system of education. From its own human resources, the society has to provide to education capable and sincere teachers, administrators and planners.

Good elements of the society should be made strong enough to sweep away the ill effects of bad elements. Education should provide additional strength and guidance to noble elements of the society to overshadow the effect of bad elements and as a consequence eliminate their weaknesses.

At the same time, education should protect itself from the evils prevalent in society and endeavour to replace the existing society with a far better one. Both these agencies should take a pledge towards a better and still better social set-up.

The future generation is the most valuable asset of every society and the latter must do its best for nurturing and enriching this asset. Society must inform itself about the negative influences which are being made by it on its children. In no case, should it pass on a diminishing legacy to the new generation. If society allows dirty elements to exist in it, then it will be difficult to save the new generation from their influence. Children must feel that they are growing up in a clean society and they will have to form a more clean society when their turn comes. An unhealthy society must make organised efforts to gain health and not in any way spoil the healthy effects of education.

If crime, corruption and antisocial activities are common in a society, it will be difficult to save the new generation from these vices. Both education and society should propose higher standards for each other. Only then will the qualitative graph of the two continue to rise.

Society has to ensure progressive trends in its own sphere and in the sphere of education. Both have to work towards building a knowledge-based world. Both of them have to see that they get more capable citizens for the future. If at any stage society finds that it is not providing a conducive environment for the growth of a child, remedial measures must be urgently taken up. Similarly, if it is found that educational institutions are not up to the mark, things must be set right without delay. Both have to come out of lethargy, if any.

A citizen should not be known as a hopeless and good for nothing fellow among others. He should not collect for his name any of the tags like, shirker, irresponsible, dishonest, mischievous, corrupt, characterless, foolish, or rogue. Everybody must be known as a humble, humanitarian, helpful, educated and wise fellow. Again, everybody should have made a mentionable contribution for the betterment of society during his lifetime.

The process of socialisation should be based on positivism, humanitarianism and evolutionism. It should emphasise the functional relationship between education and the other institutional orders of society, such as economy, polity, kinship and religion. Education has to be recognised as one of the means of promoting economic prosperity, quality of society and social cohesion. The social importance of education has to be stressed in the modern industrialised society. It fits people for increasingly specialised roles. It prepares individuals for mutual awareness, mutual interaction, cooperation, division of labour, dynamic role, progressive outlook and social control. The individuals have to imbibe the spirit of social contract to ensure for themselves the security and certainty of existence and living life under general will.

The society has to keep a watch over the infrastructure for its educational institutions and should not delay the process of making provisions. There should be a regular arrangement of updating these facilities. The expert agencies should constantly work out the list of latest equipments required.

The society will perform many functions towards education. It will establish and maintain good educational institutions. It will formulate healthy aims for them. It will control, guide and supervise them and draw out the maximum possible benefits for the students. It will provide universal education through a sufficiently rich curriculum devised by its experts. It will arrange for job-oriented, vocational, technical and professional education according to the needs and capabilities of the students. Its educational plan and expansion should be based on data so that the factor of unemployment is sufficiently controlled. It will provide finances, resources and equipments for its educational institutions so that they can work smoothly and efficiently. It has to ensure cooperation between the institutions, parents, managements and other social organisations.

The approach to education has to be futuristic, progressive, constructive and utilitarian. It will impart its rich cultural heritage to the students and enable them to further enrich their culture. Society has to ensure that education develops for its various spheres, competent and imaginative leaders and willing followers to help in carrying out necessary reforms. It has to offer ideal examples of cooperation, fellow feeling, social service and sacrifice before its new generation. It has to advocate wider attitudes so that students can rise above narrow communal feelings and attitudes based on caste, creed or regions. The society has to protect children from evil influences and provide healthy, congenial and constructive educational environment to them. It should stimulate the critical judgement among the learners so that they may evaluate their culture and traditions and modify them, if need be.

Society should form many welfare organisations which look after the welfare of the teachers, give incentives to meritorious students, give financial assistance to poor students, honour dedicated teachers, hold educational competitions among students, help the institutions for educational trips, appoint non-official experts to supervise the working of the educational institutions and report their irregularities to the concerned departments and authorities.

An educated adult also needs adult education, so that he is equipped to play his role in solving the problems of society. There should be different centres for adult education so that adults can be successfully guided to tackle their respective areas of problems.

*****

Twenty five

Education and Family

With the passage of time, in spite of our expanding knowledge of philosophy, psychology, education and sociology, we have destroyed the heritage of family and home. How can the remnants of home, now a destroyed and disfigured agency play its vital role in building the personality of the offspring? We have ourselves made the home powerless and ineffective in imparting virtues to the newly born.

A family is a group of persons united by different ties for creating and maintaining a common culture. The family can exert the most formative and powerful influence on the development of a child's personality. A congenial environment in a family gives better development to its members, whereas stress, strains and undesirable activities of a broken family create problems in development.

Family should be recognised as the original social institution from which all other institutions develop. An ideal family continues to remain a strength for other institutions. In larger interest and value, it should be nourished and strengthened by its individual members.

Apart from discharging their various responsibilities towards the family, all the members must ensure a congenial, helpful, encouraging, aspiring, productive, inspiring and creative environment in the family. This institution of family should be an embodiment of love, participation, cooperation, duty, care, cordiality, trust, better future, planning, sacrifice, respect and wisdom.

Every member of the family should be conscious and faithful about his role in the family. A single misfit in the family can spoil and destroy its atmosphere. A serious mistake by one member can ruin its honour and status. At the same time, a remarkable achievement by one member may raise the reputation and dignity of the entire family.

All the family members should strive and contribute towards the collective resources, possibilities and character of the family. None of its members should try to let down other members. High status of a family is a matter of pride for each member. It is matter of honour to belong to a noble family after all. At the same time, the poor status of a family is a handicap for every member. Belonging to a well reputed family is a reward in itself. This reputation needs to be built up from generation to generation. The members should collectively earn a shining nickname for the family.

The members have a genuine right over the resources of the family but they have a more compelling duty towards augmenting and replenishing these resources. The family is our asset and liability at the same time. We should not commit the folly of destroying or minimising its worth. Family life has got rare pleasures and contentment for its members. Quality of family life leads to the quality of life in general.

The head of the family is required to be a true leader, guide and role model. He should be a good achiever in various aspects of life. He should earn and deserve respect from other members. He should have well thought out educational, economic, vocational and social plans for the members of the family. He should make lifelong efforts to enhance his ability and competence. He should be able to develop family as a well-knit group, as an agency for understanding and free from any misunderstandings.

It is sad that we find a large number of contrary things happening in the family atmosphere such as broken homes, separation, desertion, divorce, disowning and disinheriting children from the right to family property, members fighting among themselves for the sake of property and assets, neglect of the children, the head of the family getting addicted to drugs and ruining the economy of the family, children going out of control, new generations taking delight in breaking the family traditions and family ties.

As the family is the first agency for the education of its members, it should enhance its ability to educate. Let education also try to make the home a place of real love, understanding and collective responsibility.

The intimate blood relationship between the members of a family has very rich possibilities and opportunities which should be put to maximum use. The newly born child gets its first experiences of life from the family he is born into and gets acquainted with his basic needs.

Let the family give a great and meaningful name to the young child. The meanings and significance of the name should be explained to him and he should be inspired to live up to his great name.

The family must try to provide an educative, intelligent, constructive, psychological, healthy and inspiring environment to the child. The child should be guided and encouraged to overcome his weaknesses or handicaps, if any. There should be a good number of examples in the family for the child to emulate. The family has to perform a large number of functions towards its children and there should be no irresponsibility or carelessness in this respect. There should be no occasion for the family to be blamed for neglecting its child in any manner.

If one of the members of a family happens to be a teacher, he should make an impact on the educational achievements of all the other members. Similarly, if a member happens to be a doctor he should make his contribution towards the health of the remaining members. If one member happens to rise in any field of life, for example, business, he should be able to ensure a good entry into that field for any other member who so desires.

It is very strange that some individual members do not appreciate the need of a family. Some want to be separated soon after marriage. Some others want to live apart soon after getting employment. Some insist on division of property so that they can live separately. They fail to understand the automatic benefits from family life.

The home climate should be conducive, soothing and inspiring for the proper growth and development of its members. The home is the soil in which numerous capabilities germinate. Informal education given by the home is most natural and lasts for long. A good home may also expect good neighbours who can make a valuable contribution to the development of its children.

Some notable personalities in human history got their foundational development from their homes. An educated parent is able to create an educational climate at home. With the progress of women and their education, the home is better equipped for the development of a child.

Through the medium of education there is need and hope of reviving good traditions of a home. Every member of a family must be made to realise that his healthy behaviour is a great gift for the family, and unhealthy behaviour is a great curse.

Intellectual development and language development received at home help the children throughout their education and later life. The home develops in the child, healthy and positive emotions like sympathy, affection, helpfulness, and sharing of joys and sorrows. In the present times of a confusing social set-up, the home finds it difficult to perform its functions. The home and the educational institution have to work together in this situation to achieve better results.

Some people are fond of playing politics within the family and in the neighbourhood. They spoil the environment for themselves and for their children. They should be re-educated to strengthen the institution of family. All the members of a family should be made to realise that apart from their relationships, they are close friends to one another. Just as different instruments in a symphony create a magical music, similarly well tuned members of a family create an enjoyable harmony.

Where there is a culture of learning at home, the child flourishes at school. Ogburn and Nimkoff have mentioned some major functions of the family: affection, economic, recreational, protective, and educational functions. Margaret Fuller has said, "A house is no home unless it contains food and fire for the mind as well as for the body."

Education should focus on the individual's preparation for setting up his home which may have all the desired qualities. We should be able to re-capture the essence of family life. If the family life of the members is not charming, most of the charm of life will be lost. Every home must be a sweet home in the real sense and every family must be a happy family.

According to Milton Singer, there are five factors which have affected families the most. These are education, industrialisation, urbanisation, change in the institution of marriage and legislative measures. Education has to neutralise the harmful impact of any such factors for the existence of a well-knit family. It has to especially contradict the blame that the rise in the level of education increases the percentage of those who are in favour of nuclear families. It will be one of the functions of education to prepare every individual to make his home worthwhile in the real sense.

To provide sound initial experiences to children, our homes should be free from jealousy, backbiting, strife, strained relations, immoral tendencies, unethical means of livelihood, ill-treatment, poor thinking, bad practices and dirty aims.

Every family should make a resolution that the generations to come will do better in almost all the fields like education, health, socio-economic status, harmony, contribution to society and achievements in general. The home should be in a position to instill reasonable aspirations in the child's mind regarding his academic and non-academic achievements.

The home should provide examples of good human beings around the child. It should provide formative experiences to the child to enable him to develop qualities of the head and heart.

The values in every home should be compatible with the values which we wish to develop through education. There should be perfect coordination and agreement between the two in this respect. The two should not pull in different directions in the matter of development of personality of a young learner and in the inculcation of values.

The home should give every support possible after the child is admitted to school. It should try to supplement the good ideas that the child receives at school. It should be conversant with the aims and schemes of education prescribed for its child. It should not needlessly criticise the school and create doubts in the mind of the child about the worthiness and sincerity of the school programmes.

It will be in the interest of the child if the home takes the trouble of remaining in touch with his school. If the teachers point out any serious lapses at home regarding the developmental interests of the child, the home should not feel offended but should readily correct the situation.

If the parents are not educated enough, they may not be in a position to provide the right direction to the development of their child. In such cases, the school should keep the child under its watchful observation, so that its development is not adversely affected by the shortcomings of his home.

The educated parents can certainly keep track of the academic progress of their child. They may ensure the child's regularity in his home work and should come to his help when he faces any difficulty.

If the home is expected to maintain a specific standard of environment and behaviour for the child, it should try to upgrade and reform the situation. It is presumed here that the qualities of experiences available to the child at school will be better than those available at an average home.

The home should be able to coordinate with the educational institutions at the time of the choice of subjects and vocations during the education of the child. The home should not give any wrong information to an educational institution about itself or about its children. Whenever a teacher of a child happens to visit them in connection with anything educational, the parents should offer their willing concern and cooperation.

Why should there be a chaos in the family? The joint family system, which is a necessity, collapsed long ago. Each member directly or indirectly creates tensions in the family which are not easy to resolve. The revival of family spirit and joint family system is no longer a possibility. It is a big man-made loss.

Each family has its own distinct habits of clothing, eating, talking, living, thinking, working, socialising, planning, achieving and making progress. These are the elements of a family's culture. This culture has to be preserved and transmitted by each family from generation to generation. It is the duty of a family to continue to strengthen and enrich its culture.

The age-old structure of a joint family has now been broken down under the stress of industrialisation, social, economic and political factors as well as legal compulsions. In spite of this, the importance of family as a powerful agency of education has not lessened even a bit today. The foundation of a child's future is laid by the family first. In later life, it becomes very difficult for him to demolish or reconstruct these foundations, if they are found to be unsatisfactory.

Family thus, helps in the development and education of a child in many ways such as physical, mental, emotional, social and religious development, transmission of culture, development of language, interests and habits, morality and character, innate tendencies, individuality, provision of practical and vocational education, etc.

Parents can do many things to help their children to succeed in school and life. They can build up the vocabulary of the child. The child can be taught the names of many things around him, he can be made familiar with places in his local surroundings, he can become familiar with people doing various jobs around him, and can also learn many concepts and the names of famous places. If children see their parents reading books, consulting a dictionary or surfing the internet, they will themselves feel motivated to do such things. When the child starts going to school, parents should fix time for his homework, play, entertainment, viewing TV, etc. The family should throughout perform its positive role for the welfare of its members.

Pope John Paul II said, "As the family goes, so goes the nation and so goes the whole world in which we live."

*****

Twenty six

Education and Generation Gap

It is our sacred duty to serve others and our own elders are the nearest available for this service. They are our own and by serving them, we are in reality serving our own blood. The two generations are blessed with a very sweet relationship which should be enjoyed by both as best and as long as possible.

One has varying obligations towards one's parents, elder brothers and sisters, senior relatives and any person senior to him in age. Seniors have respective obligations towards their juniors too.

Rigid adherence is expected towards a detailed set of social conventions in the inter-generation relationship. Formalised behaviour towards each other tends to prevent conflicts and makes possible a smoothly functioning family, institution and society. Everyone at his own place has to observe loyalty towards each other.

Old generation is considered a burden by the new generation. The new generation, often, disowns or throws out the old generation. These are all inhuman traditions. Family which used to be a model of cohesion for the society is losing that position today.

This generation gap between the old and the young is recognised as a source of many problems. There is no possibility of the removal of the existence of this gap. But this gap should not be widened by narrow considerations.

We can certainly make efforts to remove its loopholes and its side effects.

While dealing with their younger generation the older generation should not forget that they themselves were young once. At the same time, the younger generation should learn to reasonably adjust with the old generation, not to offend it, and try to observe and acquire the benefit of its qualities and rich experiences. The two generations should learn to live together with understanding and adjustment. There is no justification for the two to remain at variance with each other. They are destined to live and work together in every home, community, institution and establishment. There is no cause to blame each other for the adjustment problems between the two. The new generation must show due respect to the old generation and get the maximum benefit from its legacy. It should try to understand that in most cases, the old generation has made considerable sacrifices for the development and security of the new generation.

At the same time, the old generation should present itself as a respectable role model for the new generation. It should be free from weak points which may invite criticism and disrespect from the new generation. Its helpfulness and guidance for the new generation should be clear and convincing.

New generation is always in a hurry to take over and enjoy the available privileges and the old generation has a tendency to cling to these privileges as long as possible. Any clash over the privileges harms the interests of both and wastes their energies which are meant for the welfare of both.

Even when the old become physically weak, they try to tighten their grip over the younger ones, over family matters and business issues. The younger ones, instead of developing a sympathetic attitude towards the aged, start over-asserting themselves. Social changes are taking place at a faster rate. While the young ones are prepared to welcome and accept these changes, the old find it difficult to adjust to these. This further alienates the two generations from each other.

The old members think that the things would get worse when they are no more. They are proud of whatever they have been able to do for their family. They often find that the essential traits of devotion and dedication towards the family are missing in the new generation. But the young consider that their knowledge and training are comparatively more vast and up to date than that of the old. They are not convinced with the traditional style of life of the old. They consider themselves advanced and forward-looking and blame the old for their attachment with their outdated modes of living. Both the categories quite often find themselves in disagreement with each other and are unable to discover a meeting ground. Wide generation gap does not permit them to work as a well-knit family. Their illogical disagreement leads to unwanted confrontation.

The impact of a generation gap is visible among parents and children, the old and the young, the teachers and the taught, and the experienced persons and the beginners. Any two categories of people with an age gap of two decades quite often fail to have an understanding, a workable equation, fellow-feeling and a reasonably smooth co-existence. They clash on views, attitudes, values, divergent thinking and unnecessary aloofness. For many ailments of our society, and failure of our ventures, the old blame the young and vice versa. Almost every institution and agency witnesses this kind of blame game.

When an elderly member of a group is not satisfied with some of the ideas and actions of a younger member, the latter is duty-bound to rethink, discuss and resolve the issue. There is no place for having camps in any group due to age divisions.

Old age is subject to stress, strain, idleness, reduced income, physical weakness, illness and isolation. Quite often isolation and loneliness may be caused by the loss of contemporaries and loved ones. The negligence and indifference by the younger generation further aggravates their problems. Life expectancy has increased and this has further added to the problems of the aged. In most cases, old age brings many types of ailments, may make the person almost bedridden, helpless and over-dependent. At that stage of life, he needs special care and should not get neglected. An unreasonable cause for neglecting old people is neither desirable in a family nor in any society.

The government and other social agencies have undertaken various social, legislative and welfare measures to protect the interests of the old people. Old age homes have been set-up to provide physical protection, medical aid and economic security to them. Due to the new trend of nuclear families, old people are often deserted by their own children. In the old age homes also, most of them are bound to suffer from emotional problems.

The individual should prepare himself well in time for the problems of old age. He should plan ahead for an active and useful existence in his later years. There is no question for him to get dissociated from the society, nor is there any question for the society to disown him. The government and other social agencies can build a network to put the services of the aged to some constructive use. The old person should also find for himself a suitable place in society, ways and means to age gracefully, and continue his self-fulfilment till the end.

Most of the aged persons are able to do some social service. Their rich and long experience can be put to gainful use through some organisations. When they are kept usefully busy, they can tide over their emotional problems also. Let society understand that they can be useful till the end. They should not be left alone to feel isolated. The society should not allow its vast segment of old persons to go waste.

Although it is the personal duty of an old person to take good care of his health, the society will fail in its duty, if it leaves him unattended.

Education should impart and develop compassionate and natural feelings and sense of responsibility among the learners for the aged and dependent people. Everybody has to reach old age and he must insure good care for himself by taking good care of the aged when he is young.

When education aims at preparation for life, it should prepare the individual well for changing roles at different ages, that is, when he is young, his role in the family life, and also for the problems of old age. The importance of the role of older generations in family life needs to be specially stressed through education. Some of the elder members of the families behave in a condemnable manner. They neglect the younger generation in respect of health, development, facilities and education. Some of them spend more than their income and waste the resources created by their forefathers. They ruin the economy of the family forever and throw it into the pit of poverty. They indulge in drug addiction and abuse, and physically assault other members of the family. They lower the social status of the family and present a very poor and harmful picture of the older generation and are a curse as role models. We have again to empower our education to such an extent that such people become very rare.

The school should not present itself as an institution divided between two camps consisting of old and new generations. The teachers should be considered as friends by the students. The students should learn to watch the noble and extraordinary conduct of their teachers and try to learn from their outstanding behaviour.

According to Plato, "Education is an effort on the part of the older generation to pass on to the younger generation all the good habits and wisdom acquired through experience."

Education is a very purposeful link between the two generations. The question of difference of opinion, demonstration or strike called by students against the teachers and administrators should seldom arise. The two sides should be able to work in complete harmony. A number of channels should be available to neutralise the tension or conflict, if any.

There is enough justification to make generation gap a subject of educational research, in order to find out its causes and consequences. The findings of this research may provide some hints for both the generations to live and work like friends and companions.

*****

Twenty seven

Education and Adjustment

Adjustment of an individual is related with many areas like health, home, society, emotions, etc.

In fact, well adjusted personalities are very rare. Most of the people fail to fit into their social group and lead unhappy and unproductive lives. People can rarely be described as well-adjusted in every way. They can show different traits of adjustment in varying degrees. Adjustment ensures behaviour patterns that enable a person to get along well and be comfortable in his social setting. He should be internally consistent or should show homogeneous behaviour.

Adjustment indicates rapid pace of activities, energy, vitality, mobility, productivity, efficiency, enthusiasm, liveliness, serious-mindedness, persistent effort, self-control, leadership traits, initiative, optimism, cheerfulness, interest in reflective thinking, meditative nature, philosophical inclination, mental poise, faith in social institutions; freedom from (feelings of guilt, shyness, egoism, self-centredness, suspicion, fancying hostility, tendency to get into trouble, resentment, desire to dominate, and self-pity), respecting others, not getting easily disgusted, inhibited in emotional expression, resistance to fear, and less interested in clothes, style or romance.

The mental hygiene approach strives to develop well-adjusted personalities. When we talk of maladjustment, we find many people who are depressed, who feel useless and are unable to face the future. Some are under emotional stress and have a tendency to escape the efforts for adjustment. Some are unable to benefit from experience, have disregard for social pressures and are likely to get into trouble of various sorts. Some suffer from oversensitivity and complex tendencies.

There are many types of maladjustments which have to be removed and cured by education. Incorrigibility of a human being can be taken as an example. It is quite a common problem. Parents find some of their children incorrigible, teachers find some of their students incorrigible, and employers find some of their employees incorrigible. An incorrigible person refuses to listen to any advice or does not listen to his own well-wishers. He is averse to self-control and social control. With the passage of time, he becomes so rigid and stubborn that he does not allow anybody to interfere in his waywardness. Latecomers remain latecomers in spite of a lot of advice, warnings, punishments and personal losses. There can be no shortcuts to remove incorrigibility. It demands unlimited patience and persistence. We should try to win the confidence of the person by showing sympathy and understanding and giving positive help. Mere casual advice and criticism cannot show any results. Our positive approach demands that through our long process of education we should not allow any bad habits and maladjustments to settle in the mind and behaviour of the young learner.

Behaviour that is in conformity with the demands and expectations of others, peers, siblings, parents, relatives, teachers and members of the community is considered adaptive behaviour. Behaviour that fails to conform to the social and cultural norms is called maladjusted behaviour.

Maladjustment can be of two types: social and emotional. Social maladjustment makes the individual unmanageable at home causing further difficulties to the parents and their siblings. They become a problem at school, retarded in educational achievements, destructive, quarrelsome, and socially immature. They seek undesirable company or become isolated. Delinquents are a sub-group among the socially maladjusted. Emotionally maladjusted have inner tensions and show anxiety, neuroticism or psychotic behaviour.

Maladjustment requires special treatment in order to enable the person to seek personal and educational adjustment.

The causes of maladjustment can be discussed under three heads: psychological factors, psycho-social factors and physiological factors.

Psychological factors involve frustrations. When the capacities of an individual are strained or he is unable to satisfy his motives, and drives, it may lead to behavioural deviations like aggression, regression or compulsive behaviour. When he is unable to choose between a few courses of action or when the course of action chosen by him does not reduce his tensions, he reacts in an emotional way by temper tantrums, fighting, etc. In some cases, the individual is forced to perform a task which is beyond him. He becomes tense and excited and may get angry. For example, truancy is common among slow learners and retarded children. In addition to truancy, he may run away or become aggressive and hostile. Maladjustment is common among children whose parents are over-ambitious about them.

Psycho-social factors include early home experiences and social and economic aspects of a person's life. Some children tend to defy all authority, be cruel, be malicious, may assault everybody and still may have no guilt. They are jealous, deceitful to others and tend to blame others for their own faults. They are unsocial and aggressive children. They usually come from broken homes. They are deprived at an early age to form positive interpersonal attachments. Some are aggressive towards authority, but socialise within their peer groups. Some fall into the category of over-inhibited. They are shy, timid, withdrawing, secluded, sensitive and submissive. They lack friends, are over dependent and get easily depressed. They have frequent physical complaints. Such children come from families of high socio-economic status and are overprotected. The atmosphere at home may also be restrictive. Thus, maladjustment may be caused at home due to overprotection, rejection, hostility, inconsistent discipline, unhealthy relationship between the parents, and failure of the parents to meet the basic demands of the children.

Some physiological factors also lead towards maladjustment such as prolonged illness of a child, chronic disease of any type, brain damage, etc. When a child cannot normally take part in the games or activities of the peer group, he gets frustrated and isolated. Some physical, sensory or nervous disorderliness in the child may also lead to maladjustment. Such causes are defective speech, undernourishment, undersize, oversize, weakened heart or some accident.

In the case of one room homes or slums, the children are likely to face many developmental problems. Being the only child of their parents may be another cause. Having a step mother or step father may be another important cause of developmental problems in children. When the mother is also employed, she fails to pay attention to her children.

Discipline at home should not be repressive. The rules of discipline should be kept consistent. The children should not be stopped from expressing their feelings and their feelings should be duly acknowledged.

The parents or teachers should also avoid giving lavish/ excessive/undue praise to the children.

If ever the child has to be criticised, one has to target his wrong behaviour rather than to simply criticise him. The parents/teachers should also avoid giving false threats to children. The child should not be ignored when he tries to seek his parent's or teacher's attention towards some of his significant achievement.

The adjustment of children is a joint responsibility of the teachers, parents, counsellors, psychologists, psychiatrists and health officers. It requires their collective efforts.

The teacher has to detect the cases with minor and severe problems. If need be, he has to refer them to suitable experts. He has to understand the cause behind the deviant behaviour of the child. He may also guide the parents about effective child-rearing practices. He has to ensure that the school atmosphere, relations between the teacher and the taught, teacher's expectations from the child, quality of teaching, opportunities of co-curricular activities, etc. are all conducive to the adjustment of the child. In collaboration with his colleagues, the teacher should adopt good adjustment practices in the school.

There are many adjustment mechanisms to help the students in their adjustment problems. Rationalisation involves finding a logically and socially approved alternative for our past and present shortcomings. It helps the individual to avoid unnecessary frustrations. By repression, the individual is enabled to remove painful ideas, thoughts, experiences and memories from his consciousness. Regression is a mechanism which involves an unconscious back-tracking in behaviour to an earlier adjustment which might have proved successful in the past, without due regard to its suitability at the present moment.

Sublimation stands for acceptance of a socially approved substitute goal for a desire whose channel of expression in its present form appears blocked. A student who cannot do well in games and sports may find cultural activities as a substitute goal, in which he can obtain applause for his merit.

That is why it is suggested that opportunities be provided to the students to sublimate their sexual instinct through participation in creative arts, games and sports, dramatics and other co-curricular activities. In the case of identification, the individual enhances his feelings of worth and adequacy by identifying himself with the persons or institutions of big and outstanding achievements. All these mechanisms of adjustment are more useful and beneficial when used in moderation.

Education can teach a learner to adjust to different circumstances by relating itself to people's ambitions and needs of life, relating itself to production, making itself an integral part of culture, vocationalising education, making education useful for social and national unification, making programmes of social service a part of education and modernising education.

It is the duty of every individual to promote his adjustment throughout his life and he must become a medium of adjustment for others who are facing difficulties or hurdles in making adjustments. One has to get adjusted with all the new demands and challenges in life. He has to deal with new persons at different stages in life and he must be able to adjust with them amicably. Adjustment is a precondition for living a meaningful, purposeful, helpful and successful life.

*****

Twenty eight

Education and Media

At present the relationship between education and media is too thin. There is need to develop a strong relationship between the two.

The voice of the media is considered to be very powerful in the present times. This power should help in creating the right type of society and an equally right type of system of education. The media should influence the government also in the same direction. It should not compromise with substandard situation. The media should launch a campaign for the highest possible goals in education, society and government.

It is generally felt that media indulges in cheap type of entertainment for the people for commercial reasons. It may also present poor characters for the sake of a story in hand. Some of the presentations are found to be vulgar and obscene. The media should not exploit the sentiments and inferior tastes of the people. It has a commitment for the promotion of morality and values. In case the media does not stick to norms, education has to make the new generation cautious to accept and grasp only that information and entertainment which is clean. It has to accept the role of reversing the mania for cheap modes of media. People should be so enlightened about quality in art and entertainment that the media has to mould itself to come up to these standards.

Although information and entertainment will remain a top priority for the media, it should also have a wing which highlights the structure of quality education.

The media should not play a distracting role for an average student. It should offer materials for the students which are interesting and educative. All the programmes and materials of the media should contribute towards character building and the enrichment of culture. Media should avoid creating and aggravating harmful controversies. It should rather curb the elements of discord in society.

Media can certainly influence the atmosphere of a family, social climate, political climate, individual development and educational climate. It should avoid exploiting the sentiments of the people for its momentary popularity and petty gains. Its approach to every issue should be constructive and positive. It should employ itself to cast forward-looking, dignified and rich influences on individuals and society. Its influences should not be regarded as objectionable from any angle.

At one time, it was said that TV was going to replace the teacher. The TV or any other type of media should not think of supplanting the teacher, but it should serve to supplement the teacher's work. Certain portions in the media should be reserved for promoting the cause of education. It should look towards the programmes of education and play its role in popularising these programmes, enriching them and evaluating them for the listeners to create a better climate for educational services. Media should refrain from taking liberties with the norms established through education.

Different organs of media have their respective educational values which should be vigorously conveyed to the students. The experts in education and media should form a working group which may draw up a scheme of collaboration for the benefit of learners. The two should play a corroborating role towards formal and informal education. Media should now and then give critical judgement of the affairs of education and suggest better alternatives, if need be.

The newspapers are meant for disseminating news, discussing political and social issues. But, if they want to reduce the number of sad and painful news, and want a better political and social atmosphere, they should reserve more space for educative material. People have to be convinced to adopt a healthy style of living and follow rules in political and social fields, so that the newspapers can present a healthier matter for its readers. Apart from giving guess papers, admission notices, etc., the newspapers should also publish good instructional material. The newspapers may give reports about the outstanding educational institutions to provide guidelines to others.

Some institutions have special features about them. These should also be published for making those features universal. Some institutions show good examination results. The information about how they achieve these results may also be published for the benefit of other institutions. Certain institutions show significant achievements in games and co-curricular activities. Their methods for these achievements may also be given publicity through newspapers so that other institutions may also follow them. Some institutions may be suffering in their accomplishments because of some shortcomings in the infrastructure and staff. These handicaps may also be published to awaken the authorities to fulfil the needs.

Some teachers may be making exceptional achievements. Reports about their manner of functioning may also be publicised to inspire other teachers to follow their example. Similarly, reports about outstanding achievements by some students may be publicised to motivate other students to adopt them as models. Some educational administrators have a unique and successful style in running the institutions. Their style may also be publicised for prompting others to work in the same manner. Certain schools carry out projects and social service programmes. These should also be brought to the notice of others through newspaper reports. The newspapers should also highlight the problems being faced by the educational institutions for bringing them to the notice of concerned authorities. They should also comment on the expectations from educational institutions in the present circumstances and in the times to come. The public and the authorities should be made aware as to how far the institutions are coming up to the expectations. The newspapers should frequently bring out the features and editions on education.

The magazines have to present the literary material, which is at the same time educative. They should offer quality literature which can guide the readers to adhere to principles, morality and values in their individual and social life. From time to time, these magazines should also invite special articles on education, on the successes and failures of education, on the standards expected from education, on the relation between literature and education and on the visions of education. In spite of the availability of a rich and educative literature worldwide, individuals are unable to learn the desirable lessons from it. The habits of reading quality literature are also not very common among them. Even if they read something, they fail to imbibe the good suggestions offered by literature.

The dependence on radio is on the decline. Radio reserves most of its time for music. Some good lessons and discussions by educational experts may be frequently broadcasted for the benefit of teachers and students. School broadcasts are already a regular feature with the radio. Some surveys should be conducted from time to time to see that the school broadcasts and other educational broadcasts are being availed of by listeners. The radio should also record good literary, cultural or educational programmes from schools and broadcast them for the benefit of all. It can also record inter-school debates, poetical recitations and other competitive programmes on its own premises and broadcast them for all schools.

As a supplement to classroom teaching, the possibilities of radio are almost unlimited. Some day, its use as an instrument of education will be as common as textbooks and blackboards. The students can be indirectly introduced to the experts, journalists, authors, scientists, leading personalities in different walks of life and outstanding teachers through the medium of radio. It reflects on the spot current events, such as proceedings of a particular legislature, description of a catastrophe, news of educational interest and commentary of an important match. Programmes on the life of a foreign country including their way of life, their food, their economic conditions, their hobbies, their vocations, their celebrations, and their customs can be an educative experience for the students.

Radio is useful to deliver talks on different subjects like commerce, science, mathematics, agriculture, farmer's activities and teaching. By providing a variety, it can eliminate monotony of the regular classroom teaching. It can be an important medium for leisure time activities. It could also improve the language and pronunciation of the students. It gives the pupils a sense of participation when an event is unfolded before them through the radio. Radio broadcasts broaden the mental horizon and develop the sense of judgement, discrimination and critical thinking of the students. The range of the radio is unlimited. Any number of pupils scattered all over the world can listen to a broadcast at the same time. Radio possesses qualities like recency, realism and authenticity. It can be more useful in languages, social sciences, sciences and music.

Television can be more useful as an aid. It can telecast good lessons and demonstrations by experts for the benefit of all the schools of the region. It can show rare and costly equipments, which cannot be made available in each school. Some distant happenings, places of importance and events can be brought into the classroom through the medium of television. The use of television can make things more interesting, colourful and understandable for the learners. The exceptionally good work being done in some schools, by some teachers, by some managements, in some laboratories, in some classrooms, on some playgrounds, in some student committees, and on some stages for cultural performance may also be telecast for the benefit of others. The television can also arrange for a programme of healthy entertainment for teachers and students. It must present the picture of good points of educational institutions.

Television through its combined voice and picture, appeals to both, the ears and eyes. It is often called the electronic blackboard of the future. It is a versatile audio-visual aid which incorporates demonstrations, charts, models, exhibits, and chalk board. It has a wide range, because it can be viewed by a large number of students at one time. It can provide to the students the benefit of instruction being imparted by master-teachers, superior instructors and experts. It is considered a time saving device because more material can be taught in a given amount of time on television which is carefully planned, timed and uninterrupted. It offers uniformity of communication and allows excellent material for observation and discussion. No student can feel neglected. It focusses the attention of the students on the topic in hand and other distractions are removed. It can be a medium for showing inaccessible and dangerous places which are otherwise important from the educational point of view. It shares the work load of teachers. It can also fulfil the needs of distance education satisfactorily. It has a recreational value of its own type.

Some people designate the present age as the computer age. Computers are being widely used in almost all spheres of life, i.e., in the fields of commerce, agriculture, education, offices, banks, transportation, communication, space travel, crime detection, defence, administration, research and games.

Computer is called the electronic brain. It is a device which stores information on discs and magnetic tape, analyses it and produces information as required. It has the capacity of storing or memorising a large amount of information and producing or retrieving it when called for.

In education, computer is employed for the classification of pupils according to their abilities. It is used to evaluate their performance. It can allocate learning resources according to the individuals and their needs. It provides direct interaction between the student and the subject matter to be analysed, and provides opportunities for problem solving ability and creativity among the students. It is useful for laboratory and practical work and provides training through simulation. Lessons can be repeated a number of times on the computer. It also provides reliable data for guidance.

The core of computer assisted learning activity in education is the drill, practice, diagnostic testing and question and answer tutorials. It includes simulation and games, problem solving and creative activities. As teaching aids, computers are being widely used in many advanced countries. They can cope with the needs of thousands of students simultaneously. They can completely handle individualised instruction by following the individual's own pace, processing individual feedback, and sequencing of instruction. It relieves the teacher of the daily routine because the performance of learners during the course and on the tests is recorded automatically.

Computers can be used as educational aids at all levels of education starting from pre-school stage and going to colleges, universities and technical institutes.

Some of the important computer-aided learning materials are: logo for the teaching of mathematics, PLATO system for a laboratory course in chemistry, simulated cases in the field of law and medicine, computerised programmed packages in arts and humanities, and computerised programmes for languages.

In the field of education, computer is being used for teaching and instruction, drill and practice, simulation, tutorial and dialogue, data processing for research, guidance and counselling, examinations and laboratory work.

There is a cause of worry in making computer as the main source of instruction, and that is that the students get glued to the internet to such an extent that most of their time goes waste. Internet should not be allowed to interfere with the process of systematic learning.

There is no doubt that e-learning is going to give a big boost to education in the near future. It will telecast through the audio-visual medium, employing multimedia, multi-centric system to create interactive and virtual classrooms. As part of thee-learning process, students study on their computers, read textbooks, write essays and communicate via e-mails with their instructors and classmates. The e-learning system goes further by merging video conferencing with any sort of computer course programmes.

*****

VI

EDUCATION AS A LEADING POWER

Twenty nine

Education and Civilisation

Whether there is more or less material development is not the main criterion in judging development. What is essential is that reasonable men are enabled to control material conditions.

We find all around us the signs of intellectual and ethical fatigue; the decline of optimistic and ethical convictions about the meanings of life and of the universe; our superficial and narrow specialisation with its misplaced confidence in facts; increasing racialism and narrow nationalism; the growth of inhuman ideas and actions and failure to arouse their condemnation. Civilisation can be restored only through will for ethical good. Our age must recover its reverence for life. The crisis of our society has left man devoid of self-control – the power to control his emotions and appetites. Man has been degraded in respect of anything noble and sacred. The crisis is accompanied by a large number of social, economic, political, intellectual and moral problems including delinquency and crime, family disintegration, poverty, mental sickness, suicide, religious fanaticism, misdirected revolutions, terrorism and wars. Only a change towards a new sense of duty, justice, love, sacrifice and morality will release the creative forces needed for the new civilisation.

A man or a society is civilised, if truth, beauty, adventure, art, peace, the recognition for each individual, freedom of thought and action, tolerance, the use of persuasion rather than force and wisdom remain its dominant qualities.

Out of adventurous advance and a deadly lethargy of decadence, we have to select the former for the future of our civilisation. In developing civilisations, we have to bring to the forefront, admire and follow the creative personalities. We should remember that most civilisations in the past had broken down because of their own mistakes.

We need to establish a constitutional and cooperative system of world government. In economics, we need to make practical compromises between free enterprise and socialism. We have to put the secular superstructure in place of religious fanaticism.

Building and maintaining a high civilisation in which man can develop his latent potentialities should be and is our comprehensive social purpose. Progress has to ensure achievement of human values.

Education has to teach that the human, animal and vegetation worlds constitute one organic whole and we cannot prosper at the expense of others.

Dewey saw civilisation as a junction of a stubborn past and an insistent oncoming future. He explained that the social-civilisational feature has a tremendous bearing on education. The axis of the courses of study has to be focussed on the development of a civilisation.

Education will spearhead the growth of civilisation. It will provide competent experts and technical hands to carry forward the march of civilisation. Its influence on civilisation has been largely indirect. A few scientists and some other experts have provided the directions to be followed by civilisation. The fruits of civilisation did not equally benefit every individual. Some of its fruits were monopolised by a few smart people. Maldistribution of its benefits should prevail no more. Every individual must be made a shareholder in the growth and benefits of civilisation. Education has to prepare every individual to be a deserving shareholder.

Every individual should be made aware of his rights to education, livelihood, employment, health and economic security. Our civilisation has yet to ensure these rights to every individual.

One of the duties of every individual is to add to the infrastructure and to enrich the civilisation in his own way and according to his position.

It is for education to specify the goals for a civilisation and the progress of a civilisation must always be directed towards these goals.

When civilisation drives us to an excessive inclination towards materialism, we have to be cautious. Materialism is eating into most of the values of education and values of life. Materialistic outlook overshadows our learning, wisdom and desire for peace. It has introduced cut-throat competition in every walk of life. The mad race for materialism has to be softened with the help of sound thinking and reasoning. One must collect fruits of one's labour only by fair means and not by foul means. We should learn to master materialism and should not allow it to be our guiding principle. It should be made to serve our needs but not at the expense of the needs of others.

Materialism should be countered by rationalism. Irrational materialism is an abnormality which we should try to avoid. Educated people should defeat the evil designs of materialism, which has created a divide between individuals, employees, businessmen, communities, families, relatives and nations.

Richness and more richness of the civilisation are welcome. It is a happy and encouraging sign to aspire to and try for more richness. But this richness must be equally shared among all the citizens as far as possible. It does not entitle people to indulge in blatant luxuries and squander away the resources of a society or nation. All the facilities should be economically utilised, and savings should be further invested into productive ventures.

Again, this richness of a civilisation should not raise the costs of education. The facilities for achieving the highest levels of education should remain within the reach of a common man as well. If we find that education is becoming too costly, it must be subsidised at every stage by the state and the society. Merit and ability should not be allowed to go waste because of poverty. If merit is recognised and promoted by education, it will make a worthwhile contribution towards the growth of a civilisation.

*****

Thirty

Education and Culture

Education has a significant role in transmitting, preserving, promoting and enriching culture. It will prepare the individual to appreciate different aspects of culture, such as literature, arts, traditions, customs, festivals and entertainments. Education will endeavour to remove from the culture, dark spots, if any, and will enhance its glory. Cultural values will be enlisted and conveyed to every individual. Educational institutions should try to reflect the cultural heritage and offer its explanations. Cultural comparisons will be kept free from any bitterness. These comparisons will highlight the affinities between different cultures and efforts will be made to lay the foundations of a global culture. If there are certain cultural conflicts and misunderstandings, these will have to be sorted out.

Culture is full of noble lessons like truth, goodness and beauty; brotherhood, sacrifice for others, morality, honesty, welfare of all, charity, partriotism, fighting for noble causes, and following higher values in life. Education should safeguard culture from its deteriorations, if any. It has a role to play in streamlining cultural values. It has to strengthen the positive impact of culture on society. As the instrument of social change, education helps in evolving better cultural patterns.

Some crises in the society such as political instability, class conflicts, and religious fanaticism may lead to a cultural crisis which has to be removed through education. When material culture is developing fast due to scientific and technological developments, we find that non-material culture consisting of ideas, values and norms is lagging behind. The balance between the two components, material and non-material culture, is getting disturbed. Education has to bridge this cultural lag by its knowledge, activities and programmes

It is evident that modern man is getting detached from cultural values. These values have to be firmly planted in the minds of the new generation. Some people wrongly regard these values as only ornamental. Such like notions should be replaced with firm belief in the utility of these values.

Man is not only a social animal but also a cultural being. Culture is the treasury of knowledge. Education not only grasps and transmits that knowledge; it makes it more meaningful and expands it. It modernises cultural definitions for us. Our values attached to private property, fundamental rights, goodness or desirability are influenced by our culture. Education has to clarify and rationalise these values for a better social set-up.

Our goals of attaining success in life, being obedient to elders and teachers, being patriotic, attaining salvation, etc. are all set forth by our culture. Education prepares us to achieve these goals and presents before us models of these achievements.

Culture partly decides our career. It presents before us numerous career possibilites and alternatives. Education prepares us for the career of our choice and ensures our competence and success in that.

Culture provides behavioural patterns. It rewards noble deeds and punishes ignoble ones. Taking culture as the foundation, education provides development to our behaviour. Through this process of development, education does not blindly copy culture; it provides evolution to it with an eye on better behavioural patterns.

Culture moulds personality. Every culture will lead to a special type or types of personality. Education looks after the development of the personality in a more formal, systematic and scientific manner. It is capable of taking a personality to astonishing heights.

Culture provides not only for universals but also for alternatives. Still, no individual is compeletly shaped by culture. Every individual is unique and his uniqueness may be based on different backgrounds and individual differences in ability, aptitude, interests, facilities and learning. Every individual gets exposed to influences which are not completely determined by culture. He receives education, meets people of different cultural backgrounds, travels, reads books and comes under the influence of media inside and outside his culture. Many agencies shape him into a modern cultural being.

The best that has been thought and known is culture. It is regarded as a continuously changing pattern of learned behaviour. It is a complex whole including a number of aspects. It is the total behavioural pattern of the group conditioned partly by both, the natural and man-made environment. It is the total life of the people in terms of what they do, think, feel, behave, desire, fear, etc. It is the domain of styles, of values, of emotional attachments and intellectual adventures. It relates to the expression of our nature through different modes of life. It is idealistic, and stands for ideals and norms of human behaviour. It is in a continuous flux or it is dynamic in quality. It is social or it is inclusive of the expectations of others from an individual. It has unlimited vastness consisting, for example, the patterns of communication, methods and objects for physical welfare, travel and transportation, exchange of materials and services, real and personal forms of property, sex and family patterns, social controls and institutions of government, artistic expression, recreational interests and activities, religious ideas and practices, mythology and philosophy, science and technology, structuring of basic international processes, etc.

The cultures of occupational groups, religious groups, castes, social classes, age groups, sex groups and many others are designated as sub-cultures. The contact of two or more cultures leads to their interaction and mutual adaptation.

Contra-cultures are applied to designate those groups which not only differ from the prevailing patterns but sharply challenge them; a group of criminals, for example.

Culture influences education by shaping its aims and objectives, curricula, methods and techniques of teaching, textbooks and allied reading materials, infrastructure, co-curricular activities, vocational and job-oriented courses, arrangements for the physically challenged, maladjusted and slow learners, nature of management and discipline.

Educational institutions have to provide for different cultural activities in the form of a literary society, dramatic club, music club, fine arts society, social service society, exhibitions, games and sports, educational tours, self-government, celebration of important days and festivals, participating in the functions organised by the community and contributions made to the school/college magazine.

Education highlights the values of culture and enables the individuals to understand and practise those values. Culture makes a profound influence on the teacher in the form of ideals, values and missionary zeal. These traits are further transferred to his students.

*****

Thirty one

Education and Religion

Whether we believe in God or not, we should try to develop through education all individuals into God-fearing persons.

If God has created this universe, He has definitely aimed at making it a blessing for all. We should learn to avail and cherish this blessing and should not commit the mistake of squandering it away. Education will convince us that these blessings can be achieved and will enable us to draw maximum benefits from them. Even if one is deprived of blessings, he will not start cursing his fate, but will strive to achieve the best out of his opportunities and possibilities.

When we say that God is Truth, Goodness and Love; we should not forget that education is also rich in these attributes. Education and religion should not pull the individual in different directions. They have to collaborate for human welfare, peace of mind and self-realisation. They should uphold the genuine values held by each one of them.

Religion imparts to us in its own way, good behaviour, service to others, desire for contentment, faith in our destiny, doing our duty to the best of our ability, sacrifice for a noble cause, etc. Some of the functions of religion are: mental equilibrium, social solidarity, conservation of values, social control, welfare, explaining of individual suffering, enhancing importance of the self, recreation, etc. These functions indicate that education and religion agree on many avenues of individual and social upliftment. Since education has a more systematic place in the development of an individual, it has to draw upon religious elements for the welfare of mankind. Through education, religion will be used as a means of bringing people closer to humanity.

Education, religion and morality have to be brought on one platform to guide and improve the conduct of a human being. All the three act as powerful means of social control. Religion prescribes the rules of conduct and it intends to identify these rules with moral conduct. It is our duty not to be immoral and that is the same as the duty to be religious. Education has to rationalise both, moral and religious conduct. It has to convince the learner that there is no cause of clash between modern science on one side, and morality and religion on the other. If the sole purpose of religion and morality is the service of mankind then they have a strong common cause with science and education. Education has to draw for the individual rational influences from religion and morality.

The terms right and good are frequently used in ethics and morality. The word right implies conformity to some standard or that which has desirable qualities, satisfies some genuine need or has value for the human being. Technological theories hold the view that an act to be right must make some contribution to the goodness of man or mankind.

To have a moral social life we must have agreements, understandings, principles and rules of conduct. There is no human society that does not have well-established codes or rules of procedure.

Moral practices and standards depend on the stages of development, the general level of intelligence, and the knowledge available at that time. Morality grows out of life and makes an attempt to discover and live the good life. Morality is also a personal, social, economic, political and international concern.

The moral laws that a man obeys are not imposed from outside. These are the laws which are self-imposed. For example, a sense of duty and reason come from within; they are the expressions of one's own higher self.

Human beings with refined faculties are not satisfied with just the pleasures of the body; they strive for higher pleasures of the mind. Once a man has learnt to live at a higher plane, he can never sink into a lower level of existence. This is because of the sense of human dignity.

The theory of self-realisation emphasises the development of all the different functions of the person to their optimum capacity. The harmonious development of a man's personality has to be accepted as the satisfactory standard.

Reflective morality consists not only in making right decisions but also in making clear the reasons for one's decisions. Certain traits like love, honesty, friendship, unselfishness and self-control are universally approved. Some other traits like treachery, murder, and theft are universally condemned. The desirable traits are called virtues and the undesirable ones are called vices.

To meet the intellectual and spiritual demands of morality, the golden rule is "To do to others what you wish others to do to you."

Good consequences have to be achieved by the use of good means. To say that any means may be used provided the end is good would create a dangerous principle.

Morality comprises ethical, spiritual, humanistic, scientific and aesthetic values. Moral education means value-oriented education. It is better imparted through example and practice and not through rules. Morality like charity should begin at home. The attitude of service and the realisation that work is worship should be developed in the child. There should also be some provision for social service activities during holidays.

Education and Religion

The entire programme of an educational institution, its curriculum, its methodology, and its total climate should bear the responsibility for building a reflective and moral character.

The programme of moral education will be effective if it is consistent with the psychology of child behaviour and development. It should encompass the child's feelings and his constructive and creative impulses, as well as his intellectual pursuits.

In order to develop powers of moral judgement, children must have opportunities to analyse, to form and test judgements, to put selections into execution and to observe the consequences.

The religion is a source of moral and spiritual values which beautify and glorify life by cultivating a truthful heart with values. The many ills that our society and world of education are suffering from are mainly due to the gradual weakening of the hold of basic principles of religion and morality.

One should get a chance to study some selections of a universal nature from the scriptures of various religions. In a multi-religious world, it is necessary to promote a tolerant study of all religions by giving selected information about each religion. It should highlight the fundamental similarities in the great religions for the cultivation of comparable moral and spiritual values. Misunderstandings if any, about the true nature of religion should be effectively removed. Suitable reading material maybe prepared for all stages, which should describe briefly in a comparative manner, the basic ideas of all religions. Education on moral and spiritual values should be provided both by direct and indirect methods, by suggestions, by discussion and by discourses. The driving force, the inspiration and warmth of all higher conduct should come from religious education, from the faith in and love for God. Love for God leads to love for mankind.

Religious fanaticism, religious intolerance or clash between believers and non-believers are the worst lessons of religious education. The subject matter of religious and moral education should be comparative and universal. It should be linked with sound philosophy of life, human psychology and service to mankind. Essence of all religions, and their meeting points may be stressed in the lessons meant for children. Even indirect criticism of any religion should have no place in those lessons. Religious beliefs of different religions should be shown due respect. Religion is misunderstood when renunciation is taken as its message. Narrow religious considerations and practices should have no place in educational institutions. It is wrong to use the forum of an educational institution for the propagation of any particular religion.

Religious differences and conflicts have done great harm to our civilisation. Education should strive to convert narrow thinking or fanaticism into a broad concept of religion. Religion should not be allowed to create any segregation or compartmentalisation. It should generate tolerance for different religious thoughts. The common features of different religions may become mottoes of every educational institution. Religious education should not be allowed to raise new controversies.

Observance of religious rituals and dogmas and preaching of its irrational and supernatural aspects should not be stretched too far. Education has to draw guidance instead of misguidance from religion. No element or group should be allowed to exploit the religious sentiments of innocent people. Education should promote the fact that religion unites people instead of dividing them.

God sent man on earth for His experiment and we should hope that man makes this earth an ideal place to live in and his life on earth is ideal in its own way. Education has to convert this dream of God into reality. God has made man, the brain of the world which is competent to run this world independently. It is wrong on the part of man to leave everything to God. Man does not hesitate in blaming God for whatever wrong happens in this world. When he chooses to defy God in many of his actions, he has no business to blame Him for anything adverse that is happening here. Most of the problems on this earth are man-made. Man is considered God's representative but he has destroyed God's image along with his own image.

Let us agree with the idea that God is only a myth. Many people refuse to believe in Him. Even if God does not exist, His teachings exist, His ideas exist, His principles exist and His commands exist. Even if we do not believe in Him, there should be no hindrance in following His principles, ideals, edicts and lessons. Let us regard Him as an imaginary King and try to run His kingdom on His behalf and according to His Wishes.

It is often said that God punishes the evil-doer, but not always. Many evil-doers escape punishment and punishment is very delayed in the case of those who are punished. The guilty must be promptly and adequately punished. If God fails to punish them, it is the duty of the society to create a system which delivers prompt punishment. Not a single crime should go unpunished.

Education has to provide clarity about the concepts of God and religion. The puzzles must be solved for the benefit of mankind. We should be able to draw light from them instead of getting more confused and debating on them.

Prayer is an important activity related with religion. It provides peace of mind, mental strength and the power to overcome the sorrows and pains of life. It may be very difficult to secure full concentration during prayer but one can improve it with continuous practice. Time devoted to prayer varies from individual to individual. But some people correctly suggest that one can pray for twenty-four hours without ignoring the other activities of life. It will be a great blessing if one can form the habit of silent prayer without any break. It is possible and practical. After our prayer, we generally beg for favours from the Almighty. We ask for our well-being and relief from our hardships. It will be better if we beg for the well-being, happiness and comfort for all. Even if our prayers go unanswered, we should not lose hope and faith. We should understand the meaning and significance of our prayer and get attached with it after every repetition. Our motivation for prayer should be very deep and heartfelt. We should realise that prayer is making our life more sublime day by day. The prayer should not be disposed of as a ritual.

People in general, blindly follow rituals, but disobey religion in their practical life. The organised religions have caused more wars, violence and suffering in the world than any other single factor. Education has to discard such religious sentiments and their impact.

There is a religious place in a corner of a country, where liquor is presented as the offering. This custom violates the basic religious values. People should be able to disapprove and discontinue this custom. Its continuance is an insult to the sacred ideals of any religion.

Education can draw upon religion to inculcate in children the essential moral and humanistic qualities like courtesy, tolerance, sympathy, fellow feeling, equality, fraternity, selfless service, sacrifice for a cause, nobility, love for mankind, mental peace, self-confidence, and sublimation of instincts. Religion offers an enlightenment which directs the individual towards idealism and higher values. It makes him courageous enough to face the problems of life more boldly. It preserves and enriches culture in its own way. Education should develop a critical attitude among the students so that they are not blind or superstitious in their faith. They should be made to understand the unity of all religions and rationalisation of religious thinking.

Religious education should in no way create bad blood, disturb the peaceful atmosphere and break the unity of mankind. Its rigidly conservative approach should not be allowed to come into conflict with rational thinking. It should not preach an unreal attitude. Rather, it should condemn inhuman crimes and barbarities committed in the name of religion. It is not religious to arouse emotions of enmity, hatred and fanaticism. Religion has to curb inhuman tendencies. It should give real, rational, humanistic and scientific meanings to education. There is need to establish coordination between scientific researches, rationality, materialistic outlook, progressivism, modernisation and religion. Religion should not divide but unite humanity.

*****

Thirty two

Education and Politics

If politics has been converted into a dirty game, some agencies must come forward to cleanse it. An irresponsible politician definitely plays havoc with the government and society.

Everything is considered by some people as fair in politics. What a wrong and dangerous notion! If a politician does not stick to the rules of politics, he can easily change sides for ulterior motives, can be pressurised, can be purchased or compelled to compromise with his principles. In this case, he is certainly presenting a dirty picture of politics.

When we aspire for an ideal way of life, an ideal society, ideal governance, the politicians who are instrumental in achieving these ideals must be ideal personalities themselves. A person who falls below the ideal criteria has no right to become a politician.

A politician is a leader, reformer, builder and a guide. His roles demand a calibre and dedication of the highest order. He is a servant of the people. Selfless service to the society has to be a motto for him. It is strange that some politicians become corrupt, create conflicts among people, patronise antisocial elements, protect criminals, divide people for their narrow purposes, use muscle and money power for votes, instigate violence and promote terrorism. Why should a politician get tainted? Why should he be surrounded by hypocrites? He must be able to maintain respectability, trust and a clean image. He must be able to prove that he deserves to be the representative of millions of people. Why should he indulge in luxury at the expense of public money? It is very sad that politicians today require a vast security set-up for their personal safety. The way our elected representatives behave in the legislatures also does not sound very creditable.

A politician's mistakes carry far-reaching consequences for the people. Every politician must get into the habit of self-evaluation. He should never misuse his authority and should not brush aside public criticism against his policies and conduct. He should take criticism in a sporting manner and obtain directions from it for better performance. He should not give anybody a cause for continuous criticism against him.

The politicians get divided into various parties. They should adopt the parties of their choice on the basis of ideology. When they stick to an ideology, they have to be loyal to it and should enrich it. They have to work for the success of their ideology and party. Their political fight should observe the rules of healthy competition. They should desist from using unfair means to gain an upper hand over other parties. Working in the interest of the people should remain their uppermost priority.

The state as controlled by politicians, exercises various authorities over education, such as constitutional control, economic control, educational policies, administrative control, etc. The political set-up is duty-bound to provide sufficient and ultra modern facilities to the field of education, but should not in return try to impose its unwelcome ideas on this field. The possibilities of and expectations from education should not get subordinated according to the whims and selfish motives of politicians.

Rather, education should be so empowered that it supplies wise, honest and selfless persons to the field of politics just as it is to supply the right type of individuals to every walk of life. As we want every educated individual to be result-oriented in life, similarly politicians should be people with good performance skills. Politicians should accept the role of education as an agency to supply capable and trustworthy members for their group.

The tactics and tricks adopted by politicians to get elected have polluted the political system. The educational institutions should present objection-free elections on their campuses to give an experience to the would be politicians.

Politicians are required to be good orators and organisers, but more than that they should be good thinkers, planners, policy makers, executors of their plans and policies, administrators, and above all good human beings, and all these qualities should be developed in the student leaders and politicians of the future.

Our socio-political leaders have to follow and reflect in their lives and their behaviour, those values which they wish their followers to adopt. The socio-political ecology has to be purified through education from its factors like communalisation, caste and region-based polarisation, politicisation of welfare agencies, corruption, criminalisation of society and administration and repression of the opposition. In the long-run, education should aim at developing saintly politicians for society. They must believe in humility and should not exhibit any ego or pride.

Political personalities have to be made conscious that people look towards them as ideals in the matters of knowledge, wisdom, devotion, sincerity, honesty, achievement and discipline. They should not stand in need of slogans and campaigns for getting recognition and popularity but these rewards should get showered on them without asking.

Educated people especially, should not tolerate a politician if he chooses to misuse his position or tries to exploit and misguide the masses. They should come in the forefront to expose him. They should build such a strong voice and public opinion which may prevent the politicians with ulterior motives to come forward. They should be able to exercise a watchful eye over the conduct of various politicians. The undeserving persons should not dare enter or survive in the political field.

Educational institutions should make the learners aware of the qualities of leadership desired in a politician. They should not fall into the trap of unworthy politicians. They should place their destiny only in the hands of the trustworthy. The syllabi in education may refer to the roles, rules and guidelines for the would be politicians. The learners must be made aware of the need of neat and healthy political game and also the improper dealings of the politicians of the day. A stress may be laid on the behaviour, personality and characteristics of a politician.

Education should be welcome to cast its influence over politics and politicians. As far as possible, highly qualified people, professionally trained persons, experts in various academic fields, visionaries par excellence and highly motivated people only should come forward to join politics. The mediocres of the academic world cannot do justice to their duties and responsibilities as politicians. They must be able to understand and solve social, economic and political problems of the people. They must be men of action and achievement and not merely men of slogans.

The association of teachers should act as a watchdog against the intentional and unintentional misdeeds of the politicians. It should place before them from time to time the expectations of people. It should be able to condemn the insincere politicians and convince people to reject them. There is a need that the politician is reminded of his responsibility by renowned scholars and thinkers from time to time. He should remain under the influence of great teachers available in his country and the world at large.

Each country should set-up an educational institution manned by experts, which should be attended by several batches of politicians to discuss the problems and progress of their country and evolve better strategies to improve the situation. This institution should provide a forum for discussing local, national and international issues. It should carry out regular researches to foresee the problems and possibilities of the future. It should keep a watch over the level of debates in the legislatures and the nature of tools being employed to win the elections. It can keep a record of the overall contributions of various politicians. A wing of this institution can pinpoint the admirable participation of any individual legislator or a group of legislators in raising the utility and dignity of a house of representatives.

Different organs of media criticise the politicians for their lapses and try to give them right direction, but there is hardly any improvement. Therefore, other agencies have to be invited to play their part in the matter. Education has to ensure that every individual is made a man of principles and those who choose to enter politics do not suffer from any handicaps in this respect.

Intrigue, leg-pulling, backbiting, self-glorification, false criticism, bribing the media, gathering sycophants around, creating fake heroes, giving undue favours, etc., are some of the tricks of the politicians. Through the organs of education, they may be convinced to get rid of these shallow and improper attributes.

A politician must be gifted with the qualities of leadership, as he is required to lead the people towards different goals. If the qualities of a politician are noticed early in his life, there should be special provision in his programmes of education to enable him to develop the qualities of leadership.

On viewing human history, we can find that most of the politicians failed to give up to the mark performance in their respective fields. Every politician should be so educated that he richly deserves his status and authority. They are required to make a mark in life and they should not fall below the expectations associated with them. They must create a better record. They should believe in lifelong education for improving their knowledge, ideas, beliefs, commitments, achievements and services. They have to lead a result-oriented life enhancing their reputation and popularity. They should adopt methods like social service, developmental activities, fighting for a genuine cause, inspiring people to become productive and constructive citizens and making a good impression through their personal life. It is wrong for them to depend on road shows, on stirring violence, arousing directionless emotions, provoking agitations and protests and unfounded criticism of the opponents for their own popularity.

Politicians need huge funds to maintain the structure of their political party for frequently holding big public meetings, transporting people for processions, holding blockades, arranging strikes and for running election campaigns. They have to collect these funds by underhand means and have to do undue favours in return to their donors. This vicious circle continues. They should be educated to follow a modest style of personal and public life.

A politician should develop a habit of thinking. He has to constantly think of better ways and means to improve the conditions of his people. He has to think about the problems being faced by the people and his country. And he should join his efforts in the removal of those problems.

A large number of politicians become so ambitious that they become too fond of power and wealth instead of following the mission of selfless service. Many of them are bent on grooming their kith and kin for a political career. They misuse their position, experience and links for that purpose.

A politician must have made some mentionable sacrifices for others. It does not behove a politician to be a man of narrow loyalties such as loyalty towards his party, party programme and a group within his party. His loyalty should extend to mankind and the entire world.

We need to address the problem of negation of sociopolitical values, involving issues like corrupt electoral practices, criminalisation of politics, the role of money and muscle power in deciding election results and lack of voter awareness and voter participation.

It does no credit to the politicians when in their vested interest, they mislead the masses, arouse their emotions, cause divide on the basis of religion, caste or class, raise false issues to overshadow the genuine issues, consider their political career as an investment, draw maximum possible material gains through their political position, threaten internal and external peace, do not stick to one ideology, change political affiliations overnight, do not behave as servants of the people and do not keep the welfare of people as their uppermost priority. Educational institutions should play an effective role in curbing such tendencies of the politicians. They have to groom learners to produce the right type of politicians to serve society and its people.

Education and politics should strengthen democracy and should try to make it real and everlasting. It goes to the credit of political leaders that they brought about many movements, developments, prosperities and revolutions but they cannot escape the blame of creating two world wars, many other wars, big and small battles, conflicts, destruction, riots and misery.

Political leadership tries to exercise its control over education as it wants this big establishment to remain loyal to it. But this control should not amount to non-educational and objectionable interference in the affairs of education. Politics has no right to make education one of its subordinates. It has resources at its command for the welfare of the people. Education should be given its due share out of these resources. This support to education should not be counted as a favour. The political leadership should not in return spoil the system of education by tampering with the curricula, by propagating its viewpoint through textbooks, by launching its programmes through educational institutions, by appointing its own favourites to key positions in the departments of education, by promoting its own henchmen to start their educational institutions, by creating different political blocs among teachers and by dividing students on political lines. Political leadership should not in anyway, protect or tolerate incompetent and irresponsible workers in the field of education. It is bound to its duty to place education in the hands of the most qualified and dedicated workers. The state should decentralise its educational functions in favour of responsible public institutions also.

People place their destiny in the hands of political leaders who should not breach this trust to the slightest extent. Under no circumstances should political leaders adopt shortcuts for increasing their popularity or achieving their goals. They should remain honest towards the welfare of mankind and should not try to achieve the welfare of their followers at the cost of their opponents.

Political leaders have often raised armies for invasion, conquered territories and brought people under slavery, necessitating freedom struggles by the oppressed people resulting in devastation in this conflict and better situation only at a very heavy cost. In this new age, the awakened people should not allow a political leader to repeat those tragedies.

Education should develop strict and honourable guidelines for the politicians. They should be convinced to acquire education of a sufficiently higher level. A poorly educated person cannot do justice to his duties as a political leader. It is an insult to the status of a political leader when a mob instigated by him resorts to unruly behaviour, or when he himself breaks the decorum of a legislature. Democracy should not be misused by political leaders to grab power by all possible means. At the same time, political leaders should not continue with their practice of favouring their supporters and disfavouring their opponents. Due to wrong policies of the political leaders, the existence of democracy is endangered.

The democratic system of government is based upon the principles of equality, fraternity and liberty thereby emphasising cooperation, fellow feeling, service and sacrifice. Each individual is provided maximum opportunities for education and development according to his interests, aptitudes and capacities. In democracy, curriculum is organised on the principle of diversity to suit different individuals.

Political leaders are expected to attach the maximum possible importance to their duties and responsibillities instead of hankering after power, authority and privileges. They should not try to derive the benefits of publicity, self-aggrandisement, control or satisfaction of motives, but should serve the noble cause of education with dedication. They should allow education to set rules, guidelines, norms and discipline for them and follow the same honestly without regretting this subordination. The educational experts in the fields of political science, economics, sociology, religion, history, agriculture, sciences, technologies and professional courses should be invited to advise the political leaders in their respective fields and this advice must be implemented in the interest of the society and country. Educational experts should form committees at different levels to watch, evaluate and redirect the functioning of political leadership.

Nikita Khrushchev has said, "Politicians are the same all over. They promise to build a bridge where there is no river."

*****

Thirty three

Education and Government

Education and the government have to join hands for a common purpose, and for the welfare of the people. The destinies of people have to be shaped in the classrooms. Any reform envisaged by the government can be best achieved in collaboration with education.

It is the duty of the government to form expert committees to chalk out plans, programmes, goals and activities for the guidance of educational institutions. Education should be regarded as one of the premier investments made by the government. The huge expenditure involved in education cannot be arranged by the local bodies or private enterprise. If education is starved of provisions, it will lead to a great loss for the society. Even if some of the sectors of education are given autonomy, government has not to withdraw itself from related financial liabilities. Government should organise and finance education with the belief that it provides solid foundation for every development programme.

Sound policies and programmes of education will in return provide strength to the various organs of the government. If all the members of the new generation receive quality education, then every new generation will be able to supply efficient and dedicated manpower. The top and heavy government machinery very seriously needs sincere elements to run it.

It is said that people get the type of government they deserve. People should make themselves deserving enough for an ideal government or the system of education should make people deserving and righteous that only a right type of government can continue to rule over them.

Democracy was in the beginning admired as the government of the people by the people and for the people. Today, it is ridiculed in many ways like the government of the people, bye the people and far from the people. Democracy has been the latest and wisest discovery in the field of governance. We should employ the medium of education along with other relevant efforts to ensure that democracy proves to be a successful and lasting experiment in the realm of governance. According to Diogenes, "The foundation of every state is the education of its youth." The voter in a democracy has to be made mature enough to select the right type of representatives for the government.

Young children should be given the opportunity to elect their representatives for different student bodies in an educational institution. Their ability to elect deserving representatives should be watched and streamlined. Their elected representatives may be associated with the administration.

The government which ignores education is perhaps an anti-people government. The distance between education and government should be bridged to such an extent that they work hand in hand for the upliftment of the individual and society. The government should not consider education as one of its departments among many. Its role must be regarded as most crucial. The standard of education of the new generation will determine the standard of government elected in future. It should be made possible that learned men, scholars and experts are elected as representatives of the people.

The govenment may enlist its demands on education and see that these demands are adequately fulfilled. At the same time, the government should empower education to fulfil these demands. Education cannot be expected to meet big demands if it is starved of facilities or rigidly controlled.

The well-meaning government will give topmost priority to education. If education is enabled to succeed in its programmes, most of the problems of the government will automatically disappear. The self-disciplined and enlightened individuals will not be any burden on the government. They will not need any interference and control of the government in their day to day life. If such like people come at the helm of affairs in the govenment, they will be able to convert it into a people-friendly government. People will develop a faith in the government and unnecessary differences and tensions between the two will get removed.

No government should ever think of misusing education for the indoctrination of people or for the propagation of its clever designs. It has no right to exploit, misinform or misdirect people. The common man must feel that the government is working for his welfare and the two should learn to work in complete coordination for progress.

The demonstration of poor work culture in government offices and departments delivers a wrong message to educational workers and institutions also. The government should enforce efficiency and transparency in its network and expect the same atmosphere in all the areas including education. Only an efficient government can demand efficiency from different branches and functionaries of education.

Governments all over the world are not performing their functions adequately. In many cases, they have become dens of corruption, red tapism, scams, nepotism and wastage of resources. They should take the help of education to develop people who may be able to reverse the situation. Governments have to remain pre-occupied with enforcing law and order, controlling agitations, checking crime, and fighting terrorism. Thus, they get little time for developmental activities including education. They should come forward to reserve due attention to education so that the countries become free from problematic citizens.

The government has to undertake full responsibility for quality education. Even if private agencies come forward to open their educational institutions, the government has to supervise the whole system to ensure desired standards. The standards of education in any country should remain comparable even with the standards in the most developed countries. A country offering sub-standard education to its people will continue to remain backward. The government should treat education as a crucial area of investment for national development. There is no justification in borrowing an educational system from abroad, but the government must keep in touch with the latest developments in education in different countries and upgrade its own system without delay.

The textbooks in a country, the standards of examination, the nature of competitive tests, the subject matter of professional courses, the status of research work and the level of advanced literature should be at par with those of other developed countries of the world. There is need for a healthy global exchange and healthy competition in these matters. Different countries should come closer to share their experiences and vital information in the interest of education.

Ensuring cent per cent education up to a certain level is no more an ambitious target for a government. The government should provide numerous avenues and diversifications in courses so that every individual has a number of choices before him to ensure that he is employed well.

Technical education, professional education and higher education are becoming over-expensive and beyond the reach of common man. There are some educational institutions which fleece the students and parents for providing lavish facilities. The Government has to intervene to keep the cost of education within reasonable limits.

Education should make it clear to the learners that they are not only the medium to run the society and government but also to reform them. They must try to reform the government which suffers from misgovernance. In its own interest, government should make education more and still more of an effective agency. The governments should raise the quality of education and get in return qualitative personnel, system, progress and governance. Transforming education is a pre-condition for transforming mankind and all its functions.

Aristotle has said that "All who have meditated on the art of governing mankind have been convinced that the fate of empires depends upon the education of youth."

Education and government should be the sources of direction, strength and norms to each other. Put together they have to take each new generation to greater heights and a better quality of life. If one goes wrong, the other has to come forward to show the way.

The government has to appoint committees of educational experts to frame the schemes of education and their modernisation from time to time. But it has no right to misuse this authority for political interference, indoctrination or for brainwashing in the domain of education. It should promote the approach of a child-centric education. It should provide maximum possible funds for education, and should not allow education to become so expensive that it goes beyond the means of an average citizen. Its policies should ensure universal, compulsory and free education. The people, who are poor should be provided financial help for the education of their children. It must ensure that education received by any individual does not go waste for want of job opportunities. The diversification of students and admissions into technical and professional courses should be strictly based on the data of the job market. Both education and government should continue to explore new avenues in vocational life. In order to strengthen its own democracy, the government should promote democratic activities in educational institutions. The government should encourage and support educational research. The findings of research should not be allowed to go waste.

The government should not show its usual lethargy in the sphere of education in aspects like active supervision and implementation of advice of supervisors, foolproof data about educational institutions for the purposes of expansion, infrastructure, diversification, job-oriented courses, modernisation of the curricular and co-curricular programmes, self-discipline, democratic experiences, streamlining overall achievements, role of an educational institution as a centre for community, accountability of the staff and successful entry of students in society after completing their education. The government should also ensure the comparability of its educational system with those in other countries. It should see that the aims of education are being reasonably achieved in its educational institutions. It has to also ensure the successful implementation of educational reforms.

*****

VII

EDUCATION AND DISCIPLINE

Thirty four

Education and Discipline

Education is a discipline for our body and mind. It does not advocate external discipline. It stresses internal or self-discipline.

Discipline stands for an acceptable type of behaviour. It does not permit anything which is not approvable. Every single act exhibits an element of discipline in it. Discipline involves training of the mind, manners, attitudes, sublimation of emotions and development of character. It imparts qualities such as how a person speaks, how he behaves, adjusts in a group, works, helps others and becomes an example for others to follow.

Apart from individual discipline, there is need for social, institutional, administrative, religious, economic and political discipline. Only effective discipline in every sphere of life can make life worth living.

The discipline in an educational institution should be an intelligent, smooth and a non-enforcing one. There should be minimum use of any authority, orders, instructions or punishments for the purpose. The institution which has a long list of rules and regulations for maintaining discipline is a poorly disciplined organisation. An educational institution should be a model of discipline for other institutions and establishments. Education should stand for a positive instead of a negative discipline. It should utilize example instead of coercion. Discipline should be from within and not from the above. It should be spontaneous and voluntary, and governed by an inner urge and not by fear.

Discipline should be an equal concern for everybody. It should not be left to the enforcement agencies. It is a wrong idea to make the games instructor or any other member of the staff as the in charge to maintain discipline. Neither should it be left to the principal alone. It is often suggested that a discipline committee may be formed with student representatives to ensure discipline and to tackle indiscipline at their own level. But maintaining discipline should be regarded as the joint responsibility of the entire faculty and student population.

A child's initial years are the proper time for a permanent effect on the human mind through lessons about good conduct. If we succeed in establishing the idea of discipline in the mind of a young child, his mind will not permit him to go astray. Our training in good conduct should be so impressive and convincing that the learner makes up his mind to believe in good conduct. Educational institutions should seldom require strictness for discipline. The attitude of sympathy towards young learners should never be lost sight of.

We should be able to get tough with ourselves in matters of good habits and discipline. Many undesirable forces and temptations may lure us but we should be able to remain firm. Our resistance to these temptations should not become weak. The choice must remain with us. Nothing should be so powerful as to drag us against our choices. What we want, what we like and what we need are our prerogatives. External stimuli should not be allowed to have a control on us against directions and decisions which we have taken with all caution and sincerity.

A child should be constantly trained on what is right and what is wrong. It should be made clear that right is right and wrong is wrong irrespective of the situation. If required, reasons may also be emphatically given to clear the confusion or doubt, if any. The teacher, by his example and explanation, is the main source of lessons on discipline. His facial expressions, gestures, a smile and approval through words like 'fine' or 'good' convince the child that he is on the right path. Similarly, nodding of one's head in the negative is a warning for the child to be careful.

In spite of various efforts, we find that discipline is very rare in our families, society, offices and institutions. Our rules and regulations, dos and don'ts and punishments do not achieve the results. We are found indisciplined when we are on the road, in a gathering, celebration, party, fair, procession, queue, bus, joint venture, etc. We need enforcement agencies to ensure discipline at every step. We conveniently shift the blame for indiscipline on these agencies. But we must admit that education has to bear a major part of this blame and criticism.

Indiscipline causes double wastage of our energy. The originator wastes his energy on it and enforcement agencies waste their energy to control it. When we try to enlist the causes of indiscipline, we obtain an unending list. Some of these causes are – the atmosphere of indiscipline at home, in society, in the government and even in educational institutions, tendency of the individual to seek attention through pranks and due to inferiority complex, etc., tendency of the group leader to enhance his nuisance value through the objectionable behaviour of his followers, to show off in the case of a rivalry and group competition, to gain importance by challenging the authority and seniors, to gain popularity by the easy way of negative behaviour, to go against sane advice because of ego problems, to use indiscipline as a means of protest and agitation, poor common sense that fails to distinguish between discipline and indiscipline, to develop an attitude of aggressive behaviour, to feel that one is always right, or that one doesn't care for others, to attain an authority over a situation by fair means or foul, when one hates others, to have fun at the cost of others, when one happens to be pampered by others, when discipline is regarded as the headache of authorities and there is unabated prevalence of crime.

From the examination of these causes, we can easily come to the conclusion that teachers and educational institutions must provide a leading role in building the foundations of discipline in young minds. We should not allow indiscipline to go deep and grow into a force of its own kind. We have to check it at its very beginning. It should be uprooted when it is yet to take deep roots. When each one among the faculty is self-disciplined, is committed towards institutional discipline, the problem of indiscipline will seldom take any serious form. If indiscipline in an educational institution is too common, then there is a need for observing and reorienting the behaviour of teachers and the head of the institution.

As indiscipline grows out of bad habits, we should not allow bad habits to become a routine with students. These bad habits should be checked or given a positive shape by persistent persuasion and not by condemnation, punishment or enforcement of strict rules. We shall win discipline and not enforce it in our educational institutions. The teachers and principals should achieve such a respectable status that even a mild hint from them works more effectively than a rule book.

There are many other agencies which can help in the matter of creating and strengthening discipline. These are family, society, government and media. Education through its functionaries activates these agencies also. The strict law enforcing agencies cannot be successful on their own. If the minds of young learners are tuned to the need and importance of discipline, there will be no need to fall back upon law enforcing departments and fines or punishments.

Motivation is a pre-condition of discipline in educational institutions. For this we can try a number of procedures, like focussing pupil's attention on desired learning outcomes, utilising curiosity to encourage discipline, using existing interests and developing new ones, providing concrete symbolic incentives, arranging learning tasks appropriate to the abilities of learners, providing realistic goals, helping the learners in making and evaluating progress towards goals, avoiding extreme tension which is likely to produce disorganisation, inefficiency and indiscipline .

Freedom is considered essential for the complete development of a child and discipline is equally essential and important for his development. Unrestricted freedom may make a child extremely selfish and aggressively self-centred. An indisciplined and selfish person may create many problems for himself and for the society. Therefore, discipline and freedom have to exist and function in a balance. They have to be so adjusted that they become mutually supplementary and complementary. Both have to be merged together in a broader sense. Freedom has to be enjoyed so that it does not encroach upon the freedom of fellow beings. Similarly, discipline should not require any directions from outside; it should be true self-discipline. Adherence to discipline must enhance the joy of freedom. When young children are enabled to enjoy opportunities to express themselves freely, they are likely to imbibe self-discipline. In our educational institutions, there should not be any rigid and strict approach towards freedom and discipline. The repressionistic discipline should be replaced by impressionistic discipline. The right to freedom should be availed of by the students without any resort to unrestricted freedom. It is possible to achieve a desirable synthesis between freedom and discipline. There can be no freedom for indiscipline.

There should be no place in educational institutions for indiscipline that can take the form of violence, damage to property, impediments in the normal functioning of places of learning, shouting of slogans, processions, agitations, hunger strikes, etc. The hunger for power politics on the part of student leaders is an insult to the lessons of education.

Education has to counteract the impact of media, newspapers, films and television which quite often advocate permissiveness to an individual. There should not be any undue craze for fashion, excitement, novelty, speed, enjoyment and waywardness.

An important sanction to discipline in education comes from social ethos, which should emphasise reverence for elders like parents and teachers. At the same time, there should be no indiscipline and factionalism among the teachers.

In the interest of discipline, we should make the goals of education clear and attractive, we should be able to eliminate the failures of education, we should make education relevant to occupations and life, the programme of education should be rich in values and there should be a real democracy in our institutions.

*****

Thirty five

Education and Leadership

A leader may mean a person of accomplishment in various fields such as arts, science, athletics, business or politics in terms of one's unique capacities and talents or a person who influences other people. He is obeyed, listened to or honoured by his followers. He unifies people and mobilises them to move towards a desired goal.

Sprott said, "Anyone, who acts as a model to others is often called a leader."

Lapiere said, "Leadership is a behaviour that affects the behaviour of other people more than their behaviour affects the leader."

The leader acts as a group-guiding force. Some of the characteristics of leadership are: it is a bi-polar process in which the leader and the followers play their respective roles, the leader enjoys a sort of dominance over the followers, he influences their feelings, views, behaviour and actions, he has to model his behaviour according to the aspirations of the followers, the followers regard him as an authority and accept the suggestions and directions given by him. So, they accept his superiority.

There are many qualities desired in a leader: he has to share the values, attitudes and interests of the group, he should exercise moderate superiority over the other members of the group, and he should love people and be prepared to make sacrifices for the common good. He should be looked upon as an ideal person so that they can imitate him in the way he thinks, feels and acts. He should have a magnetic personality and should be a diligent worker. He should have thorough knowledge of group psychology and working of the group mind. Through suggestions, he should be able to make his followers accept his ideas and plans. He should be a good orator. His intellectual level should be higher than that of his followers. He should be able to take quick and right decisions. He should be self-assertive. He should possess integrity of character and dealings. He should also be gifted with a sense of humour. Scientific and objective attitude is also a desirable quality. He should be able to inspire and guide others. He should possess qualities like social insight, imagination, vision, judgement, flexibility, enthusiasm, lofty sense of duty, broad-mindedness, emotional maturity and sympathy. He is at the same time a planner, a policy maker, an expert, an executive, an exemplar, arbitrator and mediator, ideologist, a father figure, an organiser and a symbol for the group. He has to be a controller of internal relationships and has to be the most responsible member of the group.

While trying to identify the traits of leadership, Bird has given a list of 79 traits. The important ones are: aggressive, ascendant, dignified, expansive, friendly, honest, just, reliable, self-composed, self-controlled, sociable, suggestible, vigorous, courageous, original, self-reliant, tactful, enthusiastic, self-confident, sympathetic, an extrovert, initiator, intelligent, charismatic, etc.

The emergence of a leader is particularly demanded in situations where the progress towards group goals is blocked or when the group suffers external threats to its security. The leader will come forward to satisfy the needs of the group. He will win the confidence, admiration and adoration of the followers. With the help of his expert information, and technical competence he will convince the followers that they can depend on him for achieving their goals. His position will ensure the unity of the group and in his absence; the group is likely to disintegrate.

In the matters of an organisation, he will function as a democrat. He will carry out the mandate of the group, or better, will encourage and facilitate the carrying out of this mandate by the group members themselves. He will initiate plans for the group, will distribute duties among members, will surrogate for individual responsibility, will supervise individual members and ensure progress.

The destiny of every group, family, institution, organisation, nation, country and even the whole world depends upon wise and effective leaders. A good leader is an asset and a bad leader is a disaster.

At the level of education, we have to locate and discover potential leaders. We have to train them so that they can assume leadership in social, political, industrial and cultural fields. They maybe assigned leadership duties during education in the form of being class monitors, class representatives, prefects, secretaries of various societies and clubs, organisers of special programmes and functions, members of the discipline committees, chief scouts and guides, assistants to teachers in various duties and captains of teams. Giving them various responsibilities will train them to come in the forefront in later life.

The head of the institution should be an example for everyone to emulate, in matters of running the institution and guiding its population as a leader and in being a father figure. Similarly, every teacher is a guide and leader for his class. His qualities of leadership should be visible to the students for imitation.

People who discharge leadership duties in various fields and have a good reputation may be invited to educational institutions to share their principles and experiences with the young and would be leaders. We have already incorporated a few lessons about various leaders in the textbooks of students. Their merits and demerits as leaders should be frankly discussed with the students.

Good student leaders should be rewarded and their qualities may be explained before student assemblies. When we emphasise the qualities desired in every individual, we should get an opportunity to discuss that the leader is a super-individual and thus, he is duty-bound to acquire and develop higher qualities. A bad and incompetent leader needs to be dethroned by the followers at the earliest, so that he does not continue to harm the interests of the group. An undeserving leader should not be allowed to thrust himself upon the group. Every individual should develop an ability to distinguish between good and bad leaders. The bad leaders should be isolated and rejected without delay. Traits rather than tactics of leadership should be allowed to survive.

Research workers in the fields of political science, sociology, psychology and education should from time to time evaluate the status and performance of the past and present leaders to provide a scientific picture about them for the information of the people. It is the peoples' right to know about the credits and misdeeds of their leaders.

It will be beneficial, if educational experts are invited to set-up special educational institutions and programmes, to provide training to the existing and potential leaders. They should be made worthy of their distinctive roles in various fields. At the moment, we do not feel satisfied with their performance. Left to themselves, they seldom acquire growth in qualities and competence. The overall development of the society is largely determined by the way they provide leadership. The society suffers because of poor performance of leaders. Instead, the right type of leadership can carry a society to great heights. Through systematic training, they should be groomed to reflect appreciable results. A leader should be able to give a good account of himself while providing directions to his group. There may be an agency to earmark accountability and demand the same from leaders in different walks of life.

It is not wrong to say that history is full of examples of follies committed by some leaders. Mankind has been suffering the consequences of those follies. Let us make clear through education that a leader's blunder has very far-reaching and wide ranging consequences. A leader must therefore, be extra careful about his actions.

The potential leader should be able to provide a proof of some selfless service, and sacrifice for the group. The followers must feel satisfied that he will do still more selfless service and will always be ready to make sacrifices for his followers. The followers must be able to notice the contributions made by him for their welfare.

Education should enable the members of a group and their leaders to create and maintain high morale in the group. Every educational institution should be seen as a group with high morale. Some of the signs of high morale are: holding the group together through internal cohesiveness rather than through some external pressure, absence of divisive frictions, adaptability of the group to changing circumstances, ability of the group to handle inner conflicts on its own, produce and maintain necessary inner readjustments, feelings of acceptance and liking among group members, positive attitude of members towards group objectives and group leadership, and the desire among members to retain the group.

Sometimes, orderliness is mistaken to demonstrate high morale. A quiet classroom may be taken as a high morale situation. Such orderliness is generally brought about through the application of external pressure, through arbitrary rules and regulations or through penalties and punishments. This situation does not denote high morale.

One essential determinant of high morale is a positive goal, which acts as magnetic pole. In such a case, the aspirations of members are drawn towards a higher morale. Many people may participate in the group for self-expression, prestige and recognition. It is also necessary that every member finds a feeling of progress towards the goal.

There should be a confirmed belief regarding the equality of sacrifices made or gains achieved within the group. A sense of solidarity, identification and involvement among the members is an important factor for increasing the morale of the group.

*****

Thirty six

Education and Justice

Let us first make a resolve as individuals not to do injustice to anybody. When we indulge in injustice to others, complaints have to be filed against us; the sufferer goes to higher authorities or courts. This involves the two parties in a wasteful and avoidable process of litigation.

By becoming law-abiding, an individual honours law and its place in life and society. He earns a unique respect and satisfaction as an individual.

A person must be prepared to fight for justice in his own case and in the case of others who need his support in their fight for justice.

Justice is one of the pillars of modern society. It has to be safeguarded by judges, lawyers, law enforcing agencies, human rights groups, international body for human rights, the media, politicians and the public. There should not be any bias on the part of any agency or forum in the matter of delivering justice.

Even within families, the selfish, clever and dominating members deny rights and privileges to their near ones, and get away with a better share of the household property and facilities.

Society in general should not tolerate or give respect to the individual or the group that break laws and does injustice to the weak.

The procedure for availing justice should be kept simple, straightforward and inexpensive. Every individual should be educated about his fundamental rights and the channels which help protect his rights. One has to learn to do justice to one's duties, towards one's dependents, vocation, commitments, aims and aspirations in life, and to the cause of enrichment of society and culture. We have to do justice to various qualities demanded from our behaviour, character and personality.

Crimes or antisocial activities should not go unpunished, and there should be no mercy at the stage of awarding punishments. Crime and corruption are increasing because the judgements against them are not severe enough today. There is every justification, if the courts award maximum permissible punishments against crimes for some time to initiate the process of eliminating crime.

Even lawyers should be repeatedly reminded about the values associated with their profession and they should refrain from using their ability and the loopholes in law to protect criminals. They should avoid taking up the side of falsehood.

Sometimes people do not give equal status to others who belong to a lower class, caste or minority or to those who are financially poor. This type of discrimination is against the fundamentals of justice. Many categories of individuals such as orphans, physically challenged individuals, slow learners, children of uneducated parents, backward communities, slum dwellers, residents of labour colonies, inaccessible rural areas, and those weak in health, are often discriminated against in educational institutions, job market, matrimonial relations, and social relations. Education has to counter and eliminate discriminations of all types. The society suffers also from discriminations on the basis of sex, religion, region and political views.

The right of civil liberties, freedom of expression, freedom of worship, right to property, right to justice, etc., have also to be duly promoted through the medium of education by initiating various information programmes in educational institutions.

Giving evidence in the interest of justice is one of the responsibilities of a good citizen. But people avoid being witnesses in courts because of the inconvenience and dangers involved. Even some eyewitnesses of a crime do not want to come forward to speak the truth. An educated person should not lower his dignity by giving false evidence.

Education ensures equal opportunity of development for everybody. Even if certain individuals are not adequately responsive to educational efforts, they should be paid special attention to come up to the mark. The facilities of education are not withdrawn even from a person who tries to run away from it. Every student deserves the maximum possible attention of the educators.

There are constitutional provisions and laws to run the organisation and administration of education. Different managements have to evolve their own rules and regulations. These provisions, laws, rules and regulations have to be fair to all concerned. There should be a regular forum to scrutinise their implementation and review them in the light of experiences and discussions. Educational institutions have to be a remarkable example of the observance of rules and regulations framed for them. These rules affect students, teachers, parents, administrators, school boards, universities, institutions of technical and professional education, selection of staff, admission process, fee structure, course content, discipline and system of evaluation, scholarships, freeships, etc. There have to be rules for associations of students, teachers and managements. Rules are meant for facilitating the process of education and not to make unjustified interferences and create unnecessary difficulties in the running of educational institutions.

Let us use the medium of education to reduce the incidence of injustices made to individuals, within families, institutions, establishments and communities. The need for social justice is equally important. There should be no place for discrimination on the basis of class, caste, community or religion. Equality should be ensured as far as possible in the matter of opportunities, distribution of facilities, development, sharing of wealth, distribution of responsibilities, enjoying of privileges, and favours granted by the government.

Education should develop in the individual the firmness for and belief in justice and fairness. Individuals should always be ready to fight against injustice and partiality of any type.

*****

Thirty seven

Education and Sacrifice

One must learn to make sacrifices in life in order to improve the quality of life. For his own achievements and progress, one has to sacrifice his comforts and carefreeness. For his sound economy, he has to sacrifice his luxuries and careless expenses. For leaving behind a rich legacy for the new generation, the old generation has to forego some of its privileges. For the progress of his community, the individual may have to sacrifice some of his selfish motives.

Let us always remember the martyrs who made supreme sacrifices for a universal cause. Nations are enjoying freedom, existence and honour by virtue of the sacrifices made by many people.

In order to support children for their development and education, parents may even have to forego their necessities.

In order to do greater justice to one's studies, the student may have to sacrifice his rest, temptations for excessive watching of the television, playing games on the computer, going to movies or availing other entertainments.

Sacrifices can be made in many forms; by devoting and sparing one's precious time for others, by fighting for a common cause, by giving company to a person suffering from loneliness, by sparing one's hard earned money for the needy, by devoting time and help to the old people and by going to enquire about the health of a patient.

An individual makes sacrifices by donating one eye for a blind person or by donating one kidney to a person whose kidneys have failed. Blood donation is a regular sacrifice made by some people which helps in saving many lives. Donating one's dead body for medical research or donating the organs of the dead body for transplantation is a sacrifice of its own kind.

Wise people make various sacrifices for the unity and welfare of their family, community, nation and the world. If you keep your needs modest and under control, it is a sacrifice for the common good.

There have been many people who have forgotten everything about their personal interests and ambitions after choosing a cause and devoting themselves to it. Some people continue to do lifelong service for a cause or for the welfare of others.

For conserving natural resources like water, one may have to sacrifice some of one's necessities served with water. For helping in the ecological balance one may have to sacrifice the use of automobiles for travelling. A person who uses electricity and other sources of energy in the most economical manner is also making a sacrifice for the society. In saving resources for more productive uses, an individual may have to sacrifice glamour as well in the form of decorations and celebrations.

There are many people who are doing selfless service in the field of health, education, development, human rights, upliftment of the downtrodden, helping widows and women who have opted for mutual separation, care of orphans or poor children, running homes for severely handicapped people, setting up old age homes and playing people-friendly roles in politics. Such people have left behind an unforgettable record of sacrifices made by them for others.

Experienced people who give free and sincere guidance and advice to the needy have been doing a great service to the society by sacrificing their time for others.

Certain educational, health and welfare organisations have done and continue to do great service to the society on account of sacrifices made by their founders. Philanthropists often donate beyond their means for the welfare of people and society.

As the teacher is the pillar of the profession, his job demands many sacrifices from him. He has to work with a wholehearted commitment, dedication and devotion. The excellence of his students and their admirable roles in various walks of life will be his main reward. He will have to devote his spare time for self-study and professional growth. He may have to devote extra-time to the bright group and to the less bright group, separately. Some students' special problems may demand individual attention from him. He will have to take extra classes, if need be. The student in need of guidance should be most welcome to his place on Sundays or on holidays. He may have to stay in school after classes to look after the games and co-curricular activities too.

A writer who enriches literature and the culture without getting reasonable monetary return or honour is making a sacrifice in his own manner. A doctor makes sacrifice when he gets up at midnight to attend to an emergency. Some preachers, who have no lust for money and prestige are certainly doing memorable service and making sacrifices as well. Many astronauts have sacrificed their lives for scientific research and for making valuable contribution to the advancement of the civilisation. The police and armed forces have to sacrifice their lives or get injured while controlling criminals and terrorists.

Only those people deserve to be leaders in different walks of life, who have made significant sacrifices for others. At the same time, a person who has made any sacrifice should not claim any return for his sacrifice.

To work overtime for the sake of disposing off a day's work, without expecting any extra allowance is also a humble example of a sacrifice.

Education and Sacrifice

Some of the small sacrifices are: when a bright student helps his less bright classmate to remove his difficulties, when you listen sympathetically to the miseries and worries of others and help them as much as you can, when you do not burden everybody with the tales of your miseries and worries, when you keep your cool and remain soft spoken in spite of anybody offending or annoying you, when you live a simple life in spite of your affluence, when you smile in spite of personal worries and tensions, when you do not lose your sense of humour in spite of your problems and worries, when you share your happiness with others, when you offer your seat in a bus or train to a standing passenger who is uncomfortable due to old age, illness or some other reason, when you send new year greetings to friends in spite of some personal reason for sadness, when you give financial help to a needy friend in spite your own financially circumscribed circumstances, when you share the work load of your colleague by devoting some extra time and when you offer sympathies to an unfriendly person during his grief.

Even if you are awfully busy in your own life, sacrifice some of your time for your aged parents, children, siblings, friends, relatives, an ailing member of the family, if any, guests, neighbours and the community.

We should not expect any return for our sacrifices. Some of these sacrifices may be placed under the categories of manners, etiquette and behaviour. The habit of making sacrifices brings with it a rare joy, satisfaction and credit. Even if some of our sacrifices are not recognised and appreciated, we should not blame anybody.

Our textbooks carry some lessons about sacrifices of our martyrs and other crusaders for some noble causes. The sacrifices made in the name of religion were also for the honour of mankind, or for the purpose of freedom. We have to make clear to the students that some scientists left behind startling discoveries after their lifelong dedication to research without expecting or receiving any recognition from the beneficiaries. The world is enjoying the immeasurable benefits of those discoveries. Some philosophers, thinkers, writers, religious leaders and revolutionaries suffered very heavily for the reforms advocated by them which were appreciated only much after their demise. The mission of education remains incomplete if it does not prepare and motivate everybody to make sacrifices. A person's education and excellence is not exclusively reserved for the promotion of the self, but meant also for the welfare of mankind. If everybody adopts this attitude of making sacrifices for others, the sufferings in this world will decrease immensely.

*****

VIII

EDUCATION AS A NOBLE FORCE

Thirty eight

Education and Drug Addiction

Drug addiction became a habit with the human being in the early times, but then he was not sufficiently aware of its dangerous consequences. Now he is being warned on scientific grounds about its dangers. Still, he refuses to listen. All type of authentic information is being thrust into his ears by different agencies, but he continues to indulge in drugs at the cost of his health and welfare.

The losses on account of drug addiction are innumerable. Some of them are: irreparable damage to health, wastage of money, dying will power, lack of confidence, disaster for the family, domestic estrangement and strife, maladjustment, lack of respect among relatives and well-wishers, numbness of sensibilities, social nuisance, offence against law, slavish dependence on a drug, constant worry of disruption of drug supply, concealment, telling lies, bad manners, lack of self-control, lack of aspirations, slow poisoning, bad company, losing fertility, tendency to steal and commit crimes, irresponsibility, constant need for increasing the drug dose, adopting a new and more powerful drug after the old one fails to give adequate push, ineffectiveness of medical treatment in the event of illness, risk of losing a job, irreparable damage to vital organs, abnormalities, loss of prestige and dignity, unconsciousness, loss of self-discipline, coating one's natural beauty with ugliness, becoming a member of the network of addicts, suppliers, or gangsters, a target of ridicule, and an overall poor personality.

What are the gains of addiction to a drug addict? These are false and indefensible gains. It provides temporary relaxation, an artificial feeling of well-being, forgetfulness of worries and tiredness, getting more work from the weary and jerky body machine, a temporary relief from pain or sadness, whipping up exhausted energy and a fake cheerfulness.

All over the world, numerous agencies are engaged in checking drug addiction, but the malady appears to be spreading day by day. It is a problem which presents a horrible picture of human behaviour in many ways. The drug addict is his own worst enemy. He starts in this direction due to various reasons, some of which are: frustration, depression, failures, losses, worries, poor family atmosphere, addiction among elder members of the family, company of addicts, addiction being common in the community, lack of physical energy to work, etc. The cure adopted by the addict to offset various causes becomes a more serious cause and chronic disease.

Drug addiction is going on at such a large scale that it necessitates a class of people who enter this trade as manufacturers, main suppliers, dealers, smugglers and couriers. Most of them are likely to become the victims of the same drugs. The trade creates a huge business with a high profit margin. It creates a class of criminals who become very dangerous for mankind. They are a great curse to humanity. They cause death to the addicts, cause diseases, ruin families, cripple society, spread corruption and create all sorts of problems for the administration.

Some of the drug addicts intentionally spread the disease among their companions and relatives. They enjoy roping in others and feel happy when they succeed in hunting their targets and expanding their group of addicts.

The members of the family of a drug addict suffer uninvited torture. A drug addict causes an unending strife and tension within the family. He does not ruin himself alone, but is likely to seal the fate of all the other members of the family. Some of the family members may also catch the bad habit of addiction due to the intimate company of the addict. It is also well known that the drug addict can make his family poor. Often he cannot meet the cost of his stuff out of his regular income, he is forced to sell the precious items available at home, sell the property, borrow from all possible sources, and indulge in stealing or in some other crimes that can help him fetch some money. Drug addiction is related to domestic violence, broken homes, low income, expenses beyond sources, crime, etc.

Addiction cannot be regarded as a personal pleasure or an affair of the addict. It has to be treated as a problem for the family, as well as the society.

A large percentage of drug addicts are financially poor. They can hardly afford the drugs they need to survive. Their poverty and addiction combine into a very hopeless situation for them and their families. In the event of non-availability of money for drugs, the individual resorts to torturing or threatening the members of his family for finances or he tortures himself and ultimately, commits suicide when there is no alternative before him.

Recovery from drug addiction is very difficult; prevention is the best remedy. Recovery needs a long drawn out, scientifically structured and costly process. Recovery, if at all achieved is a glass house which needs to be protected throughout one's later life. It needs a rare self-restraint, self-watch, self-confidence and above all, a strong will power.

Bad and hopeless circumstances may be quoted as an excuse for drug addiction, but it should not be forgotten, that it will make the circumstances worse. Every drug is a dirty food and addiction is a dirty habit. It has assumed dangerous proportions and it must be faced as a serious challenge.

Bad company is one of the main causes of drug abuse. An educational institution should not allow the development of this bad force within its population. In some cases, family tradition becomes a cause. Again maladjustment of some kind may drive the individual to become the victim of some drugs. Education has to neutralise all these and other causes. It has to mentally prepare every individual to overcome this temptation throughout life. Smoking and drinking have become trends today. They are considered as permissible drugs. But they are no less harmful and wasteful than other drugs. An individual has to be enabled to realise early in life that he will never allow drugs to spoil his personality. Dependence on any drug to get more work done is a bad bargain. Education preaches in many ways that smoking is dirty, alcohol turns you into a fool, opium is cruel, and ganja dampens your senses. It is one of the big failures of education that it has not been able to control the menace. Rather, drug addiction has entered educational institutions too and is fast becoming a fashion statement among young students.

There ought to be an intelligent ban on drugs in educational institutions. Parents should be advised in time to notice the changes in the personality and behaviour of their children. If the child sits staring into space a lot, not focussing on anything, if he remains isolated for an unreasonably long time, the parents should look out for reasons. If he comes home very late and cleanses out the fridge, but there is still a marked weight-loss, or he disappears into the bathroom immediately after eating and starts vomiting and when a peculiar smell regularly keeps coming out of his room, the parents are required to thoroughly check into their child's actions. Excessive dependence on medicines for cold and cough can also be indicative of drug abuse. Pure vanilla extract, hair spray, paint strippers, nail polish remover, iodex, shoe polish, etc., are also used as drugs.

It is a very serious problem for the new generations. Through education, young minds have to be made extra cautious about this menace. Children may be forewarned and made mentally strong to resist whatever drug-temptation comes their way. To raise an addiction-free generation should be an important aim of education. The young learners should swear to observe a self-imposed ban on drug addiction.

It is really very shocking to note that some highly educated intellectuals admit their dependence on drugs to get inspiration. If an intellectual depended upon this or that drug for enhancing his creativity, he must have been a loser and not a gainer in this bargain. He could have achieved much higher levels of creativity, if he had abstained from the use of drugs. It is a great insult to human intellect to make oneself dependent on drugs for enhancing one's capacity to think.

Education should create foundations for distaste, hatred and fear of drugs. Other agencies have not been able to take this problem as seriously as required. It is creating serious emotional, financial, social and health problems for the addict. No government in the world has shown the courage to ban smoking, drinking and other drugs. This problem is an insult to our intelligence and education. These intoxicants have innumerable demerits. Any merits attributed to them are simply fake.

It has been recently reported in a study, that in our population more than 70% of the youth are drug-addicts. Education and other agencies have to jointly make determined efforts to establish an addiction-free society.

The educational institutions should develop knowledge-addiction, work-addiction, art-addiction and discovery-addiction among learners. The individual must be oriented towards higher values in life and must look upon drug-addiction as unworthy of his dignity, stature and upbringing. He should be acquainted with much finer tastes of addiction so that he is not tempted towards dirty tastes of entertainment. The individual should never crave for drugs to avail a short-lived happiness. He should be guided towards healthy activities of relaxation which are available in abundance.

If one cannot live without intoxicants, he should learn to enjoy sacred intoxicants like achievements, qualifications, merit, excellence, creativity, help to the needy, selfless service, love for Nature, mankind and meditation.

*****

Thirty nine

Education and Suicide

Suicide is an act of extreme cowardice. Killing someone else is murder and killing one's own self is more than a murder. Committing suicide is a great sin. Human life is too precious to be destroyed by one's own hands. A human being has no right to destroy himself. Suicide is the greatest failure of a human being. There cannot be a misfortune greater than killing oneself. No problem, failure or shock can be serious enough to drive a person to commit suicide. Suicide has become a serious social problem. No logic can possibly condone it. It is below the dignity of a human being to kill himself. It is a matter of running away from life and admitting defeat.

Failure in an examination, not fulfilling the aspirations cultivated by a person, being insulted in the presence of others, a failed love, inability to get admission in the institution of one's choice, denial of required finances from parents, poverty, harassment of a woman for dowry, illicit sexual relations, burden of debt, drug addiction, incurable disease, depression and many other causes lead to suicide. Even if it is not possible to eliminate these causes, we have to eliminate the events that can lead to suicides. Suicide is no remedy to these causes and no solution to these problems.

Frustrations, tensions, tragedies and depressions are a part of life. One has to be bold and wise enough to face these situations and should not decide to run away from them through measures like suicide.

It is said, love thy neighbour as thyself; that is you must love your neighbours, but before you love them, you must love yourself. When you love yourself, you cannot think of destroying yourself.

Our own existence is a great gift of Nature and we should not become ungrateful and deny this gift to ourselves. There are always a large number of people who are attached with us and we should not be cruel to them by breaking that attachment. Suicide leaves behind very harsh familial, social, economic and psychological after-effects. Its memories give unforgettable pain to all concerned.

We have not been able to improvise a yardstick to measure the value of human life. Even if a person finds that he is leading a miserable life, he is good for nothing, the situation should not disappoint him forever. It is his duty and responsibility to continue to make efforts for better times and never lose hope for a better future. It is not a small matter that life is a boon for our lifelong struggle. This struggle is life's own reward.

Suicide is a very distressing example of human nature and behaviour. It shows poor development of the ability to think. It is also a sign of poor socialisation of the individual. Such individuals have probably not been able to take even the first steps towards self-realisation. Suicide has a demoralising and depressing effect for many who come to know about it.

Today's rational individual must be able to argue for and against suicide before committing the crime. Education must develop a strong sense of rationality in the individual so that he can think positively even at the last moment. Even at the eleventh hour of his suicide attempt, he should be able to remember that he is not destined to die a premature death. Education should be able to strengthen the human mind to such a level that he can decisively resist an unnatural activity like suicide. One should be able to pause and think about the consequences, about the after-effects and miseries resulting from this drastic step. It is a negative step, which is unthinkable for a person who believes in positive approach to difficult situations in life.

Frustrations, depressions and suicides have become too common in life. Their alarming number demands effective remedies to save precious lives. Since these are mental problems, education has to provide adequate strength to the human mind so that he never falls a victim to this crime. While inviting this failure one should pause and think about his successes and privileges. He should look around and see how persons with more serious problems are bravely facing the situations. When one has a tendency to commit suicide the individual should not remain alone. He should have genuine company. He can also try to recall the suicide cases known to him and remember the agony and misery left behind for many by the folly of one individual.

There is no challenge which human beings have not been able to face successfully. Even if challenges and misfortunes get multiplied, the human being can awaken his energies to face them. It is disrespect to the human possibilities to run away from the challenges of life.

People sometimes commit suicides over petty matters. Whatever the reason, suicide is a thoughtless blunder. All justifications for suicide will get blown off with a mere second of rational thought. Education has a duty to develop a strong mind to effectively resist irrationalities like suicide.

Everyone suffers from depression at one point or the other. There are many remedies to keep it under control. Education should empower every mind to prevent and control this problem. At the same time, every well-wisher of the sufferer should be made aware of his role towards the patient. Others should not remain indifferent or unconcerned about the person in this moment of his crisis.

Suicide may also be caused by negative tendencies. Through education and other means, positive tendencies of a human mind should be strengthened to such an extent that any negative step gets eliminated. There is no justification in accepting the incidence of suicides as a usual occurrence. Our target should be the complete elimination of this occurrence. Its continuation should be counted as one of the failures of education and other agencies. These agencies should be held responsible and answerable for this. If the rate of suicide does not significantly fall, we should sit up, think over the whole issue once again, and strengthen our resolve and educational programmes to check this event.

Once in a country, where the number of suicides increased alarmingly, people approached the religious leaders to help save the situation. In a crisis of this nature, along with religion, educational institutions and teachers can definitely be of great help.

It is the responsibility of all agencies devoted to human welfare to ensure the reduction of the number of suicides to negligible figures. Education has to play a pivotal role in this endeavour. By all possible means and efforts, suicide should be made unthinkable.

In the eyes of the law, the attempt to commit suicide is a punishable offence. The court may send the offender to jail. After his release, he deserves the help of welfare agencies for better rehabilitation.

Man sometimes commits suicide of a different nature. With his own hands he destroys his possibilities of becoming a jewel of excellence and instead, becomes a worm of filth. It may be due to lack of interest in life, lack of ambition, lack of well deserved opportunities, wrong thinking, reprimand, criticism, failure, financial loss, family dispute, etc.

Emile Durkheim classifies suicide into three types: altruistic, egoistic, and anomic. Altruistic suicide results from excessive collective consciousness and social solidarity, as that of a wife committing suicide by throwing herself in the burning pyre of her husband. Egoistic suicide results from the lack of cohesion of the individual with his social group and anomic suicide occurs due to the suspension of norms in society.

The rising incidents of attempted suicide by children and adolescents have perplexed educationists, teachers, sociologists and psychologists.

When a young student is moody or has behavioural disorders he may attempt a suicide or indulge in substance abuse like alcohol, drugs, etc.

Maladaptive and dysfunctional family may aggravate the problem such as physical or child abuse, a broken family, etc. Trying to be too perfect can also lead to suicide.

Due to increased stress on academic achievement, burden of a heavy curriculum and a fast paced life some students find it impossible to come up to their expectations.

Having failed in examinations is a major cause of suicide today. Failure is associated with the loss of self-esteem and young people may develop a feeling of worthlessness. A potential suicide victim normally turns to his family, peers or a teacher he is close to when he is feeling low. All well-wishers of a failed student should give him support, encouragement and advice to sufficiently raise his spirits. He should not be neglected and left to himself.

*****

Forty

Education and Corruption

Corruption eats into the economy and development of a country. From a small beginning it has spread and expanded into an enormous monster. It has become a creed with some people. It has endangered the existence of principles and values, and has lowered the status of a human being.

Corruption is one of the social evils found almost in all the countries of the world. There are many causes for it, like materialism, mad race for money, motivation to get rich faster, socio-economic status, greed, rising cost of living, low salaries as compared to price rise, loose economic set-up, black money, tendency to enjoy luxurious living, weakening hold of social and moral values, joining the mainstream of corruption, weak character formation and development of personality, and ineffective government control and judicial system.

Corruption and organised crime very often go together. The instances of white-collar crime are more than the conventional type of crime. The losses incurred due to white-collar crimes are far higher than those of the conventional type. These crimes include tax-evasion, monopolistic controls, under-invoicing or over-invoicing, hoarding, profiteering, smuggling, violation of foreign exchange regulations, election malpractices, misappropriation of public property and funds, violations of standards and weights and measures, breaking of rules and regulations, frauds, professional misconduct, gambling and womanising, and misuse of their position by public servants and politicians. People tend to tolerate white-collar crimes because they themselves indulge in them for illegal gains. Corruption provides scope for organised crimes like racketeering, adulteration, bootlegging, smuggling, kidnapping, manufacture and sale of substandard goods and twisting law in one's favour.

Corruption generates black money or parallel economy. The social consequences of black money are very severe. It increases social inequality, creates frustration and demoralisation among honest people, leads to isolation and ridicule of honest people, favouritism, exploitation, low character and degradation of moral values. It prompts the common man to become disobedient to authority, as well as to rules and regulations. Everybody has the protection available through corruption even after violation of any code of conduct or ethics.

The law enforcing agencies, vigilance departments or anti-corruption authorities may continue to control this evil in their own way, but education has to be harnessed to build a self-respecting conscience in every individual. It should develop an aversion for the undignified practice of corruption. It should infuse strength in every mind to resist its temptation even at the cost of personal complications.

First of all, educational institutions and their human functionaries should be made to rise against this evil, which has penetrated so deep into the system that it's uprooting will require a long struggle demanding sacrifice. These institutions should at least be able to ensure corruption-free campuses. In them, there should be nothing like embezzlement or wastage of funds, demanding any extra charges from the students, fake expenses, taking commissions on purchases, favouritism, neglect of merit, not making the best use of time reserved for teaching, using institutional facilities for private purposes, and getting undue favours by virtue of one's position in the institution.

Corruption cannot be eliminated or even satisfactorily controlled, unless it is uprooted from the human mind. In order to control corruption, there is a need to raise the standards of public morality. The educational institutions, media and social organisations should create an atmosphere in which corrupt people get isolated and exposed.

Politicians and bureaucrats are largely responsible for aggravating corruption in society. Since they are the law makers and controllers of state machinery, they are able to escape in spite of their open involvement in this crime or evil. The government machinery like police, anti-corruption wings, vigilance departments and judiciary has miserably failed in checking corruption. Rather, it is expanding with the passage of time.

It is through education that we can awaken every young mind to become a responsible and strong force for protecting society from corruption. The inspired, committed and value-oriented young minds can definitely make a difference. Every individual should decide to become a crusader against corruption and then individuals should come together to form vigilant voluntary groups to decisively fight this evil. It cannot be left to government bodies to check, as the government machinery is itself deeply involved in corrupt activities. We should so educate the new generations that they may firmly believe in their ability to create a society of their dreams and aspirations. It does no credit to an educated individual when he helplessly accepts to become a member of the corrupt system. We need a fairly large number of incorruptible people to reverse the misdirected way of the social set-up. Education must aim at developing honest people in large numbers in which the dishonest minority may fail in its conniving pursuits and designs.

Under no circumstances should an educated person surrender to corrupt practices, thinking, influences and ideologies.

*****

Forty one

Education and Crime

There may be hundred and one reasons for a person to commit a crime, but if he has attended an educational institution for a few years, he must have developed the ability to resist the urge to commit a crime. Committing a crime is the action of a sick, weak, imbalanced, unsound and uneducated mind. Education must be a guarantee against crime.

There are some people who get addicted to crime. They continue to enlarge the list of their crimes and take pride in it. The fear of law and jail does not have any effect on them. They stop listening to the warning given by the mind. They become hardened criminals. Education must save a mind from getting so hardened, inhuman, irrational and cruel.

Religion has tried to preach lessons against crime in many ways. It is not out of place, if educational efforts against crime take possible support from religious sentiments of the children. Small crimes of the child may not be curbed by punishment but by some positive suggestions and moral lessons.

With the aim of establishing a crime-free society, we should be able to ensure crime-free schools. Students should be taught not to tell a lie, not to cheat, not to steal, not to quarrel and should be restricted against foul play within the school. Just as discipline is to be controlled by a committee of students, similarly there may be a students' committee to check small crimes.

Our records have labelled some of the tribes as criminal tribes. This policy should not continue any more. Let us start with the belief that nobody is born a criminal.

Through education, we may have to neutralise the negative effect of some other media which are full of crime stories. The young child should be enabled to draw healthy lessons from the criminal incidents and stories portrayed in different media. He should not be prompted to develop interest in crime stories.

The government, social agencies, judiciary and punishments have failed to eliminate crime. There is overcrowding in jails. Instead of building more jails, let us build some good schools. We should empower education and depend on it to bring down the crime rates. Let us teach that crime is a denigration of civilised life and education received by us. An educated person should not be found to be criminal, corrupt, a shirker or destructive person. Education must become a movement against crime.

Crimes, depending upon their seriousness are of three types: (1) treason (war against one's own country, giving aid to enemy), (2) serious crimes like murder, slaughtering people, forgery, fraud, robbery, burglary and rape (3) minor offences like theft, drunkenness, disorderly conduct and vagrancy.

Individuals who are social misfits and mentally stressed individuals are labelled as psychopathic inferiors. They are pathological liars, sexual perverts, tramps, amoral, misanthropes, eccentrics, and unstable individuals. Psychologists and educationists should sit together and find out sure remedies for such criminal tendencies.

Instability of social order is an important factor in causing crime. It is more common in a disorganised and heterogeneous population. Discord and general instability in the families, especially in broken homes also becomes the cause of crime.

Insane criminals commit a higher percentage of offences against human beings including homicide, assault and sexual offences. Some criminals commit a higher percentage of crime against wealth and property.

Psychoanalysts point out that unconscious motives and repressed mental conflicts are responsible for criminal behaviour. Criminals especially suffer from destructive and antisocial impulses.

Cause of crime is best sought in the adjustment of the individual to his environment. When he finds it difficult to satisfy his wants and desires in a direct and socially acceptable manner, he attempts to find substitutes to get satisfaction. Criminal behaviour is an indirect and irrational attempt to adjust to discomforting or frustrating situations. Under certain circumstances especially when normal channels of expression are blocked, an individual resorts to criminal behaviour.

Criminal behaviour is more or less a disease. The criminal needs provisions like hospitalisation, medical or psychological treatment. We have to help him learn to get social and adjust with a normal way of life. As a precaution, we have to ensure mental health of the individual to improve his ability to make personal and social adjustments. Mental hygiene helps in the prevention of mental disorders, the preservation and development of mental health and the removal of maladjustments.

Erick Erickson has outlined the characteristics of a mentally healthy personality as one who: trusts himself, is capable of controlling himself, of taking responsibility, is competent and hard working, has a clear and integrated identity, can develop relationships of trust, can grow and be creative in different ways, has ego-integrity and accepts himself as he is. Stable mental health leads to the harmonious development of a personality.

In this age of remarkable scientific development, people claim that much of the mental disease and crime are due to the fact that life for many has become intolerably dull and devoid of meaning. There is a loss of direction among men who have no sustaining values and are manipulated and controlled by unscrupulous groups. The steady increase in the crime rate is largely due to symptoms like lack of a definite lifestyle, and the change in attitude towards crime and moral offence.

The senseless criminal behaviour makes us believe that a large percentage of our citizens are moral fools or at least moral illiterates.

In many places, our learners are screened by intelligence tests and personality tests, but they do not appear to have acquired the moral values and purposes needed in full-grown human beings. Marked by more prominent adult habits that they share with the rest of the community their values remain childish, if not brutally criminal.

A basic question is whether in the value systems we are promoting, are encouraging and strengthening the animal and selfish impulses present in all of us or reinforcing and cultivating the more altruistic and creative aspects of our nature.

Delinquents of today are generally regarded as the criminals of tomorrow. Delinquent behaviour occurs in early teens. Dislocation of population, congested urbanisation and slum areas indirectly encourage criminality by increasing the opportunities for antisocial behaviour.

There are a number of causes for delinquency – the child is suffering from physical deformity and may be laughed at, he may think that society itself is responsible for his disability and may wish to retaliate and try to harm society. In case the motor and physical development of a child is more rapid or slower than that of an average child, the adjustment difficulties may push him towards crime. Low intellectual performance than the average may also encourage antisocial behaviour among individuals. Some momentary physiological disorders may also cause delinquency. There are many more social and environmental causes for delinquency such as having stepparents, a broken home, over-indulgence by any parent in unapprovable activities, loose character of a parent, mental abnormality of any member of the family, divorce or separation between parents, one room homes, unsuitable environment such as living in close proximity to a liquor shop, gambling den or a flesh trade racket; child labour; lack of recreational facilities and movies with wrong messages.

Various symptoms of maladjustment are indicators of delinquency such as nervous disorders like fears and anxiety, solitary living, timidity, depression, obsession, excitability, hysteria and amnesia. Then there are habit disorders like stammering, excessive day dreaming, nightmares, sleeplessness, facial and body tics, nail biting, rocking, bed wetting, asthma, and allergies. Also, there are some behavioural disorders like temper tantrums; destructive, defiant or cruel behaviour; stealing, lying, truancy and sexual abnormalities. Organic disorders present symptoms like neurological dysfunctioning, head injuries, brain tumour and epilepsy. There may be psychotic disorders like hallucinations, delusions and bizarre behaviour. There may also be some educational and vocational difficulties like lack of concentration, inability to carry out assignments, slow learning, retardation and irregular response to school discipline.

The delinquents should be identified as early as possible. Their environmental situations should be improved. Economic hardships, if any, should be removed. They should be given some sense of security about employment and means of livelihood. There is need for a humanitarian and sympathetic approach towards them. There is need for cooperation between the educational institution, parents, neighbourhood, community and religious organisations. Education is the medium through which we have to inculcate hatred for crime. Moral values should be imparted through all possible means like education, games, literature, religion and mass media.

Educational institutions and teachers have to improve their functioning so that maladjustment of the child or delinquency of any type is not allowed to cross the limits. The feelings of the children should be heard and addressed. Their feelings should be recognised, accepted, tolerated and tactfully modified if need be. They should enjoy freedom of expression in respect of their feelings. There should never be a need to scold children.

The mild cases of maladjustment can be dealt within the normal school set-up. Their self-confidence should be developed to encourage them to handle their own problems. Every symptom should be provided some healthy orientation. The acute cases may be referred to counsellors, psychologists and psychiatrists.

In the case of hard criminals, a constructive reformatory approach is being emphasised. The environment of juvenile delinquency centres and prisons and the treatment of the criminals should be in line with psychological principles. They should be provided with an environment of love, understanding and trust. Efforts may be made to enable them to readjust and resocialise. Severe punishment should not be regarded as the only means to reform them. Humanitarian approach may be introduced in jails. The jails may be converted into reformatories so that every criminal after release from the jail does not repeat any crime. For an everlasting change in their way of life, the help of social workers, social reformers, welfare agencies and religious leaders may be sought to ensure for them a blotless later life. Research agencies should be involved to study their causes and psychological reasons so that it is possible to adopt an unfailing rehabilitation programme for them.

A life full of crime is not proper for an educated human being and he has no right to blacken and waste his life by becoming a criminal. The remedy does not lie in giving him opportunities of criminal expression and then throwing him into jail, but by giving him timely opportunity for education, socialisation, character formation and personality development.

It is very painful and shameful that the number of crimes is rapidly increasing and the nature of crime is becoming more horrible by the day. We should learn to stop this trend. If left to the law enforcing agencies alone, the situation is bound to further deteriorate. What can be the alternative then? We have to turn to education and allied agencies for developing more determined individuals to fight against crime. Let us believe in the pious nature of a human being and remind him everyday through education that he is not to become inhuman in any way.

*****

Forty two

Education and Terrorism

The idea of terrorism needs to be uprooted from young minds by developing rational thinking through education. Terrorism is one of the most destructive activities of a human mind. Terrorism is a kind of uncivilised behaviour of some misguided elements. It is born out of acute mental derailment. It is a heinous crime devoid of all logic. It is an undeclared bloody war and human mind must have a strong hatred against any form of war. Civilised people must not indulge in terrorism. The young minds have to be convinced that terrorism is inhuman and akin to insanity. They have to be saved from this cruel and irrational behaviour.

The terrorists become victims of a suicidal tendency and suffer from the narrow vision: to kill or be killed. The noble words 'live and let live' are more binding for an educated human being. The idea of terrorism does not fit into his genius at all.

Terrorism borrows its justification from religious, economic and political fanaticism. It is regarded as a shortcut to defeat and eliminate the opponent. It has proved to be a sheer wastage which is incapable of bringing about the desired results. The history of terrorism cannot claim any remarkable achievements to its credit. It has brought suffering to itself and others.

Terrorists are a small minority and they try to make life hell for the vast majority. Their dastardly acts of violence often spread fear among peaceful people.

Terrorism is a recent phenomenon. It is still in its infancy. The situation will become horrible if it is allowed to reach maturity. The terrorist claims that he is fighting for a cause. If he is honest to his faith, why doesn't he come into the open like a brave crusader?

Terrorism is an attempt to destroy within seconds the peaceful atmosphere and the civilisation created over a long period of painstaking efforts by humanity. Intolerance and hatred are some of its supporting factors. The terrorists get so hardened that sane appeals do not work on them. They may have many excuses for the path pursued by them, but they are seldom prepared to listen to the point of view of the other side.

The cult of terrorism is the product of sick minds and perverted conscience. It sustains itself because some fanatics get distanced from sane members of the society and develop closed minds. Some shallow minded people may find adventure in terrorism. Some needy people may be attracted towards its monetary returns and other benefits. Some people get entrapped because of opportunities they may get to settle scores with their adversaries. Some criminals may join the group in order to escape arrest and jail. Some may be entrapped due to the faint hope of capturing power and authority.

Terrorists feel elated when they find that they have been able to create insecurity among important and common people. The important persons, bureaucrats, officers and politicians constantly live under the threat of militancy. They can no more enjoy a safe and normal lifestyle. It is a great tragedy that some governments are supporting terrorists in every possible way to disturb neighbouring countries.

Its threat has resulted in a huge wastage of our resources for the security of important persons and places. The security arrangements of VIPs are one of the ugly sights gifted by terrorism. Terrorism has created a gulf between the leaders and their followers. Even the so called beloved and popular leader of the masses cannot move freely among the people. The continuance of terrorism will be a misfortune for society and civilisation and a great obstacle in their stability and progress. It is a failure of human sensibilities and positive ideologies. Its growth is a challenge to our system and governance. It is spreading in many corners of the world and provides sad news everyday.

Social agencies and governments are trying to bring terrorists into the mainstream with small successes here or there. The military and para military forces are trying to eliminate or catch them. Thousands of armed forces remain alert and preoccupied but fail to handle a few dozens of terrorists. The human bombs or suicide squads among them succeed in their surprise attacks in spite of tight security arrangements. Sometimes, they succeed in destroying very precious properties. The losses inflicted by them are difficult to measure. Many a times their victims are innocent people. Terrorism leaves behind painful memories which invite condemnation. Terrorists create terror and suffer insecurity on account of that. People who become merciless deserve no mercy. The terrorist seals his own fate right from the beginning and has to remain underground.

There is no doubt that people have often to struggle for their rights, but they must be instructed for all times that they will not resort to terrorism as the mode of their fight. There are a number of alternative means which are not destructive and which can bring better results in every human struggle. There is no justification in frightening and killing the unarmed people who are least concerned with the pro and anti-proponents of the issue at stake. The young minds should be made to understand that there are numerous more civilised methods to get one's grievances removed.

Let us confirm within our mind that terrorism is a passing phase and our determined and persistent efforts will make it disappear. Terrorists want to dictate their terms but the silent majority should come forward to resist.

Our educational programmes should make the individuals so sensible in due course of time that terrorist groups do not find any new recruits. Their idea of terrorism should be contradicted through relevant lessons in the curriculum. Their blatant crimes should be made known to the young learner through supplementary literature. The reasons and procedures for controlling this crime may be made a topic of discussion among the students.

The methods which we employ through education against criminal tendencies are applicable in preventing terrorism also. Education is meant to awaken the humanitarian outlook in the learner who may boldly face the inhuman onslaught of terrorism. We shall have to enable the young minds to discuss and debate the issue of terrorism. Any so called justification for it should be thoroughly analysed and rejected.

Education should so empower every mind that everyone begins to hate terrorism. An educated and sane society cannot tolerate terrorism. Terrorists are always in a small minority and they have no right to stifle the majority opinion and try to threaten everybody who differs with them. Education has to arouse the element of reason. The idea of terrorism needs to be defeated before its birth in one's mind. Everybody should acquire a firm clarity and conviction which is seldom shaken by any amount of propaganda or false notions. Education has not to allow any learner to go astray and favour terrorism. It should exercise a rational control over its students. It should enhance everybody's mental power so that the destructive and misleading forces cannot work on him. Through education, we have to safeguard the inherent goodness of the human mind so that contrary temptations cannot take over. The noble ideas conferred by education will not get disturbed by any wicked schemes of circumstances. The cruelty involved in terrorism will destroy all the so called arguments in its favour. The terror-seeker will be disowned by society and will not enjoy any recognition.

Education should also activate other social agencies and media forums to play an effective role in fighting the menace of terrorism. The religious and political elements should be exposed, if they directly or indirectly extend any support to terrorism. Education should prepare the new generation to give a decisive fight to terrorism.

There is need to study the minds of terrorists and devise scientific means to correct them from their misguided path.

*****

IX

EDUCATION AND SYSTEM

Forty three

Education and System

Society has various systems corresponding to the sustaining system and the regulating system in an organism. Education has a concern with every system and with every branch of any system. A system is evolved for smooth functioning and convenience of every wing of the society.

There are many agencies which promote the system in a society – the law and law enforcing agencies, public opinion and the media, publicity and propaganda, the folkways and lores, coercion and punishment, religion and morality, sanctions, and above all education. In the case of a learner, it is through education that we have to activate all other agencies for the willing observance of the system.

We have to understand the structure of an educational institution as a family, society and social system. This institution attempts to function as a model of the society, for the society and as a forerunner of the emerging society. It is a sub-system of the social system. Its structural components include the collectivities sub-system, the role sub-system, the regulative norm sub-system, and the cultural value sub-system. Again, its functional components are: latent pattern maintenance sub-system (having the mechanism of socialisation with the help of which cultural pattern can be acquired and transmitted to the new generation), adaptative sub-system (it adapts itself to social and non-social environment), goal-attainment sub-system (it determines the goals of the system and their attainment) and integrative sub-system (it coordinates the efforts of different sub-groups for proper integration and optimum attainment through that integration, the sub-groups have not to be allowed to pull in different directions for any reason).

Education has to convey and strengthen the system in many ways. As a system indicates an orderly arrangement of parts, education has to enable an individual to become a befitting and reforming member of the system. A system may have its own boundaries and the individual has to be enlightened to function within those rules for the overall betterment of the society. One system may be an element or a sub-system or a vast system. The individual must honour and strengthen this relationship. The concept of system is applicable to the study of organic, as well as inorganic realities. It is used for reference to the organic realities such as the human nervous system. It is also used in the study of inorganic realities, such as the political, economic, industrial, educational, and social systems, etc. The individual has to be educated to become a worthy and progressive member of each system. He is bound by duty to obey the systems and should never become a cause for breach of any system. A system becomes more convenient and rewarding when all concerned meticulously obey it. The abuse of a system leads to various complications and controversies. If we all follow the systems, our output will immensely increase.

Take the simple case of a time-bound system. Time governs most of our activities. If everybody becomes time-conscious, there will not be any unnecessary hurry, there will be no delays, there will be no wastage of time, every time bound event will occur as per its schedule and everybody will automatically make the best use of his time.

Then we have the system of governance. There is the federal government at the top, there are state governments, there are district administrations, and there are the local bodies. If any link in this chain is not upto the mark, the system gets defeated.

The individual must understand that a system enhances the charm and utility of life. He must become an honest follower and caretaker of every system. He can convert it into a more rewarding asset.

Everybody wants the system to work flawlessly. There should be no failure in the system under normal conditions. It should work as designed and as expected. Its bottlenecks should be anticipated and redressed without delay. People should not be compelled to raise complaints against the system.

Education has the potential to become the key to all the systems. Not a single aspect of life should be allowed to remain unsystematic. Absence of system should not be taken as a sort of freedom.

The system is one of the signs and pre-conditions of quality life. As we succeed in making our systems more up to the mark, the quality of life will improve accordingly. A system relieves us from many anxieties, wastages, complications and disappointments. Observance of a system should be a pleasure for all. A system is a hallmark of efficiency and convenience. It should not be necessary to have hard and fast rules to ensure the observance of a system.

The system should cover our work schedule, wages, output, results, rates, communications, qualities, dealings, appreciations, rewards, workload, rules, norms, etc. The problem of system centres around issues such as the coordination of activities, checking upon the use of force, the containment of conflicts, the absence of confusion, clarity of aims and direction and certainty of desired results. Men appreciate the company of fellow-beings, their approval and want to participate with them on common enterprise. The exercise of social system sustains the solidarity of a society and maintains stability of relationships. The system enhances self-control and self-discipline. It facilitates decision-making. The system cannot be taken for granted. If we become careless about it, it may deteriorate. It is our duty to

Education and System

streamline it regularly. Even in the midst of differences, divisions, contradictions and conflicts, society must strive to maintain and succeed in its system.

It is wrong to enjoy individual freedom at the cost of a commonly proposed system. It is a bad habit to depart from the prevailing system just to exhibit personal importance and to show off.

Unsystematic arrangements lead to chaos, confusion, wastage of resources, unnecessary complaints and differences, poor show and poor results. Why should any situation and activity in life today be left without a system? Our advanced knowledge in management should be incorporated into every situation in life. A lot of expertise is available today which can formulate a quality system for every area. The system is needed on our roads, in our offices, factories, town planning, business, celebrations, homes, institutions, recuritments, meetings and government. There should be arrangements for the regular review and improvement of our system.

Introduction of the system in educational institutions should lead to its introduction in all spheres of life. Education should provide a strong foundation to it. An educational institution should be an example of a near perfect system. Its members must be made eager to evolve a better system. In whichever position a member is placed in a system, his performance must remain praiseworthy. He may sometimes happen to be in charge of a system, has and may have to lead it to ensure optimum contribution of each one of its organs.

Education will provide blueprints for various systems, such as the system for health, the system for cleanliness, the system for communications, the economic system, the social system, the political system, etc. The learner should be able to play an intelligent and positive role in each of the systems.

Every aspect of life is governed by a formula of behaviour that demands compliance from all of us. Orderliness in social behaviour is a universal characteristic. It depends upon a network of roles according to which each person accepts certain duties towards others and claims certain rights for himself.

An individual has to be educated to obey and improve the existing system. The concept of social system presupposes the prevalence of change. If the change is too slow or inefficient, the social system will deteriorate and decay. Human affairs operate in the complex combination of system and change. A society must evolve systems of manageable goals and enable people to achieve them. An educational institution should provide a reasonably true picture and specimen of the social system, so that individuals do not find any difficulty in adjustment.

The world as a whole is to be made an orderly place and the society systematic for everybody. The individuals should understand their social world and know the connections between their understanding of the world and their mastery over it. Education should strive towards evolving a system with global perspective. It should strengthen the system which indicates an orderly arrangement of parts, which has its own boundaries, in which features of social life are united into a coherent whole.

Different systems are often criticised for their delays, lapses or failures. The systems should be so perfected that there is seldom any cause for their criticism. The authorities responsible for various systems should remain alert about their functioning. There should be some arrangement for simultaneous research on and evaluation of the systems to remove their loopholes, if any. Everybody should advocate the prevalence of a system and should critically observe its functioning in order to be able to offer relevant suggestions for its improvement. One's day to day experience with different systems should be in the interest of both. None of the systems should be regarded as final. As we follow a system, we should constantly think of its modernisation.

*****

Forty four

Education and Planning

Education is a source of guidelines for every situation in life. To make life more meaningful, systematic and rewarding, there is need for adopting a strategy of planning at every crucial step. An individual must get the benefit of well planned education as envisaged by his parents, guardians, and teachers or guides. He will need a well planned pre-vocational and vocational education which has a market value. After entering a job, he will plan his vocational career. Then he will set-up his family. He will devise economic plans to meet his lifelong requirements. He will enhance his experience and qualification as a part of plans for better and promotional placements. He will draw suitable plans for the upbringing and education of his children. He will plan the best use of his leisure time. He will, if possible, draw up plans for expanding and acquiring properties. He will have plans for his role in social life. He will also draw some fruitful plans for his life after retirement. He would not leave these important decisions to mere fate, destiny or chance.

His lessons in various subjects will provide to him instances of planning as a key to success in life. He will get the chance of observing, meeting and dealing with many individuals who believe in a well planned life. They will be seen as enjoying good health, economic security, happy family life, good relations, a successful career and a respectable position in society.

When we look towards education as a preparation for life, it should be taken as a preparation for a wellplanned and successful life. One may occupy an important position in his profession in which he will have to draw plans for the upliftment and welfare of the society. Education must have gifted him with an ability to draw and execute plans, which give very good results.

Education should prepare every individual for a constructive, productive, innovative, progressive and creative planning in every aspect of life. If everybody stands by this value in life, society will see progress, prosperity, healthy atmosphere and happiness. People with destructive and unproductive planning should be noticed and brought on track by social agencies without delay.

The overall planning is a continuous and systematic process involving the application and coordination of social research, principles and techniques of education, administration, economics and finance to provide everyone with an opportunity of developing his potentialities. It should result in the most effective contribution to the social, cultural and economic development of mankind.

Both, education and planning should coordinate with each other in short-term, medium-term and long-term planning. Educational institutions have to guide socio-cultural changes in terms of economic development, simple living, productive expenditures, minimising the wastages and in reducing the gap between rich and poor.

Human resources development is possible through planned educational strategies. Human capital formation is possible through proper planning in education and other variables like social services, welfare services, economic resources, etc. Contributions of education for planning-oriented development are many, such as higher productivity, better awareness, better standard of living, better human relations, better citizenship, eradication of social problems, better employer-employee relations, achievement of social justice, etc.

Education develops desirable attitudes towards science and technology which guide our planning strategies. Education guides us for many planning strategies by creating a positive opinion for the small family norm, developing feelings of social cohesion and internationalism, developing scientific attitude, creating an urge for innovation, and appreciation for development activities.

There is need to diagnose the present conditions and trends so as to provide a perspective for further planning. The plan is to be translated into action and continuously evaluated to make timely alterations. Desirable planning values and strategies can be inculcated among the individuals through education. The modern set-up demands planning at every step. Education should prepare individuals, families, villages, towns, communities, regions, countries and the world for a well planned existence and future. Every organ or agency of the society should be made conscious about planning. The level of existence can be definitely raised by day to day planning, planning of resources, economic planning, planning of facilities, planning the solution of lingering problems and planning for different age groups.

Education has to provide expertise to the authorities engaged in the planning programmes of developmental bodies and state agencies. Every planning programme should be oriented towards development, progress, prosperity, better living, and concrete results. If the results achieved remain below the expectation level, the entire plan should be reviewed, made more hopeful, and implemented with greater vigour and determination. There should be no question of the failure of a plan.

Education should empower every individual to work out his personal plans, and play an intelligent role in planning for his family, village, town and society. When he happens to belong to an institution, business or organisation, he should be able to help in the introduction of result-oriented planning in them. The individuals should be motivated to change their unplanned existence into a well planned life. Man shouldn't make excuses like leaving life to circumstances and chance.

There is a happy trend towards institutional planning among educational institutions. It provides a good experience to administrators, teachers and students.

Planning in life should be a lesson taught by education. The details of institutional plan should be worked out after discussions among teachers and students. Good models of institutional plans should be visited by them to benefit from their experience. There should also be an arrangement for the circulation of good institutional plans. Training the mind to make plans should become a trait with every learner.

*****

Forty five

Educational Planning

Educational planning involves identification of the objectives and available resources, examining the possibility of optimum use of these resources, distributing the available time for achieving the selected targets and evolving the best possible methods to achieve them.

The concept of educational planning can be best understood within the framework of socio-economic planning. The planning for education has to be a continuous, systematic and a forward-looking process. It involves the coordination of educational research, the problems in the way of effective education, wastage in education, the principles and techniques of education, administration, economics, finance and manpower planning.

The process of planning requires a successive list of activities like: the classification of educational objectives, reflecting on the shape of tomorrow's society, the periodical review of the objectives, the diagnosis of the present conditions and recent trends, assessment of alternatives for overcoming the constraints which are not only physical and economic but also psychological, sociological, adminstrative and political, the manner of translating the plan into action, and continuous consultation between the various constituents in order to modify the developmental strategies without delay. Evaluation and modification has to be a continuous process and that has to be inbuilt into the structure of a plan.

There is need to ensure that education fits harmoneously into the pattern of changes in the near and distant future and is sufficiently progressive to provide necessary leadership in all walks of life.

There are a number of conditions for a fruitful, modern and result-oriented educational plan. The situation of education in the base year needs to be scientifically studied. Then a long-term perspective of educational development has to be visualised in view of the socio-economic goals. A rational pattern of priorities within the present and prospective system of education has to be worked out. The plan should be drawn with such expertise that in case the social, economic and political needs necessitate any alteration in the model midway, it should not be difficult to do so. If it fails to show desired results in the years of its inception, necessary remedies, modifications and improvements should not be delayed.

Along with laying stress on the quantitative side of facilities and figure work of examination results, the educational plan must lay down the targets of qualitative nature. There may be some programmes of co-curricular nature, tests to measure interests and aptitudes and some measures to show excellence and creativity. The plan should provide satisfying results in the overall development of personality. The post-education adjustment of the products of educational institutions should be another yardstick, that is, "How successfully have the educated people conducted themselves in their jobs and in the society around them?"

Time dimension is of crucial importance in any planning exercise. Short-term, medium-term and long-term planning should not be taken as alternatives to one another. A long-term plan is not an aggregate of a series of short-term plans. A long-term perspective is an essential prerequisite for the preparation of short and medium-term plans. Short-term planning in turn has long term implications.

It has to be admitted that the destiny of individuals and a society is intimately connected with the available system and the plans for education. Thus, we cannot treat educational planning in a casual and haphazard manner. This planning must attack the numerous problems faced by individuals and society. Some of these problems are – unemployment, exploitation, economic disparities, chaos in family life and society, dissatisfaction from political set-up, poor character development, absence of a system, lack of self-discipline, craze for luxuries, neglecting the development of one's personality and the lack of exploration and development of creativity. Maybe educational planning is incorporated as a part of the overall developmental planning, but it must not be treated as a less important part. It must be a top priority in the overall process of planning.

Every educational institution or every department in a larger institution becomes a basic unit for evolving short-term and long-term plans. There is justification in setting up planning forums for education at the institutional level, district level, state level, national level and global level. The outcomes of educational planning will be viewed in terms of educational expansion, provision of the infrastructure, improvement in the quality of education, application of research in education, production of more competent professionals, solutions to problems like student unrest and social unrest, improvement in quality of life, cultural advancement and necessary assurance for a better future.

Human capital formation is equally dependent on proper planning in education. In a broader sense, it includes initiative, resourcefulness, capacity for sustained work, right values, and human qualities conducive to higher output and accelerated economic growth. Its qualitative side includes technical skills, organisational ability, capacity to innovate, educational level and health of the population. Educational planning plays a catalytic role in harnessing human capital and other relevant factors.

Education is a venture with far-reaching consequences and possibilities and planning can empower this venture in many ways.

Educational planning should receive due attention when development plans are drafted by a country. Its planning should rather receive a pivotal position. Educational planning may be regarded as a torchbearer in the overall process of planning. Its curricula and activities should form the stepping stones for a better future.

While drafting a plan, the following factors have to be kept in view: that the democratisation of education has resulted in the explosion of numbers, lifelong education has become a necessity in the modern age, education has to be made relevant to life, society, vocation and the all-round development of a personality. There is also a need to equalise educational opportunities by removing regional, social and cultural imbalances. Education has to be made qualitative from various angles. Education has to be in the forefront in the process of modernisation.

Educational planning has to satisfy three aspects of planning. Pedagogical planning has to ensure that at a minimum cost of resources the relationship between the student and his school is made as positive as possible. Structural planning improves the relationship of a given school to the rest of the educational system including its preceding and succeeding levels. Economic planning improves the relationship of the system of education to the economy such that the products of education are most readily and usefully absorbed in the economy.

Educational planning will be cost conscious meaning that it will yield better results for a given investment or require a lesser investment to get the same results. It will ensure intensive utilisation of available resources. Instead of making additional investment, it will ensure a better return from the existing facilities. It will develop less costly techniques or produce things of higher quality at lesser cost through research and mass production. It will adopt a selective approach on the basis of rational and well defined priorities. It will deliberately utilize greater human effort to make up for the shortfall in material and monetary resources.

Educational planning will ensure the participation of community, faculty and research agencies in preparing the draft proposals. It is done by keeping in view the priorities emerging from the socio-economic goals proposed by the country, taking note of the various constraints—physical, financial and academic and concentrating on the goals of educational development. Some of its basic principles will be cost consciousness, intensive utilisation of available resources, innovation of less costly but more effective techniques, selective approach within broad areas and human effort.

Planning will become more result-oriented, if a special machinery is set-up for drawing up, implementing, evaluation and reviewing the plan. It should collect the necessary basic data, conduct research, experiments, pilot projects and exchange of ideas about the new programme. This agency should make the public, teachers and administrators more plan-conscious. It should find ways of associating them actively with the preparation and implementation of the programmes included in the plan.

Some of the aspects of the plans of education will be – the objectives, available resources, multi-dimensional approach, existing weak points, qualitative results, evolution and continuity.

The hurdles in the way of an educational plan should be anticipated and removed. Some of the hurdles are – inadequate resources; inadequate and incapable staff; undesirable political and administrative interference; lack of vision; lack of leadership; lack of coordination between different levels; agencies and institutions of education; non-cooperation between different organs of the government and society, and red-tapism.

An expert committee for educational planning should become a permanent feature. Educational planning cannot be satisfying if we set-up education commissions after gaps of decades. It cannot be allowed to remain haphazard, a hit and miss affair, delayed and outdated. There is need for a global exchange of ideas in educational planning for the future.

It does not suffice if an overall development plan of a country carries a chapter on educational planning. Planning in education needs to be vast and comprehensive enough, and should ensure the development of all areas life. It will be interlinked with all types of developmental plans and should rather make an impact on all other areas.

There is an urgent need for educational planning when we are faced with issues like, poor adjustment of people in family life, social life and work places, poor leadership in various walks of life, social inequalities, rising cost of education, poor student-teacher relations, social and emotional problems of the modern citizen, lapses in the administration and organisation of educational institutions, lack of clarity about the education of the future, and the role of devices like computer in education.

*****

X
EDUCATION AND WELFARE

Forty six

Vocationalisation of Education

Vocationalisation will necessitate diversification of courses and allocation of suitable courses to each individual. The courses will be divided into streams like humanities, medical sciences, non-medical sciences, social sciences, home science, commerce, technological group, agriculture group and fine arts. Suitable courses will have to be proposed for each student on the basis of his intelligence, aptitudes, interests, aspirations and background.

It is a fact that study for one's vocational preparation is an important means of freeing and liberalising the mind. The traditional wall between vocational and cultural needs has to be broken. Vocational education will not be limited to the mere acquisition of some job skills. Rather, it should concentrate more on the underlying principles of industrial processes and their social significance.

Vocationalisation means learning of skills or a range of skills through the study of technologies, related sciences or other practical work. It may introduce work experience related to agriculture and allied vocations, business and office management, paramedical sciences, home science and related activities, commercial art, photography, architecture, construction work, printing, driving, etc. It reduces unemployment, suits individual aptitudes, enhances social efficiency, develops moral values and increases productivity. It relates education to activity and life. It makes school life more activity-oriented, more meaningful, more satisfying, productivity-oriented, diversified and job-oriented.

The lack of emphasis on work experience is one of the major weaknesses of our education system. Work experience develops good working habits, introduces a wide range of activities of actual life, relates education with modern technology, provides a solution to the problem of indiscipline and a solution to the problems of actual life. It may also provide a wide range of vocational courses for the benefit of backward students and dropouts. The activities selected for school life should satisfy fundamental needs and needs of the modern era.

There should be coordination between educational institutions and industries. The employers should be involved in the organisation of vocational education. There should be cent per cent placement for the vocational pass-out persons. There may be provision of bridge courses for professional growth, career promotion and lateral entry into a new vocation. There can be some part-time courses for those who have adopted some vocation after general education. These courses may offer new opportunities for some better vocations.

It is a huge wastage if a person does not get into a vocation for which he has been trained. Every vocationally trained person must have a variety of choices before him. Vocational training of one type may have relevance in a number of vocations. Vocationalisation is an attempt to provide a strong vocational base to the student in his education and later life. The individual draws happiness from his vocational education while learning and after learning by getting a suitable placement. Vocationalisation enhances the work efficiency and social efficiency of the individual. It facilitates in allocating the right person at the right place and reduces the number of economic and social misfits. It encourages resourcefulness in the individual. For children of low academic achievement, vocational training is a big hope. Vocationalisation makes education more purposeful and productive. It will also excite the intelligence and check the tendency of lethargy and inactivity.

If the educated individual fails to win economic self-sufficiency, he may indulge in immoral conduct, get degenerated in his intellectual calibre and may lose interest in life, civilisation and culture. Vocationalisation of education and work experience contribute in their own way to the well balanced and all round development of the individual. It will reduce the dominating bookish nature of education and will introduce the psychological principle of alteration between mental, manual and physical activities and give suitable rest spans to the overburdened intellectual faculty. It will initiate one's acquaintance with modern technology and provide knowledge about the sources of raw materials, their specifications, their identification, process of manufacturing, physical and chemical properties and maintenance of apparatus and tools. It inculcates dignity of labour, spirit of enterprise, habit of hard work and cooperation. With the dynamic, future bound and progressive insight of work experience, a new society may emerge with deeper interest in work, economy and prosperity. Work experience provides educational and vocational guidance in its own way.

There is slow progress in the process of vocationalisation of education because of lack of seriousness, lack of training facilities for the teachers, lack of expert guidance to the planners and teachers, lack of coordination between industry and education, lack of cooperation between different organs of general education and technical education and lack of finances for required infrastructure.

To make this programme successful, there is a need for the diversification of courses to meet different interests, aptitudes, talents, needs and economic expectations. Multi-purpose schools should be started to offer diversified courses. The sense of inferiority attached with certain vocational courses should be removed from the minds of students. Educational and vocational guidance should become a regular feature of educational institutions. Timely guidance should remove the problem of wrong classification of students. Some unilateral schools may also be set-up to provide intensive training in different types of vocational courses. Suitable cottage industries may also be introduced in some schools. The type of vocational courses chosen for a school should depend upon its location, facilities available in it and the requirements of the region. Central technical institutes may be set-up in big cities which may serve the need of several local schools. There should be some institutes for part-time vocational courses. The facility of apprenticeship training should be available in a local industry.

Some forums should be set-up for exchange of experiences among parents, general schools, multi-purpose schools, vocational institutions, industries and technical institutes.

Introduction of vocational education will require clarity about the form and organisation of vocational education within the existing system, the organisation of its curriculum, the training of teachers, necessary changes in the insructional procedures, provision of laboratory and workshop equipment, educational and vocational guidance for the selection of vocational courses, administration and control, marketing of the goods produced during training, qualitative improvement in technical education, coordination between training facilities and job opportunities, post-technical education and training, creating a favourable attitude towards manual work, modernisation of technology and simultaneous research for better results.

The aim of education, according to Dewey is social efficiency. This aim has brought a change in the tenor of society by the application of science to the means of production and distribution. Dewey believed that school was a fundamental agency for social progress and reform. In his project method, the pupils are faced with some task to be accomplished. Thus, education should develop the individual into a man of thought and action.

UNESCO lays stress on vocational education and says, "Vocational education is a comprehensive term embracing those aspects of the educational process involving in addition to general education, the study of technologies and related sciences and the acquisition of practical skills, attitudes, understandings and knowledge relating to occupations in the various sectors of economic and social life. Such an education would be an integral part of general education and a means of preparing for an occupational field and as an aspect of continuing education."

Some of the other kinds of vocational training could be in: maintenance of buildings, communications, local body and related sciences, pottery, as tourist guides, in social service, and wood work, etc.

Vocationalisation adds more meaning to life thereby making it complete. An individual may satisfy his urges of construction, self-expression, and activity through his vocation. It can be further promoted through correspondence courses, post-technical education, contact with industries, and refresher courses.

*****

Forty seven

Education and Work Culture

A strong and faithful work culture should be a natural consequence of an effective system of education. Education has to develop the spirit of dedication and devotion towards one's duty. An idle individual should never take delight in his lifestyle. The parasites in society should get ashamed of their burdening dependence on others. With an attitude of doing nothing, one should not shirk the responsibility of earning one's livelihood and should not expect and desire any undeserved gains in life.

If everybody is true to his work culture, personal poverty, social and national backwardness will vanish. People should learn to work with zeal, should be prepared to work to the optimum level of their capacity, to work wholeheartedly, impart new qualities to their work, treat work as worship, be prepared not to waste even a moment of their duty hours and want magnificent results from what they do. They should feel attached to their work. Everybody should take pride in being called a workaholic.

A devoted and dedicated worker should always think beyond the traditional routine of his work. He should aspire to evolve a better approach, better techniques and more refined outcomes in his vocation.

We should be able to create such a climate at our work places and in our institutions that anyone who shirks from his responsibility is noticed and is obliged to come up to the expectations of his co-workers, supervisors and administrators.

In an educational institution, everybody including the administrator, teachers, students and other members of the staff should be hard working in their own domain. All of them should be embodiments of work culture of a high standard. There should be no need of an outside agency to be strict or impose rules; they should all be hard task masters for themselves. We should pay special attention to inculcate work culture in the new generation as well. There should be no laxity even if mankind has made substantial progress and brought about irreversible prosperity. Hard work should not become a habit only out of consideration for duty; it should become a dominant characteristic of human nature.

Hard work in teaching and learning or education demands a kind of study beyond the parametres of the normal curriculum. By hard work by students, it is not implied they should cram and be overburdened with the preparation for examinations alone. It should lead to mastery over the knowledge.

Work experience as a part of education, is going to be useful to the learner in many ways. It is going to develop in the students the readiness for some vocation, a positive attitude towards work, good working habits, self-respect and achievement, job intelligence and special vocational skills, vocational interest and dignity of labour. It partly solves the problem of indiscipline as the students have no more surplus energy for mischief. It promotes learning by doing also. It strengthens the relation between educational and vocational activities. The educational institutions and places of work come closer. It necessitates team work and cooperation. It contributes something to productivity at the national level. The work relates education with health and hygiene, food, shelter, clothing, recreation, social service and culture. It is a basis for lifelong participation in productive work at home, in a farm, in a workshop, in a factory or in any other work related placement. It may not prepare a student for any particular vocation, but this experience adds to his capability for every vocation or profession.

There are many factors which help in the development of work culture: such as personality, self-concept, special abilities, interpersonal relationships, intelligence, family, socio-economic status, social prestige and vocational guidance.

Knowledge and work are two pillars of human life. When the work is entrusted to educated hands, it should be an example of quality and superiority.

In the absence of a sound work culture our educational, social, economic and political system are doomed to collapse.

Everybody should learn to do more work than his needs. If the students consider their work as a burden, what will they do tomorrow? During education, the learner should be motivated to learn more than the requirements of his syllabus and examination. He should never feel satisfied with that much learning which just suffices for bringing him the pass marks.

Some believe that students should have no home work or examinations in the end. These ideas promote an attitude which is against work culture. Hard work should always be treated as a pleasant duty. Wasting one's time is one of the biggest sins. There is always an element of pleasure and well-being attached with our work. Honest work should become a sacred commitment of every individual. If our work along with our personal achievement results in welfare in general it is a double gain. Some people choose to work for a cause. If it happens to be purely theoretical in nature, it must be supplemented with some productive work.

Research has shown that formal schooling raises the income of even a farmer and his ability to adopt a more paying occupation. Our work culture should not be tied to monetary gains alone; there should also be some long-term targets involved as well. Work should become a mission. It should be an honour to perspire in our work. It should be our pledge to earn appreciation in our work.

There is all the more need to attach grandeur to our work. Even if we have to work like a machine, we are a machine gifted with intelligence and emotions. Machines have taken over most of our strenuous activities. In the times to come, more and more machines will be at our disposal. But that should not bring about any difference and neither should we be indifferent towards our work. We should continue to put in our best efforts to our work. Complaining of tiredness at work too often after short intervals is improper and against one's work culture. Even if the work is tiresome, we should accept it without complaint or grudge. Even if the work allotted to a person causes drudgery, the individual must honestly try to do full justice to it. If we get fixed eight hours as a schedule of work, it should be observed strictly. It should not be less even by a minute.

Industry, by the applications of science and technology has multiplied the number of occupations, which need long-term training. People have to be educated and trained for specific jobs and prior to that they have to be provided with general education. There is a need to reconcile with the processes of general education and technical training. We have to set-up more diversified educational institutions at higher levels. General education is definitely necessary to build foundations for technical and professional education.

Maldistribution of work may be discussed in educational literature and some remedies may be worked out for better and equitable distribution. Similarly, there is need to discuss disproportionate wages for different types of vocations and the necessary remedial measures to be taken for the same. We have every right to expect proportionate return from our work, but if it does not happen we should not become gloomy forever.

One may be called upon to undertake a job of any type. His devotion to the job must be taken for granted. Individuals should be educated to do full justice to whatever job comes his way. Even if the job in hand does not suit his interest, he must not show his dislike by shirking it. He should try to adjust with his job, and at the same time search for a better alternative. There is no reason for him to ignore the work allocated to him. The educated youth demand white collar jobs, and when they fail to get them, they should gracefully accept the alternative. To remain jobless is a multiple wastage.

We waste a lot of our resources and manpower for the supervision of workers at work. Junior and senior supervisors have to be detailed at different stages. Our workers should not stand in need of supervisors. The employee should consider the work as his own and should not do it only because the supervisor is watching him. He should always aspire to bring quantitative and qualitative improvement in his performance. His employer should have full faith in him and should be proud of him.

There may be some people who are rich enough to employ domestic servants and other labour to work for them. To shift our small activities to others is an unnecessary dependence. No one should choose to enjoy on the hard work of others. Everybody must contribute his share of labour in different aspects of life.

The nature of our work should not be objectionable from any angle. Quite a large number of people are found engaged in unapporvable work culture. It is wrong to use religion, social service and politics as a means of bread and butter. Human beings have adopted many means of livelihood, which are an insult to them. Some of such means are: smuggling, theft, contract killing, fortune telling, begging, cheating, prostitution and drug trafficking.

There should be a balance between work and leisure. But leisure does not mean just sitting idle, lying down or sleeping. It can be a different type of work in the form of hobbies and enjoyable activities which provide rest as well as leisure in between work sessions.

Everybody wants to get the job of his choice. But it is very difficult to provide everyone a job which they like the most. No doubt, right choice of job will bring out the best in the individual to enable him to make significant contribution to the qualitative productivity and to the well-being of the society. Even if he does not get the job according to his taste, he should not feel permanently miserable about it. He should learn to derive reasonable job satisfaction from whichever assignment comes his way in life. Education should become an inspiration for job satisfaction.

By promoting division of labour and specialisation, education brings about optimum combination of the factors of production. In every undertaking, we find specialists dealing with accounts, sales, advertising, production, supervision, auditing, management and workforce welfare which demand a widespread influence of education.

To begin with, an individual may be offerred a job below his qualifications and merit. Even then he must have learnt to do full justice to the work in hand and wait patiently for the job he deserves to get. Work well done at his present job will enhance his merit and right for promotion. In the area of jobs, one should not restrict one's options to such an extent that he leads a disgruntled vocational life in the event of not getting the job befitting his taste and merit. On the job in hand, he must be able to build his reputation so that he receives better offers.

For establishing a better work culture, we have to remove many obstacles such as, poor education, unemployment, exploitation of labour, nepotism, delay in communication, long queues, piling up of files, extending the dates of completion of projects, non-observance of specified schedule, absence of worker welfare schemes, poor examination results, illnesses, defective tools, absence of a system and drug abuse.

It is everyone's duty to improve the speed and quality of his work with every passing day. Again, everybody should be able to receive a report of excellence after the annual evaluation. The people who become rich at the cost of their workforce should change their attitude towards work. They must evaluate their own contribution and decide to share the activity which is practical and productive. Education must motivate an individual for hard work in life. He should contribute towards much more enrichment of the society much more than what he may have drawn from it.

*****

Forty eight
Education as Investment

Investment in education enriches the individual, the family, the community, the society, the country, the civilisation and the culture. Real education makes the individual an all-rounder who is useful to himself and to others. Investment in education ensures the worth and output of the individual. Society will get prosperous overnight if every individual is educated to engage in gainful and constructive activities. A large number of human beings are simply engaged in wasteful and destructive activities. They have to be reclaimed through educaiton.

Investment in education brings manifold and multi-dimensional returns. A capable individual becomes an asset for himself and for others. Education can enable every individual to lead a gainful existence. This gainful existence is confined not only to acquiring material things. The individual will so shape his orientations that he will never waste any resources at his command and will never use his own resources for the disadvantage of others. He will always remain engaged in self-evaluation and will keep his balance sheet positive. He will keep a watch over the contributions he is making every day and that which he is likely to make in the long-run. If every individual is suitably educated to make contributions, the future of mankind will be bright forever.

Every human life is a valuable return in itself. Everybody can be a source of enrichment for the society. If an individual understands that he has not got a single moment to waste, we can well imagine the resources available to mankind.

Investment in education is to be measured in terms of excellence of human behaviour. We have to receive education with this conviction that there is no limit to the excellence of human behaviour and performance.

Research studies have shown that the average income figures of persons who have more education are higher than those of the persons who have less education. Higher the educational qualifications of a person, richer is his potential for productivity and creativity.

Alfred Marshall says, "Education makes a man more intelligent, more ready, more trustworthy – it raises the tone of his life in working hours and out of working hours ... the most valuable of all capital is that invested in human being." It is through education that the constructive urges of man are aroused.

Even the emphasis on adult education will provide incentive to the masses to raise their standard of living and to move from subsistence production into market economy.

Soviet Professor Kairov declares that when the universal four-year education was introduced in the U.S.S.R., it was calculated that the benefit to the economy would be forty three times greater than the sum spent on it.

Progressive education must be planned and made available many years before it is needed.

Mrs Alva Myrdal said, "Education has, in the nations that have advanced rapidly and firmly, been rather a precursor than a follower in the time table of progress."

The study of economic growth includes investment in education, health, science, technology, agriculture, industry and above all the training of people itself, i.e., investment on human beings.

The benefit of education lies in a better future, in the form of acquisition of modern skills and improvement of capacities which may enhance future productivity and income and enable a person to enjoy a better socio-economic status.

To work efficiently and get good returns, one should possess a strong physical and mental capacity, which is the outcome of a sound system of education.

Right from the birth of a child, investments are made for him with the expectation that it will yield some fruits in the future. There are two major investments: one for his physical well-being and the other for his intellectual development.

The return on investment in education is bound to be positive as long as there is no unemployment among the educated. We have to carefully change our educational strategies keeping in view our level of development and manpower requirements.

The investment in education should not be restricted such that the urgent needs for its modernisation are made to wait. Investment in every field has to be utilitarian, productive and result-oriented and should not be ornamental or decorative. Investments in any form and all over the world should be strictly productive, as long as there is poverty in any corner of the world.

*****

Forty nine

Education and Employment

For a few decades in the early stages of organised formal education, young people after obtaining a degree or diploma enjoyed a sort of guarantee for jobs. Those who developed love for knowledge were in most cases handsomely rewarded in lieu of their extraordinary merit.

The organised system of society required men of calibre in every sphere. The qualified individuals did not have to wait for long for suitable jobs. But this happy equation between education and employment could not remain intact for long.

The Second World War created a temporary expansion of job opportunites for the educated. The need for reconstruction and development in the post-war period also helped in sustaining the job market for qualified persons.

The emergence of democracy in most parts of the world created educational opportunities for all the citizens. Almost every young man obtained a degree or diploma and then searched for a job. The job opportunities were expanded disproportionately in order to pacify the job seekers. But this was an unsound policy that was destined to fail.

We have millions of qualified people who are jobless today. The increasing population, mechanisation and computerisation coupled with certain other factors have disturbed the equation between education and employment still further. Our schemes to ameliorate the situation are proving to be unplanned and illogical.

Lescohier describes the pathetic condition of an unemployed person as, "Unsteady employment undermines the worker's physique, deadens his mind, weakens his ambition, saps self-respect and the sense of responsibility, impairs technical skills, weakens nerve and will power ... creates a tendency to blame others for failures ... saps his courage." Unemployment damages our physical, mental and moral health. In spite of the stark reality of this damaging impact, education has to develop in the young minds a never-fading perseverance, a resolve to face even the worst situation and a determination to succeed ultimately..

Some practical training may be provided to everybody along with the courses of general education, so that the individual does not remain idle while searching and waiting for his employment. Every individual should be mentally prepared to face the universal problem of unemployment. If the job opportunities are not up to our expectations and merit, we should be able enough to control our frustration. We should not compromise forever, but by making a wiser choice should add to our qualifications so that we receive better offers.

An educated person should not remain idle after obtaining a qualification. The society must ensure cent per cent employment for its people. Job opportunities should not fall short of available manpower. It is wrong to provide unemployment allowance for jobless people. This practice amounts to a double burden on the resources of the society. It is a sad situation when there are thousands of candidates for a few hundred jobs and a fairly large number of candidates are found to be overqualified than the requirements of the jobs.

The aims of education are no longer confined to preparing the learners for white collar jobs alone. Its purposes should be to remove unemployment, to prepare individuals for self-employment, to enlarge the areas of employment, to prepare the individuals to lead a constructive and productive life in whatever form, and to be able to make the best of the employment opportunity coming their way. The individuals should be educated to free themselves from the taboos and prejudices connected with certain vocations. Educational opportunities should be related with job opportunities. Educational institutions should be in a position to guide their outgoing students regarding placements.

Quite recently the slogan of job-oriented education has become a fashion. If job-oriented education also creates unemployment among the skilled people then what will be the remedy. Our human resources development should be so perfect that we train only as many people as we are likely to absorb in the jobs of each category. Trained persons should not be forced to wait indefinitely for suitable job opportunities. They should not be made to waste their training and education by accepting a job not relevant to their preparation.

The idea of job-oriented education can work only if we have a correct data about the jobs available. The educational institutions should be restricted from training the persons in disproportionately large numbers. The rule of supply and demand should be our guiding principle in the spheres of education and employment. The diversification in education should run parallel to the diversification of occupations.

If a person is compelled to accept a job not befitting his professional education and training, after a few years of working on such a job, he will forget almost everything he learnt during his education.

With industrialisation, modernisation and globalisation, and quality education the guarantee of employment has become the need of the hour. The census data, based on the need of work for the unemployed, does not give a true estimate of the huge problem of unemployment. Hidden under the labels of part-time employment, mal-employment and self-employment are the figures of massive unemployment. Such unemployed or semi-employed people fall easy prey to antisocial and anti-national activities.

There should be a sufficient number of courses to fulfil the need for inter-disciplinary specialisations. The emphasis should shift to the great range of courses in agricultural, commercial, scientific, industrial, technological and many other trades including their combinations. Students should become capable of working in multi-disciplinary environments such as, environmental sciences, biotechnology, microbiology, meteorology, agri-business management, case studies, and should have a problem solving approach.

The economy needs to be stimulated by avoiding passive investments, unproductive expenditure, and by increasing production and curbing black money. Population explosion in general and in institutions of higher learning has to be brought under control.

When the prevailing system of education does not succeed in removing unemployment, it has to be continuously planned, diversified and re-oriented to minimise the problem.

Education demands employment. At the same time, it must lead to qualitative work on any job a person happens to get. The qualified people have to employ their knowledge for better outcomes. They are duty-bound to become more efficient by virtue of experience. Along with learning from experience, they should develop their relevant knowledge by continuous study. If they can attend any part-time courses or in service courses, it will further improve their performance, show better output, bring greater satisfaction to the employer, enhance their chances for promotion and increase their opportunities of getting a better job.

The process of getting more knowledge should be continued even after getting the job of one's choice. One must actively search for innovations and better processes concerning one's job. If the job happens to be of temporary nature or contract-based, the employee has to earn permanence by virtue of his qualitative performance. The employee must be able to establish a good equation with his co-workers, supervisors and the employer. With every passing day, the employee should adjust better to the job.

It will be a matter of greater achievement if the employee, while doing full justice to the job, adds a rare qualification to the list of his initial qualifications. If he selects an area of specialisation and advances his knowledge in that area, he will become an asset for the job market and will be welcome to hold higher positions. One should not just decide to stand still on his job. Education does not only initiate employment but also boosts a person in a number of ways, provided one maintains his professional growth.

By getting suitable education, some people turn out to be counsellors. They give educational and vocational guidance to others enabling them to seek good employment. It will be all the more admirable if by virtue of his education, a person succeeds in setting up an enterprise which provides jobs to others. The teachers of job-oriented courses can also impart training and expertise to their trainees so that they can seek worthy and better placements or set-up enterprises.

*****

Fifty

Education and Economic Development

The direct effect of education on economic development can be observed in productivity, employment, competence and mobility of labour force, etc. Indirect effect can be seen in the form of thrift, savings, control on family size, right kind of attitudes and skills. The advancement in knowledge gives an impetus to the economy of the people. The higher level of education is connected with financial and non-financial rewards. Education also leads to inventions and innovations. It creates new knowledge which leads to new techniques and new instruments, which further increase the process of capital formation. In the present economy, work is based more on the mind than on the hand.

It is under the influence of education that we understand development to be utilitarian, productive, long lasting, uplifting, employment generating and humanitarian.

Development may be taken as growth plus change with the aim to improve the quality of life at the micro and macro levels. Education too stands for this.

The development of every individual or group of individuals should be based on psychological principles like the sense of achievement, satisfaction of aspirations, willing cooperation and sharing the benefits of development. An intelligent and very well-discussed decision about the developmental priorities accelerates the rate of development.

The social, political, economic and cultural systems are to be brought on rational lines to get better results through development. Education is deeply concerned in making all these systems more rational.

In the interest of economic development, education becomes a mode of arousing curiosity, developing the right interest, tendencies and values, creating necessary abilities for free thinking, contemplation, imagination, innovation and modernisation. Education can be organised as an important instrument of far-reaching and revolutionary changes.

It has been accepted that the rise in literacy and educational level was the basic cause of economic development. Educational programmes can be made development-oriented and executed after careful planning. Educational development causes development in different areas of life and vice versa.

Development in variables of standard of living can also play a positive role in checking growth rate in population, which is one of the major constraints in development. Factors related to economic development are human resources development, technological resources development and natural resources development. Education is a dominant factor in developing all these resources.

Decisions on educational priorities accelerate the economic development; for example, vocationalising of education, and diversification in education are some such priorities. Work culture and scientific attitude through education are some other contributing factors.

Investment in human resources development has directly contributed to economic development by promoting knowledge and application of science and technology to processes of production, developing innovation and research, training workers in different skills needed for modern production and building up of the right type of attitudes, values and interests conducive to higher output.

Investments on human beings are as productive and income yielding as on physical assets, machines, techniques and evaluation of results.

Educational planning, the execution of these plans and appropriate monitoring help in accelerating economic deveopment. The social skills and cultural values of human beings are the integral parts of human capital which is responsible for development.

There is need for equality in economic development. Everybody should be enabled to make equal contributions in it and avail equal return from it. It should not be an economic prosperity of a few at the cost of the poverty of many. It should not have any traces of exploitation or monopoly. It should be based on honest and fair dealings. It is through education that every individual will be guided not to adopt any shortcuts to ensure his own economic development.

By economic development, we are ultimately concerned with the achievement of better nourishment, better health, better educational opportunities, better living conditions, better social set-up, better opportunities for work and for leisure.

Expansion of knowledge does give an impetus to the economy of any country. Education may indirectly bring better returns to an economy. Gunnar Myrdal has popularised the recent economic theory of 'Investment in Man'. By investment in man, it is possible to replace the customary occupations with more sophisticated and technical occupations. For a better occupational build-up, it is fundamental to have first the basic and foundational education and then to provide vocational, specialised, mechanical, technical and professional education.

It is expected of the planners to keep a balance between educational and economic development in the country. If our mass education programmes can achieve zero per cent population growth, economic development automatically gets a boost. The attitude and trend in savings are also enhanced through the spread of education.

The investment in human beings leading to acquired and useful abilities of all the inhabitants of the country amounts to a national asset and acts as a source of economic development. Manpower forecasting with a reasonable extent of clarity enhances the chances of continuous growth.

The political system is also a socio-cultural factor which contributes towards economic development. Education can mould and activate a political system for better performance.

Through planning, diversion, multiple avenues and education, an individual has to be enabled to find a number of channels for himself. There should not be any wastage of human talent and competence.

The new growth theorists emphasise that education, learning and skill formation enhance the productivity of people. The continuous accumulation of knowledge can result in attaining higher levels of per capita income. The high growth in many countries has much to do with their investment in education.

The 1995 UNESCO report maintains that access to higher education and the broad range of services it can render to a society, is part and parcel of any sustainable development programme in which human expertise and professional skills are required.

The famous economist Marshall is of the view that economics is the science of wealth dealing with human welfare. Broadened in its scope, economics gets integrated with education which has to guide all the activities concerned with the welfare of the individual. The economy of a country influences its education and on the other hand, the return from education shapes economic planning and growth.

Because of the intimate relationship between economics and education, some scholars have started to develop a new field of study which is called Economics of Education. Education not only aims at the full development of a personality; it has also to promote the working efficiency of the citizen. Economics of education studies in depth the investment on education with the corresponding return it brings to the society in the form of material, as well as non-material resources.

Some countries have immensely increased their material wealth and attained surprising economic growth because of their successful programmes of free, compulsory and universal education. The economic prosperity of advanced countries is largely due to their investment in education. According to UNESCO, investment in education holds the same place as investment in any profitable industry.

The demand for vocational and technical education grew stronger as a result of change in economic conditions. Efforts have to be made to promote production, distribution and other economic factors to achieve financial development and economic parity between individuals. This required bringing a change in the outlook of the people for which education was the proper medium. The democratic system also necessitates bridging the gulf between rich and poor. Equal opportunities of education to the high and low income groups further improve the chances of economic parity. Education for all, technical education, education for women, and equal opportunities of education for rural areas further augment economic development and economic equality.

*****

XI

EDUCATION AND THE WORLD

Fifty one

Education and Environment

There are different views about the extent to which a person's skills, abilities, talents or intelligence are inherited through genetics or are determined by environmental factors. Jean Piaget is noted for saying that anyone can learn anything if properly taught. But Jensen thought that intelligence was 80 percent inherited and that teachers should concentrate on students with high intelligence and leave the remainder to learn vocational skills.

But the influence of the environment on the development of an individual is so deep that it has to be manipulated to his best advantage. It has been seen that savage groups which have come in contact with the civilised groups become civilised and equally advanced. The Murray Islanders had no words in their language to count beyond six, but after receiving training at the hands of Scots who occupied the island, developed as good a mathematical ability as that possessed by any civilised people. W N Kellogg performed an experiment of educating a ten month old chimpanzee along with his seven-month-old son. The chimpanzee made remarkable progress and learnt to eat with a spoon, drink out of a glass and at the end of a nine month long experiment, understood over 50 words or phrases. It has been found that children who are sent to the nursery earlier than other children show an increase of 4 to 5 points in their intelligence quotient. Herbart believed that human improvement solely depends on education, which is dependent on the environment. He says that it is the environment which mostly helps in the development of the child. According to Huxley, the environment is everything in the development of a child. Locke believes that environment and education may mould the child in any form. Candolle studied the lives of distinguished academics of Europe and found that they had become great scholars because they got rich environments. The environment definitely influences our intelligence quotient, diverts and determines the direction of development and hence, gives shape to our personality. Clark has gone to the extent to say that the cause of superior intelligence is environment and not heredity. Total personality of the individual is more significantly influenced by the environment rather than by heredity.

But in the long-run, we have to agree that heredity gives us the capacities to be developed and opportunities for the development of these capacities must come from the environment.

The ultimate goals of environmental education will be to foster the awareness of and concern about economic, social, political and ecological environment, to provide knowledge, values, attitudes, commitments and skills needed to protect and improve the environment, and to create new patterns of behaviour of individuals, groups and society towards the environment.

In order to draw the maximum possible educational advantage from the environment, we have to consider it in its totality – natural and man-made, social, economic, moral, political, technological, cultural, historical and aesthetic. Its influence should be accepted as a lifelong process, beginning at the pre-school stage and continuing through all formal and non-formal stages. We should adopt an interdisciplinary approach to the environment, drawing upon the specific contents of each discipline in making possible a holistic and well balanced perspective. Its minutest details should lead us to its total picture. The learner must get the experience of active participation in observing, understanding, learning, and appreciating the environment and also in preventing and solving its problems.

He should examine major environmental details and issues from local, regional, national and international points of view, so that he receives insights into the environmental conditions in different geographical areas. He should focus on the current and potential environmental situations keeping in view the historical perspective. He should consider environmental aspects in the plans for education, development and growth. He should grasp the complexity of the environmental problems and develop critical thinking and problem-solving skills. He should learn the value and necessity of local, national and international cooperation in understanding the environment and to prevent and solve its problems. He should utilize diverse learning environments and a broad spectrum of educational approaches to learning from the environment with an emphasis on practical activities and first-hand experiences. He should understand the relationship between environmental sensitivity, knowledge and problem-solving. He should discover the educative material from the environment and also the real causes of its problems.

Some of the various disciplines to be incorporated in the environmental education are ecosystem, which relates to energy flow, nutrient cycling, carbon and food cycling. Man makes an impact on the ecosystem and he is capable of altering the system of the earth. The second discipline relates to population; involving population structure, age grouping, causes of population explosion, the impact of population on the environment, migration of population and its consequences, the shortage of resources due to increased population, lifestyle of different populations, the birth-death rates, health and hygiene, population policy and social, ecological and political implications of a growing population. The third discipline relates to economics and technology, which will include production and distribution of goods and services desired by individual and society. Some of the businesses and industrial plants create environmental problems like pollution.

The economic system depends on raw materials, manufacture of goods and agricultural production. The interdependence of the economic systems of various countries is an important issue. It should emphasise the relationship of the environment with the levels of production, population growth and degree of urbanisation. The fourth discipline may refer to environmental decisions. These decisions are related to social, economic and political aspects. It will also include the possibilities of alternative decisions, policies and actions to make the environment more human-friendly and educative. There is need to reduce environmental abuse. These decisions may be adopted or reshaped by various groups to improve the social life through better environment. The fifth discipline may incorporate the environmental ethics. If we exploit Nature and abuse the environment it will be difficult for us to survive. When we protect the environment, it will protect us in return. The sixth discipline may be about considering the environment as a natural heritage. Only when our life is guided by respect for the environment, we shall be able to live in harmony with it.

Environment combines social, moral, economic, physical, political and intellectual factors which influence the development of an individual. Along with the physical environment we are rapidly polluting the environment in many other ways. For example, through gaps in the socio-economic structure, through corruption, irresponsible politicians, drug abuse, antisocial activities, gambling, exploitation, poverty, class system, unhealthy competition, adulteration, crime and terrorism. There is pollution in the fields of psychology, philosophy, sociology, religion and even education. For example, the philosophical theories like "eat, drink and be merry" have eclipsed many worthwhile and healthy theories of philosophy. On the part of some thinkers and ideologues, it has become a fashion to challenge the age-old virtues and replace them with workable formulae. Intellectual pollution is also dangerous for an individual and social life. The clever intellectuals create unwanted confusions, controversies and conflicts. They misuse their intellect to misguide innocent people. They invent arguments to cause doubts about what is wrong and what is right. The media and propaganda are also employed to strengthen unfounded doubts and beliefs.

It is through education that we have to purify the environment from its physical, social, economic, religious, intellectual and political pollutions. Only then will the environment be a healthy source of education and development. When education and environment pull the child in different directions, he gets confused and cannot proceed speedily on his path of development. Let us create an environment which is rich in truth, beauty and goodness. The child should get an environment which is calm and peaceful, healthy, rich in wonderful experiences, displaying an atmosphere of cooperation, brotherhood, like-mindedness, affectionate relationships, development, fellow-feeling, helpfulness, justice, work-mindedness, commitment, devotion, solidarity and stability. It should be a growing, advancing, rectifying and inspiring environment. There should be a sort of perfect harmony between people and their environment. It should remain a medium of new experiences, challenges, satisfactions and innovations. Its educative, informative and modernising possibilities should go on enhancing with the passage of time. It should not dishearten and disturb the citizen in any manner. It should not be poor in any aspect. The citizens should feel proud of what the environment can gift them with.

Education and Environment

Environment is the aggregate of external forces, influences and conditions which affect the life, nature, behaviour, growth, development and maturation of the living organism. The natural environment consists of air, water, land, forests, sunlight, rivers, mountains and animals. All these components of the environment are vast sources of knowledge and facilities. Our education and style of life should help us in preserving, improving, beautifying and enriching it. Students should be enabled to know the immediate and distant environment, biotic and abiotic environment, interdependence between human beings and the environment, the limited resources, conservation of resources, utilization of resources for optimum development, unplanned use of resources, appreciation of natural resources, global environment, inter-disciplinary approach to environment, local, national and international aspects of the environment, sensitivity towards the environment, to develop an interest in society and mankind, and for the problems occurring in the environment.

Education should enable the learner to recognise and solve the problems of the environment. There should be motivation to visit and understand the environment of different types. The use of co-curricular activities and media may be made to enlarge his awareness. In what way we are spoiling our environment and how we should make it more worthwhile and educative are some important issues before us. We should focus our studies and researches on different aspects of the environment and on what should be done by us for enhancing its value and how we can draw from it more education and facilities.

Projects and social service for the environment should become a regular feature of every educational institution. The institution should make its campus a good example of the environment. It should also examine the shortcomings of the area covered by it and draw some action plans for its upliftment. It should try to activate the local people and organisations to carry out plans to enhance the quality of the environment. The students should be reminded about their duties to the environment so that they accept them as a lifelong routine. Frequent cleanliness campaigns will be educative and rewarding in many ways too.

*****

Fifty two

Education and Environmental Pollution

The World Health Organisation Commission on Health and Environment submitted a report entitled 'Our Planet Our Health' in 1992. The report highlighted the effects of environmental pollution as: the shortening of life span, the creation of disability or impairment among people and the lack of the full biological potential of an organism.

Pollution is defined as the presence of one or more contaminating particles in the air, water or soil, the concentration of which has reached a degree harmful to human beings, animals and plants.

The rapid material progress has no doubt made life easier and happier but has created a crisis in the form of degradation of environment due to pollution. We literally live in and breathe filth. It is beginning to threaten our health, our happiness, our civilisation itself. The man walks with his head swathed in dirty brown smoke that stings his eyes and irritates the throat and lungs. He fights his way through mountains of trash and garbage. Man has created not only great cities but disgusting slums too.

Polythene, shopping bags, and wrappers are a serious threat to our environment. They provide breeding places to deadly germs. Industrial effluents, municipal waste, etc. cause diseases like dysentry, diarrhoea, typhoid, cholera, etc. The vectors which breed in polluted water cause diseases like malaria, dengue fever, hepatitis due to flies and cockroaches, plague due to fleas, relapsing fever due to body lice, and soft ticks, scabies due to scabies nutes, trachoma due to face flies.

Left to Nature, the different components of the environment keep themselves in balance but man has disturbed this balance for his vested interests. He is exploiting the natural resources to the maximum; for example, forests, underground water, minerals, petroleum, etc. Some kinds of environmental pollution are – air pollution, water pollution, soil pollution, thermal pollution, nuclear pollution, noise pollution and solid waste pollution.

Some air pollutants can be listed as – dust, metal dust, cotton dust, soot, fly ash, fluorides, lead, cement, aircraft emissions, pesticides, insecticides, pollen grains, spores and cells of fungi. Various unburnt hydrocarbons react with oxides of nitrogen and cause respiratory problems.

The burning of coal and other fossil fuels releases harmful sulphur compounds like sulphur oxides in the air. Partially oxidised combustion products are discharged by automobiles. These discharged products are harmful hydrocarbons and nitrous oxide.

Cigarette smoking, domestic heating, cooking devices, industries and motor vehicles are common sources of carbon monoxide. Its concentration leads to health problems like exhaustion, headache, disturbance in psychomotor functioning and cardiovascular system. There is always a cloud of smoke hanging like a layer in which breathing becomes a problem. Air pollution creates symptoms like coughing, irritation of the eyes, nasal discharge, nausea and vomiting, chest pain, shortness of breath, sore throat, lung damage, poison in the stomach, and poison in the blood stream.

A child born in an industrial area is likely to weigh one kg less than one born in the model town area. The effect of air pollution on animals is the same as in the case of human beings. In polluted air, the leaves cannot grow well, the cells in leaves decay and the leaves dry up.

At our own level, we can reduce air pollution by fuel selection and utilisation, changes in our equipment and processes and some zoning and site selection. It should become a matter of pleasure with every individual to walk or use cycle for short distances. Either the government should impose restrictions on excessive use of automobiles by people or people should accept these restrictions on their own. Educational institutions should come out with a determined campaign to make cycle compulsory as a mode of conveyance for students. The status of the cycle needs to be restored.

Sulphur dioxide and nitrous oxides released by burning of fossil fuels react with moisture, oxidants and sunlight to produce sulphuric acid and nitric acid. These come down to the earth in the form of rainfall and snow. This acid rain can destroy aquatic life and forest life. It may adversely affect buildings and the human body too.

The depletion of the ozone layer and concentration of carbon dioxide is increasing due to burning of energy resources resulting in global warming. This warming may cause melting of the ice cap region, will raise the sea level, will lead to poor agricultural production, drought conditions will prevail due to poor rainfall, will cause infertility of soil, forest fires, the withering of plant life and health problems for animals. Global warming is affecting the ecosystem, ocean currents, prevailing winds, fresh water supplies, fisheries, industry, transport, urban planning and demographics. There are risks of heat hyperpyrexia, heat exhaustion, heat cramps and heat syncope.

Pollution of water is caused by some foreign organic, inorganic, biological, radiological substances, highly enriched, over productive biotic situations such as waste materials from sewage and fertilizers. The water poisoned by toxic chemicals kills living organisms. Many other polluting substances are: infectious agents, plant materials, exotic organic chemicals, inorganic minerals, chemical compounds, sediments, and radio-active substances. A major source of polluting substances is the sewage and industrial effluents discharged into rivers, streams, canals and lakes. Detergents and fertilizers pollute water with chemicals like phosphates, nitrates and ammonium compounds. Dust, clay and soil particles are the inert suspensions which pollute water. Plant protection chemicals also pollute water. Some other pollutants are effluents from dairy farms, slaughter houses, breweries, tanneries, paper mills, oil spills and washing of automobiles.

Polluted water can totally destroy aquatic life. Human beings can fall victims to diseases like cholera, dysentry, amoebic dysentry, etc. Gases spread; offensive odours come from polluted water which may corrode materials and metals. Plants cannot grow in a soil irrigated by polluted water. Birds fly away from a source of polluted water. The human beings who consume polluted water regularly suffer from many bodily defects. Hard water is unsuitable for domestic and industrial purposes. The people, industries and cleanliness maintaining agencies should be adequately educated to avoid polluting water. Necessary treatment of sewage and industrial effluents is very essential. It is a technical process involving mechanical process, biological process and advanced biological, chemical and physical processes.

The soil is polluted by throwing garbage at every place. Some other pollutants of soil are: (i) pollutants washed out of the atmosphere (ii) pesticides and biocides and (iii) artificial fertilizers. Both, factory wastes and fertilizers make the soil alkaline and poisonous. The food which we obtain from polluted soil causes many diseases for living organisms.

The problem of noise pollution is increasing day by day due to the increase in the number of vehicles, the use of microphones and sound systems, machines, construction and production work. Noise pollution affects the hearing ability of people. It can also affect the nervous system, digestive system and the circulatory system. It affects pregnancy and causes malformed babies. It creates a rise in blood pressure, an increase in heart rate and breathing, an increase in perspiration, giddiness, nausea and fatigue.

Neurotic people are more sensitive to noise. Workmen exposed to higher intensity of noise were often found to be irritated, visually disturbed, short-tempered, impatient and more likely to resort to agitation and disrupt production. Noise is most harmful to the aged, patients and students. It may also create simple headache, neural-humoral stress, mental stress, frustration, task interference and loss of efficiency. It causes sleep interference, difficulty in communication, invasion of privacy, damage to artifacts and promotes the habit of talking loudly. Some of the nuisances it can cause include; one's enjoyment is ruined, concentration is affected, meditation and recreation are all affected. It may also create social conflicts at home and at work. There is a need to make efforts like industrial noise control and community noise control. We should learn to enjoy everything peacefully and quietly.

Radiation pollution is another serious problem. There are two types of harmful radiations: (a) non-ionising radiations and (b) ionising radiations. Non-ionising radiations are the natural components of solar radiations. Much of these radiations are absorbed by the ozone layer of the atmosphere. On the earth's surface, it is absorbed by water, pigments of plants and proteins, ribonucleic acid and deoxyribonucleic acid in living organisms. A skin disease known as xeroderma pigmentosum is caused by ultraviolet radiations.

Ionising radiations are of two types: x-rays are artificially generated while cosmic rays and rays released from naturally occurring radioactive elements are examples of natural ionising radiations. Radioactive elements release three types of radiations: (1) alpha particles (2) beta particles and (3) gamma rays.

Nuclear fallout releases radioactive elements which are harmful for human beings. Their concentration in the human body is harmful for white cells, bone marrow, spleen, skin, eyesight, reproductive parts, etc. They also cause tumour and cancer.

Ionising radiation may cause physiological problems, genetic changes, mutations, tumours, cancer, short life span and other developmental problems.

The chances of radioactive materials spreading in the air have increased as a result of discovery of artificial radioactivity, development of atomic bomb and the techniques of harnessing nuclear energy. Radioactive contamination is passed on to the vegetation and living beings through the nourishment they receive from soil and water. Some other effects of heightened radiation are: radiation sickness, acute radiation syndrome, leukaemia, etc.

In this age of rapid population growth and urbanisation, environmental management is a complex problem; in the form of crowded colonies, poor water supply, poor sewage facilities, indoor air pollution, lack of food safety due to bad storing, domestic vectors and storage of toxic and hazardous chemicals in the household. The depletion of ozone layer is due also to the excessive use of air-conditioners, chemicals like perfumes, room freshners, shaving foams, etc.

People have no choice but to insist on zero pollution. Pollution has become an interdisciplinary problem necessitating joint efforts by educationists, psychologists, ecologists, lawyers, social agencies and government. Every individual can also play his role by economical use of vehicles, cleanliness of his surroudings, and proper disposal of garbage, restricted use of air-conditioners, safe cooking devices, noise control and minimising the withdrawal of ground water.

Man himself is a major cause in the pollution of his own environment. We have to reduce our greenhouse gas emissions. Let us grow more plants and trees to lock greenhouse gases. We should adopt agro-forestry for diversification of agriculture and plant multipurpose trees on all vacant land and institutional land.

We should be more worried for maintaining a healthy environment as compared to the rapid pace of development and industrialisation.

For the success of any movement for the environment, public attitudes have to be moulded through education and awareness. From lower to higher educational institutions, we can take up non-formal environmental education programmes like seminars, lectures, debates, symposia, exhibitions, and cleanliness drives. Mass media should be associated for creating awareness.

The study of the environment can be experience-based, interactive and action-oriented. The topics of study should relate to the learner's home, neighbourhood, school, region, country and global environment.

Education has to act as a purifier of the environment. Health education, hygiene, scientific knowledge, risks of pollution, balance in the physical world can motivate the learners for creating and maintaining a pollution-free environment. Students should be taken on field trips to make them aware of the menace and dangerous consequences of the problem. They should get the opportunity to discuss about the pollution in their neighbourhood and what they should try to do about it.

The students should be so convinced and motivated that after their education and after starting their life, they come forward to form voluntary organisations to handle the problem of environmental pollution.

*****

Fifty three

Population Education

Population explosion is the biggest of all problems. The growing population is no more regarded as an asset. It is a big burden now. UNESCO says, "Every new generation should be given a firmness to play its role in controlling population ... population education is an educational programme which provides for a study of the population situation in family, community, nation and world with the purpose of developing in the students rational and responsible attitudes and behaviour towards coping with the situation." A seminar on population education says, "The objective of population education should be to enable the students to understand that the family size is controllable, that population limitations can facilitate the development of a higher quality of life."

More population means more pollution, food shortage, poor nutrition and health, overcrowding, unemployment, poor standard of living, dearth of facilities, non-fulfilment of needs, dearth of resources for development, housing problem, maldistribution of resources, rising prices, etc.

The population of the world doubled during the last few decades. If it increases further during the few decades in future, it will become unmanageable. In that case, most of our systems are bound to collapse and there are many risks involved.

The most effective single factor that could achieve population control is the spread of education. We have improvised various slogans for population control. Some countries have brought in legislation for this control. Education is a positive approach for it. Well educated people will exercise voluntary control in this matter. Education will obviate the need for harsh laws and punishments to achieve it. It is due to ignorance that we have multiplied our numbers.

Our target should be a negligible growth in population. The economy and prosperity of the people will improve automatically. Population control will be a great service to mankind. We should understand the necessity of creating a balance between our material resources and the size of population. It is necessary to keep in mind the ecological disturbances.

There should be some counselling system about family planning. We should remember that scientific advancement has given us healthy and effective methods of birth control. We should incorporate them in our life. If the population continues to multiply, we are ourselves to blame for it. It will show that people continue to be irresponsible in the matter. In that case, our energies will go waste in making provisions for the growing population. The public policy on family planning and its desirability should be comprehended under the counselling system in formal education. The population data may be conveyed to schools from time to time in order to convey the right message to the coming generation. The problem has already been solved by many countries and it is not difficult for others to solve it. Multiplication of population cannot be justified by any logic. It makes life on earth miserable. We should not allow miserable conditions to persist.

The breadwinner of a family has the responsibility to provide necessary facilities to all his dependents. Why should he increase his own burden disproportionately by having too many children, and drive the whole family to a wretched existence? We can easily count on a large number of benefits of birth control for parents, families, society and mankind.

The merits of population control and demerits of population explosion should be firmly settled in the mind of every learner. There is need to strengthen our educational efforts so that people achieve the targets by self-control or persuasive education instead of coercive laws. The use of harsh rules should be the last resort.

With an increasing population various facilities get diluted and in controlled population they get concentrated. In the event of a manageable population it will be possible for the society to achieve optimum development of every individual. The needs of expansion of facilities will get replaced by opportunities of qualitative improvement in educational services, health services, communications, nutrition, housing, etc. Expansion in quantity will get replaced by enhancement in quality.

Overcrowding in educational institutions will give place to manageable numbers. The teacher will be in a better position to pay individual attention and keep in touch with the progress of every individual learner. The learner will not get lost in a crowd, he will get special attention.

Similarly, in the hospitals, the doctor will not be in a hurry to dispose of the crowd of patients. He will be able to afford sufficient time for every case and prescribe medicine after careful thought.

Too many competitors in every situation create confusion and judicious selection becomes difficult. When the number is reasonable, merit can be determined with sufficient accuracy.

If there are too many children in a family, it is not possible for the elders to give due care and attention to them. This deficiency in affection may cause maladjustment in them.

Population explosion has necessitated deforestation leading to less rainfall and harmful climatic changes.

When there are too many complaints before a deciding authority, the officer may lose his patience. Instead of going through all of them and trying to redress them, he may adopt the easier course of throwing them all in the waste-paper basket. In a controlled population, the number of complaints is also likely to fall and remain within manageable numbers.

It is the quality of the population which is more important than the number. The educational courses may include topics like dynamics of population, causes of its growth, repercussions of uncontrolled increase, etc. There is a logical need for a deep study of why, what for, and how to control one's family size for improving its standard of living

Research scholars may carry out research studies on the effects of population growth on health, education, welfare, communication, employment, standard of living and the overall progress of individual and community. The researches should work out the existing and desired relationship between population growth and socio-economic development.

All the teachers should be provided with orientation programmes in population education. The schools should also orient the parents through PTA meetings in respect of new trends in population control. The illiterate and orthodox people have to be educated to change their attitude towards family size and quality of life. The institutional libraries may be equipped with suitable reading material on the subject for the parents and others.

Population explosion is a depressant to development. This problem can be further explained in the context of ecological balance. Moreover, there is a complete imbalance between material resources and the size of the population. Through the cooperation sought from the newer generations, we must be able to escape from this flood of population for the sake of our own existence.

We find a complete imbalance between material resources and the size of the population. The existing situation leads to misery, exploitation and absence of social justice.

Since this is a man-made problem, it can and should be tackled by the determination of the people. Some of the countries, with a negative or almost zero rate of growth, are doing a great service to their future generations. Other countries should emulate their example without much delay.

It is also a fact that population growth in affluent countries is putting a disproportionately heavy load on the environment. A citizen who belongs to a developed country is responsible for a much higher level of pollution, whether of air or water on this earth.

The birth rate is affected by social customs, cultural traits, racial, social, economic factors, structure of families and level of education of its members. A strong and deeply rooted factor is the injunction for the parents to leave a son behind. Most of the parents want to have more than one son and many in these attempts are instead blessed with a good number of daughters. In earlier times, death of infants and children was very common. Couples used to feel secure about having a large number of children, so that there remain at least one or two sons to take care of them in old age. As we find now, children are disowning their old parents, and ample facilities like old age homes are coming up. These changes may weaken the trend of having large families. Early marriage and low level of education of girls are also some factors in keeping up the large family norm. The cost of raising a child is very low in poor families. A large number of children in the lower income groups are more of an asset than a liability as every child earns by seeking some work in the unorganised sector.

Uneducated people suffer from social lethargy and lack the will for self-help and for planning their lives. They develop an attitude of depending upon the government for solving their problems and for improving their lot. Favourable conditions are lacking for the development of a simple attitude that with smaller families the standard of living can be improved and a happy life can be ensured.

There have been many studies which depict that lower degrees of social and economic development are positively related with bigger family size.

There is need to highlight intellectual, moral, social, economic and ethical purposes of population education. The contents and methods of population education will vary from country to country and sometimes, from area to area within the same country. Population education should be taken as a much wider programme than family planning and sex education. It is an exploration of knowledge and the attitude about population, problems related to population explosion, and effective steps for its control.

Neol David Burleson has said, "The history of the 20th century becomes more and more a race between number and the quality of life. If we are to utilize our intelligence in our present population dilemma, we must make our education system relevant."

Efforts should be made to promote inter-disciplinary research on population explosion and its problems. Some of the areas of research can be: population growth in terms of census figures, population and economic development, population and social development, population growth and environment, population and nutritional standards, population growth and social justice, population growth and governance, education as the solution for population explosion.

Population cannot be treated merely as a quantitative phenomenon. It is the quality of the population that is more relevant as an end product of growth. We have to know the nature and meaning of the process and characteristics of population, the causes and the consequences of this change, and its effect on the individual, his family, the society and the world.

Population education is an important factor to speed up the process of economic development. It is also relevant in improving the quality and level of education for every individual. Its courses will need reference to human reproduction and family planning. These components of sex education may be taken up as a part of biology courses. Precautions to be taken with respect to population education can be conveyed through literature and other means.

*****

Fifty four

Education and Globalisation

In many respects, people globally share a common fate. And that is why we have a joint responsibility to curb calamities like global warming that cast a shadow over our collective future.

For better or worse, we are now living in a global age. Globalisation is the theme of our times. It refers to the increasing interdependence of world society. It has been advanced not only because of economic and communication factors, but by political developments too. Creating cosmopolitan nations with an overall identity, but happy in their diversity is the main approach in which an effective international agenda can be forged and furthered.

Globalisation is a welcome opportunity. It should be made a grand success. Education should play an effective role towards globalisation and vice versa.

The expanding means of communication are turning this world into a big village. Education has to mentally prepare the new generations towards globalisation being a sacred cause.

No doubt, there still exist very serious hurdles in the way of globalisation. Education has to explain ways and means of overcoming these hurdles. It has to provide material for inter-cultural, inter-nationalities and inter-religious understanding among people. Modern history should highlight the currents flowing in favour of globalisation.

The advanced regions of the world should guide and help the advancing regions. The less advanced regions should not expect perpetual help from the advanced regions. However, the advanced areas should not hesitate to share their knowledge, experiences and expertise with the less fortunate ones. In spite of genuine efforts, if there is poverty and deprivation anywhere, it should be taken up as a common problem.

Globalisation can facilitate the introduction of a worldwide system of education, global aims in education and a common core curriculum. There will be worldwide cooperation in the researches for global welfare. The misunderstandings, if any, will get resolved. The students, teachers and research scholars will enjoy ample opportunities for exchange. There will be regular provision for translating important literatures on education into different languages of the world. Innovations being successfully tried in one part of the world will be transmitted to every corner. There will be some global competitions between students, teachers and educational institutions spread across the world.

To make globalisation more effective, educational authorities from different countries will sit together from time to time and remove from the syllabi, objectionable material, if any. The objections may be from a religious point of view, racial considerations, caste factors, prejudices, majority-minority situations, economic disparities, historical perspectives, etc.

A brief geography and history of the whole world may form a part of the syllabus of every learner. The interdependence of countries and regions may be highlighted. At some stage of the individual's education, there should be provision for the learner to study world literature.

There is need and justification for establishing a global organisation for supervising and guiding education. The good elements of educational programmes of various countries should find a place in the scheme of global education. Every country should provide for the study of important languages prevalent in the world.

Education should take a lead in the globalisation programmes pursued by politics, economy, industrialisation, scientific research and cultural exchange. The programme of global education will concentrate its attention on the common and serious problems facing mankind such as global warming, poor rainfall, pollution, shortages, epidemics and natural calamities.

The visa rules for tourism should be made flexible. Tourists should be found moving freely around the world. When different regions of the world are equally advanced and equally populated, there will be no problem of illegal immigration.

Real globalisation will achieve neutralisation between the boundaries of countries. In the long run, the individual countries will find no need to raise armies for defending their soft borders. At the most, there can be one army under the command of the UNO. This army will compose of regiments from all the countries. It will maintain discipline between countries and will restore status-quo in the event of boundary violations by any country. When the world is genuinely free from armed conflicts, it will be in a position to save huge funds which are now wasted in raising armies and manufacturing armaments. With this saving, the prosperity of the world will rise manifold and there will be all-round development.

To begin with, mankind may concentrate on three priorities: the elimination of global poverty, the stabilisation of world population and the reduction of military expenditures by different countries. Let us seriously think of creating a world without borders.

Textbooks all over the world need to be rewritten in the light of new emphasis on international understanding and globalisation. There is need to hold conferences at the international level in various educational institutions.

Students, teachers and people should be encouraged to develop bonds with their counterparts in foreign countries.

UNESCO has prepared a programme to educate mankind for the need of establishing a world community which has been conceived in the charter of United Nations. The new generations should be acquainted with the contributions of different nations in establishing the civilisation in the world.

Roman Rolland said, "The two global wars with their terribly devastating results have at least established the fact that the narrow bonds of sordid and aggressive nationalism must be smashed through, and an unwalled, unhedged federation of mankind should be brought into being for fostering human relations on the plane of love, pity and sympathy."

We should be able to set-up worldwide internet access, with all kinds of knowledge digitized and available to everybody, and a completely global economy with free markets in which anyone can trade with anyone else without any interference from states or governments. The opposition to global economy is likely to come from developed countries in which the spirit of economic supremacy still continues to dominate. The people enjoying a sort of monopoly over world economy must be convinced to share their excessive privileges with less privileged sections of mankind.

The need for setting up a global community has promoted the global communication system. The first step in the establishment of a global communication system was taken up in 1965 with the launching of the world's first communications satellite. The communications capability of telecommunication satellites is enormous and will increase with every generation. The emergence of a global communications system is a notable achievement in international relations and sharing of knowledge. Man is now trying to create a central nervous system for the entire world, linking its diverse and distant parts directly to one another. Once all men are interlinked in terms of communications, it will generate intensive involvement of people in global affairs and dissemination of information and knowledge across the globe.

*****

Fifty five

Education and International Understanding

Education is a strong and effective agency which can help a lot in creating a suitable environment conducive to international understanding.

There are a number of obstacles to international understanding: high level of frustration all over the world, support for distorted beliefs about others, dominant role of leaders in different countries, vested political and social interests, dependence of international relations on national politics, the lack of prerequisites for international unity, basic ideological conflicts and unpleasant historical memories.

There is a need for understanding and respecting everyone, every culture and civilisation, values and ways of life, awareness of the increasing global interdependence, abilities to communicate, and the common heritage of mankind. There can be no proper education for citizenship without an education for international understanding. The curricula should incorporate the knowledge of the whole earth, main religions of the world, and world history. There should be conferences, meetings, exchanges at the international level. Every effort should be made to remove the doubts, scepticism and disbelief from the minds of people in different countries.

Education should create awareness of global interdependence, abilities to communicate with distant people and readiness of the individual to participate in solving problems of the world at large. There is need for re-fixing the aims of education, which would consist of developing the spirit of tolerance and cooperation, developing a concern for the welfare of all, the will and courage to place the common good before one's own immediate interests, a capacity to think clearly, independently and without prejudice, respect for persons of every class, race and colour.

The educational institutions should create an ideal compact human society. They should represent the best elements of our world culture. They should celebrate all festivals of the world. The UNO day, the Human Rights day, the World Health day are a few examples. Teacher and student exchange prgrammes, international youth festivals and international exhibitions will create the spirit of world citizenship. It has to be made clear that throughout the ages, moral, intellectual and technical progress has grown to constitute a common heritage. There is need of translation of literary works into different languages of the world too.

The leaders of the French Revolution raised the slogan of liberty, equality and fraternity. Kant argued for the federation of all nations into a league, which should break through the narrow walls of nationalism. The ideologies whether religious, social, or national should be broadbased. Unless steps are taken to educate mankind for the world community, it will not be possible to create an international society. The problems existing in any corner of the world should receive worldwide attention.

All the nations have to depend upon each other economically, socially and politically. All nations—backward or advanced constitute one interdependent family.

Personal ethics and state ethics rise and fall together. Personal ethics has three dimensions, discipline, development and dedication. One should seek the virtues of great men, and note in one's diary some great precepts and maxims. Have a globe in your room, and also pictures of great men of the world. Through education give to society, men with strong minds, great hearts, true faith and ever working hands.

The UNESCO general conference has recommended the following guiding principles for international understanding: (a) an international dimension and a global perspective in education at all levels and in all its forms (b) understanding and respect for all people, their cultures, civilisations, values and ways of life including domestic-ethnic cultures and cultures of other nations (c) awareness of the global interdependence between people and nations.

The ideal of education for international understanding is, in fact, inherent in all true education. UNESCO says, "One of the chief aims of education today should be to prepare boys and girls to take an active part in the creation of world society." Education should highlight how all the nations have benefitted from the advancement of science and technology. The subjects of civics, and economics should emphasise the need of world citizenship. Music, art, philosophy and psychology have their own unique role in bringing people of different nations closer to one another. Organisation of inter-country games, sports, cultural meets, celebration of festivals, pen friendship, etc. can help in international understanding.

International understanding promotes knowledge explosion, worldwide relations, trade, sharing of research findings, sharing of advantages of scientific and technological advancement, sharing of burden of calamities, stability in the governments all over the world, strenghening of democracy, world peace, freedom from inter-state conflicts and strifes, huge saving by reducing armies and armaments, more strategies and resources for development, and relief from many types of tensions.

In this world, there are nations with different cultures, histories, customs, traditions, colours, races, religions and languages, but the inner feelings, soul or spirit is the same in all.

In today's world, no nation can boast of its self-reliance and self-sufficiency. The nations have to depend on each other for numerous requirements, which necessitate communication and trade. And communications and trade cannot be a one-way traffic.

UNESCO provides opportunities to thinkers, scientists, teachers and artists to meet and exchange ideas and put forward plans for promoting international understanding, world peace and justice. It also encourages research on these issues by giving financial help and other facilities to researchers. It provides facilities to students and teachers for foreign visits, exchange views and gain experience in international living. It also organises art and literature exhibitions at the international level to promote love and understanding.

Every national plan of education must make specific provision for developing international feeling. It should generate a liberal, sympathetic and kind-hearted attitude towards other cultures.

Nothing new happens in any corner of the world which does not affect other countries. In order to create an international community in which all the countries help each other, cooperate in their development and technological progress, maintain good relations and strengthen world peace, it is essential to cultivate a spirit of international understanding.

Oliver Goldsmith has indicated, "Internationalism is a feeling that the individual is not only a member of his state, but a citizen of the world." Narrow patriotism has to be replaced with the love and care for humanity. The welfare of the entire human race should be made the goal of all the citizens of the world.

One of the resolutions of the UNESCO states, member states of UNESCO in accepting its constitution have agreed that the purpose of organisation is to contribute to peace and security by promoting collaboration among the nations through education, science and culture in order to promote universal respect for justice, for the rule of law, for human rights and fundamental freedom.

We have to observe all nationalities, cultures and communities as equally important people inhabiting this earth. All the nations of the world depend on one another economically, politically and culturally. A synthesis of all cultures is going on and a world culture is gradually coming into being. All the nations feel duty-bound and morally obliged to promote the welfare of all others. Geographical limits cannot delimit human qualities like love, sympathy, cooperation and friendship. The physical, political, economic, religious, linguistic and psychological barriers in the way of international understanding have to be softened with the help of educational efforts.

Independent and broad based thinking, inculcation of spiritual and moral values, broad view of patriotism, the need for interdependence, elimination of irrational fears from individual and social life, social consciousness, preparation for corporate life, and to give practical shape to good ideas need to be strengthened through education to translate the vision of international understanding into a reality.

The curriculum may incorporate essential attributes of all religions of the world, the philosophy of life of different people, ways of living, and patterns of behaviour of different sections of the world population and may emphasise on them. It may review all international welfare programmes and notable achievements of all the nations in the fields of human civilisation. The scientific discoveries and contributions in literature, art and music by different nations may be given a prominent place in the curriculum.

Social aspects in the teaching of science and technology should be emphasised to show that their advances lead to the welfare of entire humanity. Family norms should be stressed on, to fight poverty, shortages, diseases and other problems of the world. Literature should have a universal appeal. Geography can highlight the universal sense of understanding and responsibility. Human geography may inform about the living conditions and different problems of the people of the world. Commercial geography can talk about the economic interdependence of all nations. History should develop international understanding, cultural synthesis and interdependence in all aspects of life. History of international cooperation during worldwide diversities, national and international calamities and crises should be narrated to students. Teachers should develop a liberal and wide outlook about the world and convey the same to the students.

Mass media, journals, magazines and documentaries of foreign countries may be used to promote the spirit of international brotherhood.

*****

Fifty six

Education and World Peace

This world has not been created to become an arena of world wars. Let us educate ourselves to a firm conviction that there will never be a third world war. All the previous large scale wars and the two world wars have enough lessons for us. We have to stimulate the constructive tendencies to such an extent that destructive tendencies do not get a chance to raise their head. The idea of peace should be cultivated as a motivation in every human mind. The seeds of violence should be weeded out from the mind of every human being. Human nature should be empowered to control its instinct of aggression. Quarrelling should be categorised as animal behaviour. Everybody should be educated to channelise their egoistic tendencies.

It is the human mind in which the idea of war happens to grow and it is the human mind in which the idea of peace has to be firmly established. Peace is a sign of maturity of the human mind.

The developments achieved over a number of years gets destroyed within seconds in a war. The world should be beautified from corner to corner so that nobody ever thinks of destroying it.

The entire population of the world should be made peace-loving so that no government or no leader thinks of waging a war. Whenever there is any conflict in any corner of the world, people should be able to raise a strong voice against it and see that the conflict ends without delay. People should make world peace a common cause so that the governments do not engage in creating, joining or strengthening blocs. People should not allow themselves to be divided into blocs. Any government which thinks against world peace should feel isolated. Governments have been creating an unending history of conflicts which need to be given a different turn in the future.

Every individual should be made conscious that he is an organ of world peace. Education should develop peace-loving individuals, enthusiastic to play a significant role towards world peace and willing to make any sacrifice for world peace if the circumstances so demand.

World peace is one of the basic needs that a human being should realise today. It should be made a desire and habit with everybody. The young children should forget to quarrel among themselves, and they should be guided to find better methods to resolve their tiny conflicts. Peace is being disturbed by local conflicts in various corners of the world. The voice of the people should be made so powerful that it does not allow these conflicts to spread. The peace-breaking situations of the past should be looked upon as human follies and failures and should receive a justifiable condemnation. People who disrupted world peace did a great disservice to the society and civilisation. There is nothing wrong if they are exposed and condemned. When the public raises a strong voice for peace, then a few misguided elements will not be able to disturb it.

There are many individuals and organisations which are engaged in the establishment of world peace. Peace should become the voice of the people. Those who try to disturb peace should be reduced to a negligible minority. They should be isolated and made harmless. Education should join hands with other agencies in the search for peace. Even if a misguided person happens to be in the chair and tries to preach violence, he should be reduced to a non-entity because of strong public opinion and the force of different agencies, including education.

After the Second World War, the UNO was formed with a great hope to establish world peace. But this great organisation has also been helpless in certain situations. The voice of the people should strengthen the instruments of the UNO so that it can stop the conflicts, if any, with immediate effect. The governments should be convinced forever that they will have to think and pursue better means to resolve their disputes.

Globalisation of education will be a good effort towards world peace. Education should be empowered to become an effective agency for world peace. The new generations should be taught to believe in non-violence and to raise their collective voice to persuade the governments to reduce their armies and armaments. The voice of the people should be effective enough to stop for ever the game of power blocs. The resources thus saved can revolutionise the process of development.

There is not a more dangerous maxim in the world of today than "My country, right or wrong." The spirit of rigid patriotism should be replaced with the spirit of love for mankind. An individual is no longer a member of a community or a country alone, he is a member of the world community.

Different terms are being employed to strengthen the desire for world peace, such as world citizenship, international education, mankind education, education for peace and security, world government, and world society. The old barriers must be made to break down. Mutual understanding is a must to save the weak from the fear of threats received from the stronger nations.

Bertrand Russell said, "Education is the only agency through which it is possible to develop the feeling of internationalism". Education is a strong and effective weapon which can help in creating a suitable environment for world peace.

UNESCO says, "One of the chief aims of education today should be to prepare boys and girls to take an active part in the creation of world society." As suggested by the UNO, the World Peace Day should be observed in all parts of the world.

There is no such thing as a holy war, and war is worse than an irrational solution to a conflict. With the use of devices like atomic bombs, those on the right side may be destroyed as completely as those on the wrong side.

The problem of international tensions lies in a tendency to concentrate too exclusively on conflicts among nations at the expense of attention to the individuals who make up these nations. Most people are compelled to take part in a war despite their own lack of desire for it or even strong opposition to it. The relationships among nations are manipulated by a small number of leaders who wield enormous power in determining the policies and actions of their respective countries.

There are many other causes of tensions among nations, such as conflicting interests and objectives, urge of dominance, vague borderline, mutual suspicion, fear, hatred, difference of ideologies, etc.

However, there is an evergrowing world-mindedness among the people, who very well realise that most frequently, an open conflict or war sows the seeds of future conflict and tension.

Even when a nation itself is not directly engaged in international conflict, the existence of tensions in other parts of the world may influence its internal conditions. Also, the disturbing events within a single country may upset the international equilibrium. Civil wars threaten to disturb a stable international system. International tensions are not merely tensions among nations; they are also tensions among racial, religious, economic and ideological groups.

The problem of international tensions is ultimately a problem of the psychology of the individual. War is declared and fought by individuals; peace and international unity are the products of the feeling and actions of individuals. The manner in which economic, political and other such influences work in international tensions is psychological. These influences become effective through the needs, perceptions, beliefs and attitudes of the individual. Whether international tensions are heightened or diminished depends upon the psychology of the individual leaders.

The needs underlying international tensions are manifold: frustrated needs lead to aggressiveness, needs for some direct gain, need for power and prestige, patriotic and nationalistic needs, needs for resolving ambiguous crisis situations, needs for group belongingness and conformity. But most of these needs are capable of being satisfied in better ways than through conflict.

Apart from the needs, there are beliefs and attitudes of the individual which justify international conflict. They are ethnocentric beliefs, stereotyped beliefs concerning other nations, negative attitudes towards other nations, predominance of nationalist over internationalist attitudes, oversimplified perceptions of causes and cures of international tensions, belief in the inevitability of war and wishful thinking about the outcomes of war.

The programme of reducing international tensions requires the skills of political science, economics, law education, history, etc. The educator can advise the young minds on matters relating to human behaviour, need perceptions, beliefs, attitudes, principles of group functioning, morale and peace-loving leadership.

The preamble to the constitution of UNESCO asserts, "Since wars begin in the minds of men, it is in the minds of men that the defences of peace must be constructed." We must aim at developing individuals who can effectively control and eliminate conflicts.

For promoting world peace, we shall require a greater degree of international goodwill, mutual confidence and a felt need for world peace. There is need to reiterate endlessly to the young minds the evils of war and the joy of international peace. The programme for peace can be strengthened by reducing frustrations of people, making democracy real and effective, improving mental health, education for international understanding, broadening attitudes, improving leadership, providing positive views for the unity of mankind, reducing ideological conflicts, bridging gaps between religious beliefs and forgetting the idea of war forever.

The educational and social agencies all over the world should set-up a common platform for international thinking and evolve some common lessons to be taught to the children throughout. Different viewpoints from different corners of the world may be narrowed down to common and acceptable points of view. If certain conflicts still persist, they may be discussed in the world bodies to clear the differences and misundertandings. New generation should be made to understand that they have to make world peace a commitment and reality.

There should be emphasis on love for peace and prosperity, a spirit of tolerance, broad mindedness, open mindedness, love for humanity and highlighting of the evils of conflict and war. Mutual distrust is wasteful, destructive and suicidal.

Through the commitment to world-state, humanity will be free from the fear of war and mass homicide. Mankind today stands threatened by terrorism, fundamentalism, religious bigotry, ethnic egoism, and neoimperialism. To bring about world peace, we need an international cadre of committed anti-militarists. Millions are being spent to keep the war-machines of nations in a state of readiness, while millions of human beings go without safe water, food, shelter, education and medicine. Mankind is under threat due to the problems of political pollution, crisis of character, overpopulation, unemployment, lack of education, lack of sound leadership and absence of peace.

War starts in a part of the world and as a consequence millions of people die of famine in another part and millions more find themselves uprooted from their homeland. If we can eliminate war, we get rid of one of the greatest causes of mankind's sorrow.

Education is the main agency through which it is possible to develop a commitment to world peace.

Nations that explore, understand and enjoy one another's culture will be too busy to spare time for thinking about an engagement in war.

Andrei Sakharov said, "The strategy of peaceful co-existence and collaboration must be deepened in every way".

Phillip Jessup said, "Unless the world achieves some form of international government in which a collective will takes precedence over the individual will of the sovereign state, the ultimate function of law, which is the elimination of force for the solution of human conflict, will not be fulfilled."

We can accumulate the losses of two world wars and other wars like the Korean War, Vietnam War, Indo Pak Wars and many more, and bring these figures into the notice of students. Also, the annual defence budgets of all the countries may be added together to give the idea of this huge avoidable expenditure.

The idea of world war is becoming obsolete. Traditional reasons for going to war such as the acquisition of new territory, dominance over more people, enslavement of neighbours, expansion in authority, the prestige of military victory all increasingly lack relevance and appeal today.

The plans for education must create a hope that ancient class hatred and warfare will ultimately disappear from this earth. The individuals must be made to understand forever that the victories of peace are greater than the victories of war.

*****

XII
EDUCATION AND EXCELLENCE

Fifty seven

Education and Development of Human Resources

Franklin said, "An investment in knowledge pays the best interest."

George Eliot said, "Better spend an extra hundred or two on your son's education than leave it to him in your will."

Human capital is a vast treasure, which is prepared, maintained and updated by education. Human factor is the most important factor for every type of development in the world. Unlike other resources, human resources have unlimited potentialities. There is a greater hope, when suitable climate is created for human resource development. This climate has to be mainly provided by the educational institutions.

Human resource development is needed to create a dynamic and growth-oriented society. While development of physical resources is a means to an end, the development of human resources is an end in itself.

Every human being is a valuable asset. He has great potential for development and his potential can be increased with the help of suitable climate and education, and his development can take place at any time. Everybody is creative and he can be made more creative through suitable programmes of education.

The process of human resource development will include potential appraisal and development, performance coaching and feedback, career planning, intensive training, development of the organisation, quality of the work situation, employee welfare and appropriate rewards.

A worker can work efficiently, a businessman can set-up a flourishing business, a farmer can enhance his production, an administrator can run a transparent and efficient administration, a head can take all his subordinates along, a leader can inspire and win the confidence of his group, all through the positive impact of education.

Labour is an element of capital and education enhances the productive ability of trained and skilled workforce. Economic development depends not only upon the growth of physical capital, but also on the growth of human capital. Of all the human resource development factors, education has a catalytic role. It improves other human resource development factors also.

There is need to create a central agency in each nation to develop human capital and ensure its investment in the development of the economy. Professionals in human resource development should be called upon to manage the integrated mega functions from a holistic point of view throwing up creative solutions.

The scientific approach for human resource development involves identifying objectives and available resources, examining the implications of alternative courses of action and making wise choices among them, deciding on specific targets to be met within the specific time limit and finally, developing the best means of systematically implementing the proposed choices.

Prerequisites of an educational plan for human resources development will involve a scientific study of the situation of education, visualising a long-term perspective of education in the light of socio-economic goals, working out priorities, drawing up a contingency plan and introducing an in-built system in order to modify strategies and techniques, if necessary.

The planning of education is based upon social demands considering education as a consumer goods. It links education to economic development. It also relates to the stock of educated people and the flow of students completing education at different levels directly to the output of goods and services. It takes into consideration such factors as the scale of development considering the availability of specialised manpower, the scale of development needed to absorb the backlog of manpower and the new entrants to the workforce, the pattern of investment priorities envisaged in the planning and the broad economic, social and educational goals of developmental planning.

Education for human resources development has been silently revolutionising traditional subjects like growth economics, labour economics, international trades and public finance. Education like any other developmental activity has been broadly accepted as an industry. It is a means by which a country organises its human ability for the purpose of national effort. A major proportion of the growth is attributable to education and other residual factors like efficiency and organisation which are also dependent on educational attainment. All the acquired abilities of the individuals are a part of the capital of the community. Unlike material capital human beings instead of depreciating with age often improve with age and experience. The process of human resource development unlocks the door to modernisation as well.

Sometimes, the planners are apt to think that economic development just means the expansion of transport, power, irrigation, coal, steel, fertilizers and machinery. Undoubtedly, all these are necessary but by themselves they do not constitute a sufficient condition for economic growth. In the final analysis, it is the human being who has to intelligently and efficiently operate these instruments of production. The process of education has however, to be shaped in different ways in different economies.

The acquisition of any skill is not to be considered an end in itself. Everyone has to be properly motivated, through education or other similar agencies because without motivation no skill can be employed up to its maximum advantage and output.

Jerome B Weisner has said, "A good educational system may be the flower of economic development but it is also the seed."

It is necessary to forecast and work out future manpower needs and relate the educational programmes with them.

High levels of per capita income will require proportionate investment in education and health. Manpower approach links education to economic development through professional studies like agriculture, medicine, engineering, etc.

People once educated, will devise ways and means to effectively solve their economic, as well as other problems. No change would be as effective for a rapid economic growth as the means of improvement in schools. Individuals with good education, improve their economic prospects through better job opportunities and higher wages.

Education is the main source of skills and talent. The overall production does not include only the material objects of economic welfare, but psychic welfare as well.

Education is an industry, the production cycle of which is longer than that of most other industries. It produces the skills, attitudes, personalities and social set-up which form the basis for modern technology and its organisation. It yields a very high margin of profit, both direct and indirect as it aims at modifying human beings rather than materials. Education can be called the industry of industries as it turns out men who visualise, plan, create and run the industries of various types. The product turned out by educational institutions is definitely superior to all kinds of products manufactured by various industries.

Education should aim at developing resourceful men. Every individual should claim mastery over a number of resources. Even if his resources have not been developed for an unexpected situation, he should not become helpless. He should exercise his potential to bring a new resource under his command to meet the situation.

People should learn to pool their resources and transform them into collective resources. The capability of collective resources will be found many times more effective than the individual resources.

They should also get the experience of employing their resources for some cause or a common cause. That will be a commendable use of one's resources. If a person reserves his resources for any mission, it will be a greater contribution for the good of the society and mankind.

The individual is bound through duty to develop his resources to the level that can match unforeseen challenges, problems of life, fulfilment of all types of needs, the responsibilities of social life, the struggle for all-round achievements and progress, the required merit in this competitive world, the strength for fighting injustice and antisocial elements, the urge for upholding the values and curbing the vices, the qualities expected of a true human being, and to perform the necessary leadership role when the existing leadership is disappointing.

Through education, the human being is to be convinced that there is no limit to his potentialities and resources. He has to maintain the development and growth of his resources throughout his life. It is for this growth and many other benefits that lifelong education is recommended for him. He has to continue with his physical, mental, intellectual and emotional exercise to gain strength throughout. When he continues to expand and strengthen his resources, he will make his life more worthy of living. The purposes of his life will get fulfilled and he will be satisfied. When a person succeeds in developing resources in surplus, he becomes a greater asset for the society.

*****

Fifty eight

Education and Modernisation

Modernisation involves the ongoing changes in a society's education, economy, politics, traditions and religion. Education, especially pertaining to the fields of science and technology, provides the basis for modernisation. At the same time, modernisation of education will provide added impetus to our efforts towards overall modernisation.

We must believe that we possess a vision and thus, we shall be able to draw a future-oriented plan for education. We shall be able to foresee the needs of life, needs of social life, and vocational life and provide required education well in advance.

Becoming modern necessitates acceptance of new ideas, curiosity for latest knowledge, adoption of new techniques and methods, emphasis on the present and future, a practical approach in everything concerning life and the world, faith in scientific attitude, faith in change for the better, faith in rational thinking, benefitting from knowledge explosion, industrialisation, faith in modern values, desire for better standards of living, realistic attitude, humanistic outlook and continuous march towards a quality life.

Universalisation and democratisation of education, research in every field, scientific and technological advancement are some of the signs of modernisation. Education is a fundamental instrument of modernisation. It will have to adopt modern approaches to its aims, curricula and methodology. It has to modify the attitudes and aptitudes of the people to make them better professionals and to make them familiar with modern values.

There are some obstacles to modernisation which need to be removed. Some of them are – lack of united effort, narrow beliefs and faiths, illiteracy, outdated cultural traditions, closed system of society, and gap between ideals and reality.

The individual in a modernising society has a mobile personality. He has a psychic urge to have more and more enlightenment and higher material amenities. He believes in a balance between the rights and duties and follows the right line of thought and action. His qualities of hard work, integrity, consistency and efficiency are his special assets. He makes wider participation in a variety of divergent roles. Rationality influences his choice of goals and means. He is achievement-oriented, works faster and harder, is motivated not by rewards but by a feeling of self-fulfilment. He has immense faith in the desirability and possibility of progress and realises that the social, economic and political disciplines are essential prerequisites for growth. He puts off immediate and short-term satisfactions and focuses on long-term goals and satisfactions.

A society composed of such individuals radiates the attributes of modernity in social life and social institutions. Such a society believes in cooperation, coexistence, unity and consensus rather than in unhealthy competition and conflict. It is a reflective society attuned to adjustment between accelerated change and rich heritage. It develops higher attitudes to wealth, work, savings and risk taking but with overhead maintenance of social, economic and political discipline.

Modernisation presupposes certain infrastructures such as, sound political ideology and its effective implementation, viable economy, educated population, open personalities, skilled manpower, values and motivations, concerted and cooperative efforts. All these forming a part of infrastructures are the direct or indirect gifts of education. Education has to broaden mental horizons, arouse interest and ability in innovation and encourage experimentation.

Training leaders for various walks of life and activities is the noble task of education. The creative leader becomes the role model for the masses. From the educational system emerge the thinkers, scientists, technocrats, planners, administrators and workers who pledge themselves to the task of making this world a better place.

Future political leaders, industrialists, engineers, writers and reformers are very much a part of educational institutions today. Education will enable learners to believe in common values and goals for the world community.

To lead the process of modernisation, education has to be modernised in a planned manner. There will be need for a permanent forum for educational planning. It may evolve year-wise and through five-year plans. Education has to be kept well ahead of the times.

As life is likely to be more complex in the future, education should cater to the preparation against and removal of the likely complexities. Education will develop productive and progressive individuals. The investments and results of education should be regularly evaluated. There is need for additional stress on humanistic and moral education.

It is just possible that with further mechanisation an individual's labour is reduced. People should not take things easy as a consequence. They should be prepared to adopt alternate physical activities for themselves. Hard labour should continue to remain the motto even under expanded mechanisation.

It is wrong to understand material progress and abundance of facilities as the true signs of modernisation. Permissiveness in character, pre-marital sex, habits like smoking and drinking, fashionable dressing and leading an aristocratic lifestyle should not be counted as attributes of modernism. Education should provide for it a better definition and interpretation. In fact new thinking, progressive ideas, better behaviour, more satisfying relationships, achievement-oriented culture may be regarded as steps towards modernisation.

Modernisation is represented by positivism, empiricism and rationalism. It includes social mobilisation and specialisation among individuals and institutional activities. In the political field, it stands for democratisation. In ecology, it is characterised by advancing urbanisation. It also stands for literacy and secular education and a more complex intellectual and institutional system for the cultivation and advancement of specialised roles based on intellectual disciplines. It is an emergence of a new cultural outlook, characterised by emphasis on progress and improvement, on happiness and spontaneous abilities and feelings, on the development of individuality and efficiency. It also signifies the emergence of a new personality orientation, traits and characteristics, greater ability to adjust to the broadening horizons; some ego-flexibility, widening spheres of interests, growing empathy with other people and situations, a growing evaluation of self-advancement, a growing emphasis on the present as the meaningful dimension of human existence, a growing awareness of dignity of others, a growing faith in sciences and technology and a growing awareness that rewards should be according to contributions alone. Modernisation implies the ability of the society to develop an institutional structure capable of adjusting to continually changing problems and demands.

Education is the most important instrument of modernisation as it brings direct change in the system of attitudes, beliefs and values and enhances the acceptability of modern technology and its organisational and operational framework. It also lays the foundations of institutions and organisations which could assume responsibility for innovation and technological growth according to the needs and problems.

Education provides alternatives to tradition. It broadens mental horizons, raises expectations and predisposes people to make experiments. It can help in obliterating attitudes and behaviour patterns that are dysfunctional programmes of modernisation. Modernising elites are generally the products of a modern school or university system. Large scale programmes of modernisation demand specialists of several types at different levels and look to the education system for a steady flow of technocrats, planners and managers to head various organisations. Education can be harnessed to promote attitudes and ideologies required for the adoption of modern technology and its associated values and organisational premises, to provide personnel to operate and sustain the programmes of modernisation and to create capabilities to adapt to new technology.

Research in different parts of the world has shown the positive impact of education on the process of modernisation.

*****

Fifty nine
Education and Social Change

Social change is in fact an evolutionary phenomenon. It will never cease. The present day society is the product of this evolutionary nature of social change. Education is the dominant factor among the factors of social change as it positively affects every other factor also.

The socio-cultural factors like political system, social system, cultural system and economic system are mutually affected by factors related to resources. These factors are mainly human resources, natural resources and technological resources. Education is a dominant instrument in bringing about a positive change in these resources.

Education can initiate a non-violent revolution for the progress of mankind. Its important instuments of change are: objectives of education, subject matter and system of education, its programming, its human stuff and professional accomplishment. The pace of change all around is remarkably fast and education has to remain a forerunner of this change. Education has to be more progressive than the progress around. It has to be radically new and modern.

Knowledge continues to be power in spite of the emergence of some problems due to the haphazard growth of technology. It is again through education that we have to neutralise the effects of these problems.

Education has to be regarded as the gateway to an improved social set-up. It has positively affected even our customs and traditions, manners and morals, religious beliefs and philosophical principles. In modern industrial societies, educational organisations have become innovators. Societies are marshalling their resources and talents to make advances in arts, sciences and technologies through educational organisations.

Student movements have often been the major force demanding social change in many societies. The students are still the most progressive group in any society whether they are less or more vocal in calling for social reform or change. They are capable of creating public opinion in favour of desirable changes. Individually or collectively, they have often become the originators of reform movements. Right thinking elements among them always aspire and attempt to take the society to a state of perfection. It is one of the functions of education to develop such like elements in fairly large numbers. The student of today has no reason to believe that the society he has inherited is ideal for him.

Education can accelerate social change by bringing about a change in the outlook and attitudes of citizens. Its effort of imparting empirical knowledge of sciences, technology and other specialised fields helps in this direction. Relevant changes in educational system initiate economic progress and provide better skilled manpower required for technical jobs and social change.

Education creates political awareness among common people. They become instrumental in bringing about desirable political changes leading to social upliftment. The conservative contents of education are regularly modernised, so that it may prepare the citizens to provide leadership in social change.

Educational institutions have to offer a model sub-system within the overall system of society. Their functionaries are interrelated and inter-connected for the common cause of social change. They have to coordinate the efforts of different sub-groups for the optimum attainment of the goal. They have to socialise cultural beliefs and values for the benefit of the social system. The forces of integration as developed in the educational institutions must be made strong enough to reconcile the differences between different subgroups for the sake of common good and welfare.

When the role of education is positive, constructive, productive, creative and wise, it can provide optimum level of development to citizens who can creditably meet every requirement of the society. Many educational programmes such as performance, evaluation, feedback, counselling, judicious work groups, proper training, and work culture make definite contribution to prepare the citizen for his duties. Educational planning, execution of these plans and then, appropriate monitoring develop scientific and technological knowledge resulting in the improvement of production in various areas. This improvement is one of the signs for social change in the right direction.

Changing the attitudes of the people through education towards issues like fate, destiny, traditions and religion will mentally prepare the individual in the matter of opportunities, possibilities, achievements and well directed social progress. Let us be very clear about the shape and type of society we want to set up. Then we have to prepare people with a firm resolve and commitment to build the society of their dreams.

Apart from individual and social aims, education for social change must incorporate other relevant aims, which can be vocational aim, planning for a better future, preparing citizens for a better society and developing aspirations for social change.

Social change demands modification in the ways of doing, behaving and thinking of the people. We find that changes, whether upward or downward are continuously going on in a society. Upward changes are considered progressive changes, while downward changes indicate deterioration or downfall. The agency of education has to initiate upward changes and concentrate on them and simultaneously, see to it that downward changes are not allowed to continue. It has to always remain an instrument of upward social change. Human capital developed through education should function as the sum total of modern ideas and skills, initiative, sustained work, right type of interests and all other human qualities conducive to higher output, accelerated growth and desired change in the society.

Attitudes for a healthy environment have to be inculcated through education so that environmental problems do not pose a threat to the very existence of the human race. For a right type of social change, the existing political system, social system, cultural system, system of production and system of consumption can be analysed and suitably modified through education. The necessary values of democracy, egalitarian social order, modernisation, and internationalism can be inculcated through educational strategies.

The teacher has to play an effective role in bringing about desirable modification in the social behaviour of the student. He has to make use of every subject for inculcating this kind of behaviour in a student. He should lay stress on the sociocultural values of each subject and design learning experiences which may enable the students to internalise these value systems. For example, development of rational thinking, ecological thinking, attitude for conservation of natural resources, respect for new innovations and technologies, etc. can be internalised through different subjects that are taught in school. The teacher has to help learners to acquire inquiry skills and attitudes which may enable them to solve existing problems of social life. He has to provide a social, emotional and intellectual environment in the class so as to enhance the skills of the students towards a desirable social change. There will always be a need to plan our learning experiences in the light of prevailing scientific and social issues. The use of various stimulation techniques may be made to involve the students in discussions that promote the levels of thinking.

We need education to evolve a new social order, as the old order suffers from degeneration. We have to create a society where man lives for mankind, where there is no tension, where there is happiness in abundance.

A society cannot enforce any rigidity, discipline, blind conformity, unquestioned obedience and absence of difference of opinion.

Education for citizenship is required to avoid chaos and disorder. A scheme of education for citizenship would include love for children, good ability for communication, introduction of self government in institutions, co-curricular activities, inculcating good habits, developing skills, building ideas to live by, good sense of judgement, moral principles and team work.

Social change demands variations in the prevalent mode of life. The enthusiastic response to this change has now become a way of life. Let us always think of striving for and evolving a new civilisation which is more satisfying under the existing circumstances.

Education evaluates the process and results of social change and lays down the standards and criteria for it. Again, education removes obstacles in the way of desired change. It removes complexes and doubts in the minds of the people which may obstruct the progress.

Educationists, educational administrators and educators have to prepare suggestions and guidelines for social change. It is a continuous process affected by the physical environment, scientific inventions and researches as well as educational efforts. Education has to neutralize the factors which resist social change, which are; a cultural inertia, fear of a new set-up, vested interests and extent of isolation.

We find our society suffering from divisiveness, indiscipline, non-cooperation, unhealthy competition, strife, class conflicts, lack of direction and wasteful tendencies. Education has to rid the society of these and many more social evils. The rising tide of immorality and unethical ways of living are unacceptable situations in this age of knowledge and awakening. The UNESCO report of the International Commission on Education has suggested four pillars which can help in social change. They are – learning to know, learning to do, learning to be and learning to live together.

Computer technology, genetic technology, genetic food engineering, increasing exposure to the outside world, living in a multicultural society, increased stress and stress-related diseases, pollution, radioactive waste, threat of nuclear war and globalisation are some of the future trends towards social change for which education has to prepare the new generations. Our society suffers from many tensions between global and local, rich and poor, tradition and modernity, long-term and short-term considerations, universal and individual, competition and equal opportunities, and knowledge explosion and human capacity to assimilate. Education has to relieve the individual and society from these tensions.

In the emerging postmodern society, every citizen cannot avoid questions such as what our society should be like, are the schools doing satisfactorily, what the people want them to do. Among many factors of evolution of a better society, education is the dominant factor which activates other factors. The functions of education involve the awareness component, as well as the developmental component.

Technological resources and economic activity are developing by virtue of the contributions of technical and professional education. But there are still many shortcomings in the technological and economic areas. For example, the problem of pollution of the environment due to industrial revolution has become very serious and dangerous. It should have been anticipated long ago and remedial programmes should have been initiated well in time. Even now, the remedial programmes that are being undertaken are proving to be ineffective.

The social environment is deteriorating day by day. There is a continued erosion of social, economic, moral, political and cultural values. Education has failed to provide value orientation to eliminate exploitation, repression, fanaticism, violence and fatalism.

The policy and system of education should envisage the picture of society to emerge for the next generation and the generations to come. It should be effective and comprehensive enough to prepare the citizen of the future.

Education should strive for an ideal society where social norms are willingly accepted by all, where social conflicts are missing, where social commitments are a part of character, where the governance does not require authority above authority, where breach of law is non-existent, and the individuals are free from crime, fraud, drug addiction and violence. Where there is a peaceful atmosphere conducive to development with an unending craze for intellectual flights and discoveries.

There are a number of agents for social change. For example, the political system, government, educational institutions, media, religion, etc. Education is the leading agent among them all. An educational institution has to function as a model society and a society that has a vision for the future. Its programmes make the students aware of their rich cultural heritage and their responsibility towards that culture. It also gives an opportunity of comparative study of various cultures and social systems. The learners are enabled to notice the shortcomings of their own social system and evolve a better alternative. When education becomes a lifelong process, it broadens their vision and enhances their possibilities in their role towards society.

Education brings about the development of resources which create significant changes in the material and non-material aspects of society. The values of materialism, modernisation, a welfare state, patriotism, democracy and internationalism have to be specified, brought within permissible limits, shaped, implemented and inculcated through the instrument of education.

Education prepares the ground for the advancement of society through the development of knowledge in varied forms. Modern education has broadened our vision about our possibilities and commitments in matters of social change. There is a constant need to modernise the conservative content of education so that it may prepare individuals to become leaders in the social change. Every school and college may be developed into a social system like a goal-directed society. There is a regulative norm system which controls, governs and directs the sub-system for smooth and productive functioning within the larger system.

There are quite a large number of things which need to be established in the society to achieve social change. Some of them are: quality education, true democracy, good governance, economic development, good standard of living, brotherhood, peace, co-existence among nations, care for the aged, affordable communication facilities, price control, mutual respect, sympathy for sufferers, opportunities for the physically challenged, an all-round welfare for the mankind and discipline.

Again there are quite a large number of things which need to be eliminated from the society to secure social change. Some of them are: inequality, injustice, insecurity, red-tapism, terrorism, fanaticism, crime, corruption, unemployment, broken homes, strikes, agitations, strife, pollution, adulteration, shortages, inhuman tendencies, narrow loyalties, and political instability.

Education is a single factor that can develop awareness for bringing about changes contributing towards social change and eliminating the elements which resist social change. Teachers should lay emphasis on the socio-cultural values of each subject and should also design experiences which a learner can internalise in the form of values like rational thinking, thinking about ecology, conservation of natural resources, respect for innovations, new technologies and modernism.

Social change should signify positive modification of any aspect of the social process, social relations and social organisations.

There are some factors which help the process of social change. These factors are: the physical environment, scientific inventions and researches. Ogburn emphasises that in the first instance, change occurs in the material culture and then in the non-material culture. When material culture changes and non-material remains static or lags behind, it is called a cultural lag of society. Education is the only means to remove this cultural lag.

Technology and values are both, essential bases of social change. Both actively interact and bring about social change. Education perpetuates eternal values. If eternal values lose their hold due to social change, society begins to decay and degenerate. Education has to protect, preserve and promote these values. Education prepares people to welcome and adopt desirable social change, both easily and willingly. It provides a conducive environment for social change. The social change is evaluated from time to time by the educational experts to determine its desirability or otherwise, with reference to required standards and criteria. Education strives to eliminate social evils and irrational customs and traditions through various reformatory projects, social movements and social service schemes. By advocating desirable social reforms, education works as a motivator, initiator and director for many social changes.

When conflicts arise between various social groups, education tries to resolve them by advocating thoughts and feelings which bring about unity in diversity. It has to act as a creative and effective force to patch up the situations of disunity and discord. It widens the vision of people against inertia for social change through deeper investigations and researches. Education prepares people to become leaders in a way that they become social reformers.

*****

Sixty

Quality Education

Quality education will match the conditions, problems and expectations of the future. It wil be a dynamic and vision-oriented enterprise. These visions will comprise of the practicable dreams of mankind.

Since education is the most precious investment made by a society, it will be free from wastages and losses. There will be no wastage in the matter of qualifications acquired by an individual. Educational planning and programmes will be so perfect that they will not suffer from any loopholes. Education will have to be made a most profitable investment.

Education has enjoyed the benefit of lofty aims, ideals and principles for a number of centuries but its results have not been satisfying. If the future proposes still better aims and principles, their realisation not should be left half way.

Quality education has to be an all powerful and successful agency. Its impact on every individual will be so deep and sustainable that he will never divert from the path of righteousness. Society is suffering heavily at the hands of weak individuals who are driven to corruption, crime or evils. The process of education must ensure that it produces and develops only such individuals who turn out to be strong and capable to resist, fight and conquer the evils. At present, only a small percentage of the people are fighting against the evils. Quality education will develop every individual to be upright and capable to safeguard the society from evils.

It has to provide competent reformers for various sectors like religion, politics, governance, justice, etc. It will ensure the supply of competent, dedicated and honest workers for all types of occupations. It will follow the doctrine of quality education for all.

There is need for qualitative improvement in all aspects of education. In order to stop the wastage of higher education, the intake of institutions of higher education will have to be controlled. The syllabi of quality education will equip learners with all types of qualities expected of an educated person.

There is no top in quality education. The planners may devise targets for the near future. There should be an upward revision of the targets from time to time.

Most of our trained teachers are ill prepared for the job of quality education. The colleges of education should prepare them to enter their job with full confidence. The needs of quality education demand from them high standards of performance in every aspect. The colleges of education should admit as trainees after thorough screening only those who will be able to fulfil the new demands.

The schools for quality education will provide a rich, motivating and modern environment. The syllabi and programmes will be given a new shape. The workload may increase as many new and latest ideas will have to be included.

Just as society demands qualitative services in every sphere, it should demand quality education also. It should also be prepared to contribute towards providing the required infrastructure to education. It should also regularly watch the performance of educational institutions and ensure that the desired results are achieved.

The government should be prepared to afford extra expenses on buildings, equipments, laboratories, libraries, workshops, co-curricular activities and better qualified teachers. Every new institution should satisfy the demands of quality education as soon as it is opened.

Quality education is an instrument for qualitative growth and development. It will certainly preempt many problems of the individual and society. It will make the life of people qualitative in every possible way.

There can be a number of programmes to promote quality education, such as setting up of advanced study centres, specialised development of universities and colleges, professional and intellectual growth of teachers, organisation of summer schools, seminars, refresher courses, orientation programmes, research assistance for teachers, extension services, teacher exchange programmes, new evaluation techniques, accountability of teachers, administrators and managements, well planned and need-based diversification and recognition to merit. Examinations may be modernised to include internal tests, oral testing, new type tests, short answer type tests and comprehensive essay tests. The focus of testing should be on what and how much the student knows, not on what he does not know.

The provision of quality education to all should be accepted as a target by the governments, legislatures, planners, framers of budgets, educationists, parents, teachers and students.

There should be a regular worldwide survey to determine the lapses in quality education from country to country and from region to region. It should not be accepted that the quality of education is bound to vary from place to place. The world bodies should come forward to share the responsibility of providing quality education in all corners of the world. Equality in quality education all over the world will lay down the foundations for quality in all spheres of life.

Quality education should not be judged in terms of palatial buildings of educational institutions, air-conditioned classrooms, costly student uniforms, five star hotel type hostels, rich decorations, expensive furniture, high fee structure, heavy fines and magnificent equipments.

Some of the signs of quality education can be: a competent administration, highly qualified and dedicated teachers, absence of wastage of time and resources, rich curriculum, a well-stocked library, good quality textbooks, studious habits, imparting of ideals, history of the institutions in terms of outstanding achievements and contributions of students, a peaceful educative and inspiring atmosphere, healthy competitions, aims of excellence and development of great personalities, cordiality between all the members of the institutional population, multidimensional co-curricular activities, admissions to be made purely on merit, self-discipline, extra study by the teachers and students, professional growth of the teachers, absence of punishment, required training in manners and character, no unrest among the staff and students, the administrator and teachers should be true models for the students, there should be no complaints from the parents and the community, absence of undue disturbance in the schedule and also mentionable achievements in different activities, inter-institution competitions and examination results.

*****

Sixty one

Education and Vision

Education should be made to play its role in broadening the vision of learners. Educational institutions should be in a position to turn out visionaries for different walks of life. Visionaries are needed in every home, community, institution, religion, public office, profession, area of social upliftment, field of policy making, position of authority, political set-up, literature, art and every type of research area.

If every individual is a visionary in his own activities of life, he will be in a position to suggest and implement changes for the better. He will ensure his own progress, the progress of the set-up under his charge and progress of the society at large. There is a place of pride available to the visionaries in their respective fields. They deserve the credit for opening up brighter regimes for the future. In comparison, a person without vision should not entertain any inferiority complex. On the other hand, he should expand his studies, enrich his experiences, observe the work of the visionaries and try to join their rank.

It is the gift of vision, that mankind has benefitted from astonishing progress and is every day receiving new ideas and materials for a better life.

The natural gift of genes can make an individual a scholar, an inventor, a philosopher, a poet or a genius of any type. Education has greater responsibility towards the empowerment of an individual. Innate abilities grow and express themselves under the effect of education. Without education, many innate abilities may remain unexplored and unexpressed. Let us proceed with the belief that every individual prossesses a unique and extraordinary ability, which needs to be discovered and developed. It is likely that by getting special education in that ability, the individual may turn out to be a visionary in that domain. Every individual must get the opportunity of being directed to his horizon.

Broadening one's vision should be a characteristic feature of a truly educated person. The syllabi of education should highlight the contributions of visionaries in different walks of life. When information leads to knowledge, knowledge leads to wisdom, then wisdom should further lead to vision and much more. We can see that there are just a few amongst the total population who are recognised as visionaries. But every individual has a right and obligation to try his best to join that distinguished lot. He must remember that many like him have been able to change impossibilities into possibilities.

Henry Giroux said, "Radical pedagogy needs a vision – one that celebrates not what is but what could be, that looks beyond the immediate to the future and links struggle to a new set of human possibilities," and there is no end to human possibilities. Schools in his view should be institutions of cultural production and transformation rather than reproduction. They should be agencies of empowerment and emancipation for individuals and groups.

There is need to bring genuine quality to redress the bad times we witness everywhere. We are surrounded by poverty, despair, hopelessness, joblessness, and stigmatisation, the waste of generations of young, mediocrity, greed, commodification, chauvinism, sex, racism, materialism, dehumanisation, militaristic ideologies and urban colonialism.

Critical pedagogy of Giroux needs special mention here, which is not simply a matter of classroom methodology, but the development of an emancipated citizenry. He proposes several principles for critical pedagogy; some of which are – restructuring schools as democratic institutions; ethics to be given a central position; questioning practices of education that perpetuate inequality, exploitation and human suffering, a language that embraces several versions of solidarity and politics; several scripts, several curricula, several versions of education which need to be critically interrogated; the curriculum, a cultural script should be susceptible to critique; and politics requires an affirmation of diversity and of the rights of oppressed groups for recognition in education. In postmodern times, Giroux finds a way of reclaiming power and identity for subordinate groups. He says that the school is a crucial place for developing critical citizenship; the task of education necessarily moves beyond the sole sphere of schooling. His work holds out the hope of a better life for us all. His work is profoundly humanitarian, that is as unsettling as it is optimistic. Hence, education needs its visionaries.

The schools have to provide a vision so that people would know who they are, where they are and the direction in which they are heading.

With the passage of time, we have broadened our aims of education. There are still higher aims which are going to be incorporated in the process of education in future. Education has come up to the level of a large number of dreams of mankind. It will be saddled with more and more responsibilities as its capabilities are unlimited.

Education will also be required to enlarge the vision of the learner. He should be enabled to include in his vision experiences beyond his day to day experiences, knowledge beyond his syllabi, thinking beyond his personal problems, finding new paths beyond the beaten tracks, and taking life as a rare opportunity to become extraordinary from an ordinary being.

It may not happen that everybody becomes a visionary, but every thinking individual should aspire for a visionary outlook. He should try to become a searcher and seeker of vision. Thinking big should become a habit with everybody. We should not limit ourselves to narrow boundaries, rather we should broaden our outlook in everyway. One should think of making possible the things which look impossible at the moment. One should look forward to making those situations pleasant, which are unpleasant in spite of our efforts.

*****

Sixty two

Education and Creativity

Education has generelly become a means of economic development, linking degrees with jobs. Now we have to provide education with vision, and create opportunities to promote new channels, facilitate multi-disciplinary approach, and sow the seeds of innovation, ultimately enabling education to meet the challenges of the future. The domain of higher education should especially encompass creativity of a rare depth.

Our academic education is mostly anti-creative. The unchallenging classroom work fails to inspire the interests of creative children. Divergent thinking is regarded as irrelevant and wasteful of time. Teachers prefer the less creative who are peaceful, content and patient. Free thinking is the prerequisite of creative thinking. Creative people are found to be more self-actualising. The academic achievement of students is positively related to verbal and non-verbal creativity. When we talk of special schools for the gifted, we should prefer to determine the gifted nature of the child on the basis of his creativity test scores. In addition to the conventional intelligence tests, tests of creativity are more relevant in educational planning.

Creativity is the phenomenon by which a person finds and communicates a new concept. It involves the element of uniqueness or novelty. It is the capacity of a person to produce compositions, products or ideas which are essentially new or novel. It is a sort of adventurous thinking, getting away from the beaten track and showing a new path. The primary traits related to creativity are fluency, flexibility, originality and elaboration. It is characterised by usefulness, rejection of some previously accepted ideas, intense motivation and persistence and clarification of a problem that was ill defined.

Creativity is a comprehensive term which includes all types of creations whether it is painting, sculpture, architecture, design, literature, scientific or technological discovery. New things and ideas are created when there are streaks of imagination in the mind of a scientist, engineer, doctor, philosopher, writer, architect or artist.

Creativity is present in everyone, but in varying degrees. There is need for testing the level and nature of creativity possessed by every individual.

A creative person is blessed with many traits. He prefers complexity and some degree of apparent imbalance in phenomena. He is more complex psychodynamically. He is independent in his judgements. He is more assertive and dominant. He rejects suppression which is a mechanism for the control of impulses.

While many creative thoughts come as sudden insights, such flashes are more likely after hard thinking.

Measuring and developing creativity should become one of the uppermost concerns in education. In the case of creative people, knowledge is power not only to interpret reality but to change, develop and expand it. Creative people are curious and adventurous. Their interests should be located and they should be guided to develop interests in many different subjects and fields. They should be motivated to read widely and actively seek new experiences. They should think positive to be able to enhance their creativity. They need a broad and rich knowledge base. There seems to be no substitute for hard work at the preparatory stage. It is important that the educational institution tolerates and fosters independence in their case and employs a non-conforming environment for them. The use of analogies may be encouraged to help in the recognition of similarities between a new problem and an old one or between a new solution instead of the one that has worked before.

To develop creativity, stress should also be laid on the factors like: mastery of a discipline, striving for something new with hope, confidence, enterprise, independence in thinking, eagerness for originality, courage for conviction, vision, willingness to take risks, and novelty instead of routine.

Educational institutions should provide to the students, opportunities of expression and development of their creativity. Some of these opportunities are: poetic competitions, storytelling contests, singing competitions, painting, quiz contests and writing for the institutional magazine. There is also need to devise some scientific and vocational activities which involve creativity.

The society should create a system and programme for education which can encourage and develop creativity. The society should also be eager to welcome the fruits of creativity and draw maximum possible benefits from them.

In progressive education, according to Rugg, there is commitment to individual creativity. There is need to introduce activities which aim at developing each child's creativity and intuition. Also, there is need for a programme centred on the rise and consequences of industrial society and based on the demands of modern living. Nothing short of genius on the part of a student could create an ordered understanding of modern life.

Piaget has said, "Education for most people, means trying to lead the child to resemble the typical adult of his society (whereas) for me, education means making creators."

Israel Scheffler said, "Critical thought is of first importance in the conception and organisation of educational activities."

"Rationality ... is a matter of reasons, and to take it as a fundamental educational ideal is to make as pervasive as possible the free and critical quest for reasons, in all realms of study."

Jean Francois Lyotard said, "Post modern knowledge is not simply a tool of the authorities; it refines our sensitivity to differences and reinforces our ability to tolerate the incommensurable, its principle is not the expert's homology, but the inventor's paralogy."

Lawrence Kohlberg said, "The acquisition of knowledge results in an active change in patterns of thinking brought upon by experimental problem-solving situations."

Thinking is a way of removing obstacles and reconstituting experience. There are no limits to the material of thought, whether it is the case of a common man or a scientist. Reflective thinking enables man to carry on the trial and error process mentally.

There is recognition and demand for the creative individual's contribution to society. There is a great loss of talent as our educational programme does not recognise and promote creativity in children. The unchallenging classroom activities fail to inspire the interests of creative children.

Nurturing creativity, should become one of the most important objectives of present day education. Man can ensure its existence and continue to make progress by virtue of the work of creative individuals. They are the people who achieve self-actualisation and optimum heights for mankind.

Scientists, research workers, writers and various types of artists have discovered their domain of creativity and dedicated themselves to that. Everybody should try to discover his line of creativity and do something marvellous in that area. Along with development of productive capacity of the human body, education should develop creativity of the mind. Our methods should appeal to the child's active powers, to his capacities in construction, production and creation. These methods should be inquiry-centred, related with problem-solving, and capable of creating something new for life and society.

The idea of a learner being a mere conditioned organism ignores the distinctive human need, the capacity to project purposes, pursue values and create novelties. At a mature level, learning by doing would involve struggles of the creators of literature, science, art and philosophy. The educator's task is to develop strategies that will lead students to see their world with new meanings and reconstruct their experiences.

*****

Sixty three

Education and Happiness

Through education and allied agencies, we should create a world which has few sad songs, sad stories, tragic novels, few tragedies in reel and real life and very few sad faces.

There is a small state which believes in the happiness index and not the per capita income for measuring people's well-being. You will find that life moves easily there and people have patience. Time is money is a very sound idea but a style of life with more hurry than patience is not to be regarded as an essential practical form of that idea. After a day's work, happiness comes from spending time with each other – playing some game, attending a club or contemplating at the local temple. In the happiness index, materialistic happiness is one of the many things. The goods do not provide happiness, especially when we are dissatisfied all the time, as we do not possess what our neighbours or acquaintances possess.

Happiness has to be derived from factors other than wealth. One should not feel inadequate and then compensate for that by consuming more and more of expensive things. While simple living preserves the environment and promotes happiness, the modern craze for luxuries does the opposite.

It is difficult to say if one is happier today than one was yesterday, so why worry about the past or the future, just look at the present with hope and confidence.

One can say with certainty that if one makes someone happy, he would be happier, but since it is not possible to make everyone happy, at least make your friends happy and enjoy the happiness in return for making others happy.

Human happiness is the aim of most of the agencies concerned with the welfare of human beings. Everybody wishes for happiness but most of the people fail to achieve it. Happiness for all should be made a possibility. There can be no shortcuts to happiness. It will require sustained efforts and strong resolve for its establishment.

We can certainly learn to strive for our own happiness and for the happiness of others. If everybody's happiness becomes a concern for every individual, then conditions will to a large extent, take the shape of favourable circumstances for all.

It shows our poor character when we take delight in creating unhappy conditions for others and enjoy seeing others unhappy. To a large extent, we are responsible for creating unhappiness for ourselves and for others. We waste our possibilities and energies for creating unhappy conditions for others and consequently for ourselves.

Happiness is also dependent on a feeling of contentment. It is through education that we can learn a few lessons for contentment. Religion emphasises that one can remain undisturbed and happy under all circumstances, if he develops a control over his emotions. If such a magic incident happens in the life of a person that he is unable to forget it, then he is bound to deny himself the chances of being happy. We should therefore, learn to forget our painful memories.

There are many routes to happiness. Education should provide clues to all of them and enable an individual to select and pursue his own path to happiness. At the same time, education should make the individual aware of the pitfalls in every path. These pitfalls are unavoidable but everyman should become so optimistic about his happiness that he regards these pitfalls as temporary.

Happiness is not to be sought at the cost of others. Every individual should be made so selfless that he is readily prepared to share his happiness with others. He should be generous enough to distribute his own stock of happiness among the less privileged ones. There is no question of monopoly over happiness. Rather, people who are lucky to be happy must learn to share their happiness with those who are less fortunate.

A happy person should feel perturbed over watching any unhappy person. He should immediately offer his services in order to alleviate the conditions of the unhappy one.

If all of us get determined to share happiness, to do our little bit in reducing the unhappiness around, to help remove the general causes of unhappiness, we can certainly enhance the wealth of happiness for mankind.

Education should offer lessons in happiness, in sharing of personal happiness, in removing unhappiness and in adding to the wealth of happiness. Creating happiness for all can be an objective of education. In the situation of a growing percentage of educated people, it is a contradiction if we find a large percentage of people unhappy.

Our mind is made for happiness. We should not burden it with sadness. It is our natural responsibility to be happy. Happy and smiling faces are liked by everybody. Sad and gloomy faces are not welcome. Happiness begets happiness. The learner should be enabled to learn the meaning, needs, secrets, methods and the possibility of happiness for all and his role in creating happiness for himself and others and sharing his happiness. Let everyone contribute his share to the general feeling of happiness. We should not look towards unhappy people with a sense of pity but with a sense of responsibility to make them happy.

There is need to evolve games, activities, competitions and programmes in educational institutions which develop the ability of students to imbibe a good sense of humour. Let us not get accustomed to fake and artificial laughter. Making others laugh is an art that should be developed in everybody. Making others laugh is a great service to others. For instance, the media has its own role in promoting genuine laughter.

Education has to enable the individual to earn happiness for himself and for others. Happiness demands many prerequisites, towards the fulfilment of which education will play an adequate role. Some of the prerequisites of happiness are: optimum level of education, a good merit in the competitive situation, a job that suits one's qualifications and interests, necessary attitudes for job satisfaction, adequate income for simple living, a helpful society, satisfactory opportunities for progress and excellence, well deserved appreciation in society and work places, peaceful atmosphere in the system, absence of injustice, hope for a better future, effective governance by concerned authorities, opportunities and recognition for professional growth, cordial relations within the family and society, availability of welfare agencies and services, moral and material support from the society whenever anybody is in distress, and due respect of the individual.

Some habits of people can give them joy: such as punctuality and regularity, hard work in whatever capacity one is placed, sacrifice, kindness, sympathy, cordiality, affection, respect for others, helpfulness, humility, devotion, good character and high morale. A happy individual can render his best possible services to society. One should learn to draw pleasure from work.

We have misinterpreted the gains and losses in life. We have made materialistic benefits our supreme gains. Similarly, loss of materialistic baggage is treated as the biggest loss. Perhaps happiness is the highest thing to achieve in life and sadness is the greatest loss. Happiness can be enjoyed in spite of materialistic setbacks. Losses can be covered when we can share our happiness with others and make others happy.

Rousseau believed that human happiness and human welfare were the natural rights of every individual. This human happiness could be realised by a proper type of social organisation and education.

Aristotle says, "Education is the creation of a sound mind in a sound body. It develops man's faculty, especially his mind, so that he may be able to enjoy the contemplation of supreme truth, goodness and beauty in which perfect happiness essentially lies."

There can certainly be some training that can be imparted as the art of happiness. There is need to discover this art, develop it, impart it and make possible a kind of happiness that becomes an attitude which everybody can own.

*****

XIII

THE HOPE

Sixty four

The Hope

Freud regards education as the hope for future. Education is concerned with the planning of manpower and preparing the progeny for a better future. Education is the agency of making good citizens and cultured personalities. Freud forewarns that the instinct would break all bounds and laboriously created structure of civilisation would be swept away, if education does not perform the task of restraining the instinct through the development of superego. Sublimation, interjection, projection and identification are the mechanisms by which instincts are modified and made socially valuable.

Education can bring to us hopes as high as we wish and will aim towards obtaining them. It has brought us to marvellous levels of civilisation and it has enough potential to take us to still higher levels. In spite of the advancements made so far, human life is not as splendid as it should be. The human being conveniently commits follies and inhuman behaviour that we are stunned to notice. Why should he stoop so low within the environment of an uplifting system of education? The human being has himself denied the benefits of education to him. He chooses to forget education when he wishes to indulge in sub-standard behaviour. If he constantly keeps in mind what has been taught through education, he will most probably be saved from evils. A mind that is distant from education becomes a devil's workshop. The individual should remember the teachings of his education forever in order to remain on the right track.

The Hope

Education has the inherent capacities to bring to fulfilment our material, intellectual, emotional and spiritual hopes. We have evolved fairly high aims for education and there is no bar on evolving still higher aims. When education nears the attainment of its aims and objectives, human personality will approach its fulfilment.

To attach our hopes with education, we shall be required to create qualitative environment and practices in our educational institutions. Our institutions should no more suffer from problems, handicaps, lapses, defects, narrow ideas, unpsychological atmosphere, shortcuts to achievements, and poor reputation. Their functioning should be systematic, positive, productive, constructive, imaginative and futuristic.

Through education, we should be able to attack the problems from their roots. Their uprooting requires a determined remedial programme. The hopeless situations have to be converted into hopeful ones. The new generation must be equipped with a postmodern outlook in life and should proceed with a firm resolve to see the end of the hopeless situation. Hopeless situations exist around us in the form of unmanageable government set-up, political bankruptcy, the disobedience of social norms, apathetic human relations, religious fanaticism, taking delight in creating problems, absence of commitment to national spirit and international understanding, shirking allotted work and responsibility and a mad race for material benefits.

Almost all the other agencies have created hopeless situations and belied our hopes. It is through education that we have to educate new generations to reverse the situations. Education will produce a trained army of citizens who understand the nature of every hopeless situation and who never agree to compromise with such circumstances.

Education will have to churn out individuals different from, and more capable than the existing population. They will continue to bring changes for the better in the circumstances till the process of change is complete.

The agency of education will not be allowed to fail where other agencies have failed. Since it is the ultimate agency to enter the fight for a big overhaul, there will be no slackness, half-heartedness or withdrawal in its approach. It is a difficult responsibility, which will not be abandoned at any cost. Education possesses the resources and strengths to come up to expectations in the matter and there is no reason for it to leave the struggle halfway. It must play a decisive role in finalising this task.

Education has to complement agencies like family, society, media, religion and the government. In the long run, it will make all these agencies powerful enough to achieve the desired results.

The human being has not reached excellence in spite of the present advanced stage of civilisation. Education has to ensure excellence for human beings in every possible way.

A large section of the human population is engaged in antisocial activities. The sane lot, which is in minority, feels suffocated. Who will save mankind from all these and many other vices? The functionaries of government are helpless, because they themselves are slaves to many antisocial activities. The governments set-up quite a large number of departments to control these activities. The society has also set-up various non-government bodies to check these activities, but it is equally helpless. The family is a small agency and it cannot succeed where powerful agencies like the government and society have failed. The human mind is also helpless in developing a strong aversion against antisocial activities. Education has to focus on developing the human mind against all types of vices. When the human mind is awakened and his will power is strong, man will develop self-control against every type of antisocial behaviour. Controlling antisocial behaviour will no longer remain an administrative or social problem. Education will destroy the evil from its roots. It will make the government functionaries and social activists so alert and effective that any kind of antisocial behaviour will find no place to exist and flourish.

The problems which defy solutions at the hands of the government and society will be tackled in a different way by the agency of education. Through education, the human mind will be purified from vices and it will be made so clear and strong that no vice will ever originate from it. The human mind will develop an unshakable aversion against antisocial behaviour.

But the big question is, whether education can become capable of these foundational tasks. If we want education to lead the way, we shall have to empower it with necessary force and quality. All other agencies have to recognise the power and position of education. Education will always function in the interest of mankind and all other agencies if it acquires a powerful role. If education continues to suffer from vices, who would spearhead the reforms? If education becomes what it should be, it can certainly work wonders. Qualitative education can develop individuals with excellence, families with the desired harmony, a qualitative society, system and government.

Education should be regarded as the leading agency which can reshape and rebuild the individual and other agencies towards a different and better future. It can create a well organised life in which there will be no possibility of any problems arising in future. The problems will be anticipated and necessary precautions taken well in time. As soon as something of any kind is found going astray in the society, the new generation will get well prepared to offset the trend.

When most of the other welfare agencies continue to play a hopeless role, education has to become the main centre of hopefulness. The agency of education must interfere with the situations and turn the hopeless into hopefulness.

In spite of the efforts made by many agencies, the problems are multiplying. Education has to be invited to bring about an all-round reconstruction. Let us take care of education, and education will take care of us. We have failed to give due importance to education. It should no longer be considered less important than religion, economy and governance. It should be accepted as an agency that would tower over all other agencies.

Education has to show the way to children coming from different families, different socio-economic stratas of society, different religious backgrounds, communities, and sometimes children of different nationalities. Children from different groups are made to sit in the same class and receive similar education. It can do its job effectively only if education is accepted as an agency with greater influence than divergent influences of families, socio-economic groups, religious groups, etc.

Education must be a strong force which uproots the personal taboos, social taboos, prejudices, social complexes, illogical customs and traditions, caste-ridden notions, and irrational beliefs of the society and its people.

Education has to set the things right which are found to be wrong in our homes, our social groups, our institutions, our governments and in mankind. It has to rectify the mistakes being committed by all other agencies.

It is wrong to make education a tool in the hands of society, religious groups or the government. It should be the master tool or the agency to show the way to all other agencies and set-up norms and standards for all of them.

Education should be more progressive than philosophy, psychology, sociology, and religious, economic and political thought. It should be regarded as the most modern of them all and no other agency should be able to challenge it.

The Hope

Every new generation must be an improvement over the previous generation in every way. There should not be a single instance where we may be inclined to say with sorrow that things are going from bad to worse. Things must be kept growing from better to still better situations in every way.

Our priorities are wrong when we give more significance to anything other than education. In our budgets, policies, development programmes, social, national or international goals, education must be a top priority.

The best brains should be reserved for educational planning, management of education and teaching.

Religions, politics, societies and ideologies have divided mankind. Education can possibly unite it. Let us give education a fair trial. The unity of mankind must be cultivated as a great hope achievable through education.

No positive goals should remain impossible for the people who have received quality education. They should understand, transmit and universalise education as a reliable hope for the upliftment of mankind in every way.

*****

Index

Academic education, 369
Acid rain, 311
Acute radiation syndrome, 314
Addiction-free society, 236
Adjustment problems, 158, 167
Adulteration, 32, 100, 244, 305, 359
Aesthetic life, 120
Aesthetic values, 17, 28, 188
Aggression, 30, 165, 334
Agitations, 98, 199, 205, 214, 359
Aims of education, 11-15, 46, 75, 208, 292, 329-330, 336, 367
Air pollution, 310-311, 314
Aircraft emissions, 310
All-round development, 44, 96, 98, 272, 325
Amnesia, 251
Anarchy, 35
Anticipated problems, 115
Antisocial activities, 100, 146, 223, 305, 382
Antisocial behaviour, 3, 62, 250, 382-383
Antisocial elements, 57, 88, 106, 194, 346
Anxiety, 251
Aristocratic lifestyle, 349
Aristotle, 50, 207, 378

Artificial radioactivity, discovery of, 314
Asthma, 251
Atomic bomb, development of, 314
Audio-visual aid, 174

Backbiting, 153, 198
Backward communities, 223
Bad company, 232, 234-235
Bad habits, 82, 105, 164, 213, 234, 263
Bad society, 122
Bed wetting, 251
Begging, 285
Behavioural disorders, 242, 251
Behavioural patterns, 183
Benefit of education, 289
Biological necessities, 71
Bizarre behaviour, 251
Black marketing, 32
Black money, 21, 32, 243-244, 294
Bootlegging, 244
Brain storming, 88
Brain tumour, 251
Bribery, 100
Broad-mindedness, 4, 19, 217
Broken home, 105, 151, 165, 234, 248, 251, 359

Bullying, 41
Burleson, Neol David, 321

Candolle, 303
Capitalism, 32
Carbon and food cycling, 304
Career promotion, 277
Caste and region-based polarisation, 196
Caste ridden society, 80
Character development, 15, 271
Character formation, 76, 87, 243, 253
Cheating, 285
Child behaviour, 189
Child-centred education, 12, 207
Cholera, 309, 312
Civil war, 35, 337
Civilised life, 248
Classroom methodology, 367
Cleanliness campaigns, 308
Co-curricular activities, 42-43, 87, 94, 106, 110, 141, 167-168, 171, 185, 228, 307, 356, 362, 364
Code of conduct or ethics, 244
Cognition, 6
Communal tension, 30
Communication gap, 97
Community hygiene, 130
Community life, 87-88, 90
Compulsive behaviour, 165
Computer-assisted instruction, 107, 175
Conation (psycho motor), 6
Conducive environment, 146, 360

Conferences, 104, 325, 328, 330
Constructive educational environment, 148
Constructive imagination, 105
Contentment, 13
Contract killing, 285
Contra-cultures, 185
Correspondence courses, 104, 127, 280
Corruption, 3, 32, 39, 88, 100, 106, 146, 196, 205, 223, 233, 243-245, 305, 359, 361
Corruption-free society, 39
Cosmopolitan nations, 323
Counselling system, 317
Cramming, 109
Creative children, 369, 372
Crime-free schools, 247
Crime-free society, 113, 247
Crime rates, 248, 250
Crime stories, 248
Criminal behaviour, 249-250
Criminalisation of politics, 200
Cripple society, 233
Critical pedagogy of Giroux, 367
Cultural advancement, 271
Cultural development, 15
Cultural environment, 6
Cultural lag, 183, 360
Cultural values, 19, 182
Cultured personality, 380

Day dreaming, 251
Debt, 54, 99, 238
Defiant or cruel behaviour, 251
Delinquency, 178, 250-252

Index

Delinquents, 165, 250
Delusions, 251
Democratic system, 202, 300
Demonstration or strike, 162
Dengue fever, 310
Depression, 32, 233, 238, 240, 251
De-schooling talk, 89
Desirable traits are called virtues, 188
Developed countries, 206, 320, 326
Developmental planning, 271, 344
Developmental priorities, 296
Developmental problems, 166, 314
Dewey, John, 27, 50, 52-53, 67, 75, 90, 112, 179, 279
Diarrhoea, 309
Diogenes, 10, 204
Discriminations, 3, 6, 173, 223-224
Distance education, 126
Dramatic club, 185
Drill, 175-176
Drinking, 82, 235-236, 349
Drug
  abuse, 234-235, 286, 305
  addict, 233-234
  addiction, 3, 32, 88, 129, 161, 232-236, 238, 358
  peddlers, 135
  trafficking, 285
Durkheim, Emile, 241
Dysentry, 309, 312
Dysfunctional family, 242

Eclecticism, 11
Ecological balance, 227, 319
Economic crisis, 30
Economic development, 36, 90, 266, 296-300, 319, 321-322, 344-345, 359, 369
  equality in, 298
Economic disparities, 271, 324
Economic fanaticism, 254
Economic planning, 272
Economic problems, 8, 96
Economic system, 37, 45, 261, 263, 283, 297, 305, 352
Economics of Education, 299-300
Ecosystem, 35, 133, 304, 311
Educated parents, 152, 154
Education
  contributions of, 266
  failures of, 215, 235, 241
  formal, 2, 317
  free, 207
  functions of, 153, 353, 357
  global, 325
  globalisation of, 336
  individualising, 65
  in-service, 126
  job-oriented, 293
  modern, 46, 359
  moral, 26, 76, 106, 188-190, 349
  part-time, 127
  post-technical, 279-280
  real function of, 5
  religious, 21, 189-190, 192
  safety, 130-131
  secular, 350

society-centred, 52
society neglects, 145
special, 366
techniques of, 266, 269
universal, 147, 300
value-oriented, 188
vision-oriented, 115
Educational adjustment, 165
Educational administrators, 45, 99, 171, 356
Educational and vocational counselling, 73
Educational apparatus, 52
Educational attainment, 344
Educational broadcasts, 172
Educational climate, 152, 170
Educational competitions, 148
Educational courses, 36, 319
Educational development, 270, 273, 297
Educational devices, 70
Educational goals, 344
Educational philosophy, 22
Educational planners, 45
Educational planning, 269, 271-274, 298, 354, 361
Educational priorities, 297
Educational reform, 43, 45, 208
Educational research worker, 115
Educational seminars, 89
Educational tours, 77, 104, 110, 185
Educational values, 21, 28
Educative material, 171, 304
Egalitarian social order, 355
Ego-integrity, 249

Egoism, 27, 163, 339
E-learning, 176
Election malpractices, 243
Electronic blackboard, 174
Eliot, George, 342
Emotional
  adjustments, 131
  attachments, 184
  development, 38, 156
  maladjustment, 164
  temperament, 48
Enforcement agencies, 211-212
Environmental education, 303-304, 315
Environmental problems, 304-305, 355
Epilepsy, 251
Erickson, Erick, 249
Erosion of values, 19, 22
Ethical discrimination, 60
Etiquettes, 38, 79
Everett, Wilter G., 17
Evolutionism, 147
Exploitation of labour, 286
External motivation, 24
Extrinsic value, 16

Family atmosphere, 44, 151, 233
Family disintegration, 178
Family dispute, 241
Family planning, counselling system about, 317
Fanaticism, 3, 190, 193, 358-359
Fancying hostility, 163
Favouritism, 244
Fears, 68, 251

Index

Fine arts society, 185
Fire extinguishers, 131
First aid facilities, 131
Formal education, counselling system in, 317
Fortune telling, 285
French Revolution, 329
Fuller, Margaret, 153

Gambling, 82, 244, 251, 305
Gangsters, 135, 232
Gardner, Howard, 10
Generation gap, 157, 159, 161-162
Global communication system, 326
Global cooperation, 35
Global economy, 326
Global poverty, 325
Global warming, 311, 323, 325
Glorification of the self, 20
Goal-directed society, 359
Goldsmith, Oliver, 331
Groupism, 41
Guilt Feeling, 163

Habit disorders, 251
Half-used mind, 129
Hallucinations, 251
Happiness index, 374
Harassment of woman for dowry, 238
Harmonious development, 11, 15, 28, 188, 249
Health education, 128, 130, 315
Health problems, 129, 236, 310-311

Hepatitis, 310
Heredity, 79, 83
High status family, 150
High thinking, 95, 139-140
Hoarding, 32, 243
Honesty, 17, 19, 77, 89, 103, 182, 188, 196
Honour board, 87, 91
Human behaviour, 81-82, 113, 128, 184, 233, 338
Human bombs or suicide squads, 256
Human capital formation, 266, 271
Human-centred development, 12
Human development, 4, 90
Human resources development, 266, 293, 297, 343-344
Human Rights Day, 329
Human welfare agencies, 32
Humanism, 11, 14
Humanistic society, 57
Humanitarian approach, 252
Humanitarianism, 147
Hunger strikes, 214
Huxley, 303
Hygiene, 87, 128, 130, 282, 304, 315
Hypnotherapy, 68
Hypocrisy, 19, 41
Hysteria, 251

Illicit sexual relations, 238
Immoral tendencies, 153
Incorrigibility, 164
Indoctrination, 205, 207

Indo-Pak Wars, 340
Industrial civilisation, 126
Industrial effluents, 309, 312
Industrial revolution, 357
Industrial societies, modern, 147, 353
Industrialisation, 153, 155, 293, 315, 325, 347
Inflation, threat of, 35
Insecticides, 136, 310
In-service education, 126
Insightful learning, 65, 110
Inspiring environment, 151, 306
Institutional libraries, 76, 319
Institutional system, 350
Intellectual development, 152, 290
Intelligence and aptitudes, 91
Intelligence quotient, 302-303
Intelligence tests, 250, 369
Interest clubs, 88
Inter-institute competitions, 20
International Commission on Education, 357
International conflicts, 337-338
International tensions, 337-338
Internet, 176
Inter-school competitions, 87
Inter-school debates, 172
Inter-state educational tours, 110
Intoxicants, 130, 236-237
Intrinsic value, 16
Ionising radiation, 313-314
Irreparable damage, 232

Job opportunities, 292
Job-oriented education, 293
Job satisfaction, 125, 286, 377
Joint family system, 155
Judicial system, 40, 243
Judiciary, 138, 245, 248
Juvenile delinquency, 129
Juvenile delinquency centres, 252

Kairov, 289
Kant, 10, 27, 66, 329
Kellogg, W. N., 302
Khrushchev, Nikita, 202
Knowledge-based society, 146
Korean War, 340

Language development, 152, 156
Lapiere, 216
Latecomers, 164
Learned behaviour, 184
Learning by doing, 110, 282, 373
Learning by experimentation, 110
Learning through games, 110
Learning through observation, 110
Leibnitz, 66
Lescohier, 292
Leukaemia, 314
Lewis, C. I., 16
Life expectancy, 160
Lifelong necessities, 126
Locke, 303
Luxuries, 120, 139-141, 195, 226, 271, 374

Luxurious living, 139-140, 243
Lying, 62, 64, 251, 285

Mad race for money, 32, 243
Majority-minority situations, 324
Maladaptive and dysfunctional family, 242
Maladjusted behaviour, 164
Maladjustment, 53, 79, 114, 129, 139, 163, 166, 232, 235, 252, 318
  causes of, 165
  symptoms of, 251
Malaria, 310
Maldistribution of work, 284
Mal-employment, 293
Malformed babies, 313
Man of principles, 102, 198
Manic-depressive psychosis, 68
Mannerism, 57
Manpower forecasting, 299
Marital frustration, 19
Marshall, Alfred, 289, 299
Mass education programmes, 298
Materialism, 5, 19, 180, 243, 358, 366
Materialistic outlook, 180
Materialistic things, 13
Medical sciences, 276
Mental deficiency, 67
Mental development, 67, 71, 132, 156
Mental hygiene, 163
Military and para military forces, 256
Modern psychology, 66

Modes of adjustment, 79
Money and wealth, 16
Monopolistic controls, 243
Montessori, 52
Moral education, 76, 188
Moral standards, 22
Moral values, 16, 19, 251
Morality, 187-188
Motivation, 72, 213
Multicultural society, 357
Multi-disciplinary environment, 294
Multi-purpose schools, 278-279
Multi-religious world, 189
Municipal waste, 309
Murderers, 135
Murray Islanders, 302
Music club, 185
Myrdal, Alva, 289
Myrdal, Gunnar, 298

Nail biting, 251
National adult education programme, 107
National development, 206
Neill, A. S., 52
Nepotism, 205, 286
Nervous system, 66, 83, 313, 326
Neurol-humoral stress, 313
Neurological dysfunctioning, 251
Neuroticism or psychotic behaviour, 165
Nightmares, 251
Nimkoff, 153
Nitrous oxides, 311

Noise pollution, 310, 312-313
Non-ionising radiations, 313
Non-material culture, 183, 360
Non-violent revolution, 352
Nuclear fallout, 314
Nuclear family, 153, 160
Nuclear pollution, 310
Nunn, T. P., 51
Nutrient cycling, 304
Nutrition, 32, 34, 316, 318

Oakeshott, Michael, 111
Observance of religious rituals, 190
Obsession, 251
Ogburn, 153, 360
Old age homes, 160, 227, 320
Organic disorders, 251
Organisation of inter-country games, 330
Organisation of traits, 79
Organised crime, 243-244
Orientation programmes, 319, 363
Outstanding academic performances, prizes for, 91
Over crowding in educational institutions, 318
Ozone layer, 311, 313-314

Parallel economy, 244
Parent teacher association, 106, 319
Parker, Dewitt H., 16
Part-time
    courses, 277, 294
    employment, 293

Peace-loving individuals, 35, 335
Peace of mind, 62, 68-70, 186, 191
Pedagogical planning, 272
Pedagogy, 367
Peer groups, 166
People-friendly system of justice and governance, 42
Personal
    cleanliness, 130
    ethics, 329
    glorification, 21
Personalised student instruction, 107
Personality
    development, 79, 83-84, 87, 253, 272, 299
    tests, 250
Pesticides, 310, 312
Peters, R. S., 127
Phobias, 68
Physical development, 156, 250
Physiological
    factors, 165-166
    needs, 72
    problems, 314
Piaget, Jean, 52, 302, 371
Plague, 310
Planned educational strategies, 266
Plant protection chemicals, 312
PLATO system for a laboratory, 175
Plato, 10, 16, 161
Poetical recitations, 172

Index

Political and racial repression, 133
Political fanaticism, 254
Political instability, 35, 182, 359
Political leadership, 200-202
Pollen grains, 310
Pollutants, 312
Polluted water, 312
Polythene, 309
Pope John Paul II, 156
Population
  control, 316-319
  education, 316-317, 319, 321-322
  explosion, 39, 132, 294, 304, 316, 318-319, 321
Positivism, 147, 350
Post-education adjustment, 270
Postman, Neil, 91
Postmodern society, 357
Potential leaders, 218-220
Powerful vices, 61
Prayer, 191
Pre-vocational and vocational education, 265
Problem-free society, 29, 116
Problem-solving skills, 304
Processions, 199, 214
Professional
  courses, 20, 40, 202, 206-207
  education, 147, 206, 224, 284, 293, 298, 357
Programmed learning, 88, 107
Progressive education, 289
Prostitution, 285
Psychoanalysts, 249
Psychological aspect, 6

Psychological factors, 116, 165
Psychological needs, 72
Psychological principle of alteration, 278
Psychomotor functioning, disturbance in, 310
Psychoneurosis, 68
Psycho-social factors, 165
Psychotic disorders, 251
Punishments, 24, 61, 164, 191, 210, 212-213, 220, 223, 247-248, 252, 260, 317, 364

Qualitative life, 136
Qualities of good teacher, 102
Quality education, 19-20, 45, 99, 113-114, 120, 136, 169, 203, 206, 293, 359, 361-364
Quality of life, 132, 134

Racketeering, 244
Radiation
  pollution, 313
  sickness, 314
Radioactive
  contamination, 314
  elements, 313-314
  substances, 312
  waste, 357
Radio broadcasts, 173
Rapists, 135
Rationalisation, 167
Raymont, 75
Recreation values, 17
Recreational interests, 184
Red tapism, 205, 273
Reflective society, 348

Reform in education, 44
Refresher courses, 10, 104, 280, 363
Regression, 165, 167
Regular courses, 127
Religious
  beliefs, 190, 339, 352
  development, 156
  differences and conflicts, 190
  education, 190, 192
  fanaticism, 178-179, 182, 190, 254, 381
  problems, 8
  sentiments, 190, 192, 247
  values, 17, 25, 28, 192
Research workers, 219
Resentment, 163
Result-oriented
  educational plan, 270
  life, 199
Rolland, Roman, 326
Rousseau, 52, 59, 64, 378
Rugg, Harold, 52, 90, 371
Rules of conduct, 187
Russell, Bertrand, 18, 336

Sadness, 120, 229, 233, 376, 378
Safety education, 131
Sakharov, Andrei, 340
Sane society, 257
Scheffler, Israel, 371
Schizophrenia, 68
School discipline, 251
Schools of thought, 15, 22
Scientific development, 249
Second World War, 291, 336
Security arrangements, 255-256

Self-actualisation, 18, 83-84, 116, 372
Self-centredness, 19, 27, 163
Self-consciousness, 7, 67, 83
Self-discipline, 25, 138
Self-employment, 44, 292-293
Self-expression, 7, 38, 109, 122, 280
Self-glorification, 198
Selfless services, 3, 192, 194, 199-220, 227, 237
Self-realisation, 7, 15-16, 18, 27, 38, 52, 97, 188, 239
Self-realisation theory, 188
Self-respect, 122, 244, 282, 292
Self-study, 37, 74, 99, 109-110, 136, 228
Sewage, 311-312
  treatment of 312
Sex
  abnormalities, 251
  abuse, 76
  education, 131, 321-322
Shakespeare, 6
Shallow scholarship, 41
Shaw, George Bernard, 129
Shopping bags, 309
Show-business and
  extravaganza, 21
Shyness, 163
Singer, Milton, 153
Sleeplessness, 251
Slow learners, 38, 116, 165, 185, 223
Slum dwellers, 223
Smoking, 82, 235, 349
Smuggling, 243-244, 285

Index

Social advancement, 144
Social and political tensions, 88
Social change, 42, 88, 158, 182, 352-360
Social development, 156, 321
Social disintegration, 35, 133
Social efficiency, 276-277, 279
Social ethics, 133
Social fragmentation, 19
Social inequalities, 274
Social institutions, 149, 163, 348
Social justice, 18, 224, 266, 319, 321
Social maladjustment, 164
Social mobilisation, 350
Social participation, 11
Social problems, 8, 238, 266, 382
Social solidarity, 186, 241
Social system, 37, 45, 260-261, 263-264, 283, 297, 352, 354-355, 358-359
Social welfare organisations, 134
Socio-cultural factor, 299, 352
Socio-economic
  development, 319
  goals, 270, 273
  planning, 269
  status, 140, 154, 166, 243, 283, 290
  structure, 305
Sociological aspect of man, 7
Sociological habits, 7
Socio-political ecology, 196
Soil pollution, 310
Solid waste pollution, 310
Sovereign values, 28

Special vocational skills, 282
Specialised development, 363
Spinoza, 66
Sprott, 216
Stammering, 251
Stealing, 62, 234, 251
Stratification, 80-81
Structural planning, 272
Student agitations, 98
Student assemblies, 219
Student community, 98
Student exchange prgrammes, 329
Student leaders, 196, 214, 219
Student movements, 353
Student-teacher relations, 274
Subconscious mind, 68
Sublimation, 167, 380
Suicidal tendency, victims of, 254
Suicides, 32, 238, 240-241
Sulphur dioxide, 311
Syllabi, 10, 96, 197, 324, 362, 366-367
Systematic
  learning, 176
  society, 3

Tax-evasion, 243
Teacher welfare schemes, 105
Technical education, 206
Temper tantrums, 165, 251
Terrorism, 30, 35, 132, 178, 194, 254-258, 305, 339, 359
Textbooks, 10, 20, 42, 44-45, 76, 104, 111, 173, 176, 185, 201, 206, 218, 229, 325, 364

Theory of morality, 50
Thermal pollution, 310
Trained person, 197, 277, 293
Trained personnel, 38, 40
Truancy, 165, 251
Typhoid, 309

Ultra-violet radiations, 313
Unburnt hydrocarbons, 310
Under-invoicing or over-invoicing, 243
Undesirable ones are called vices, 188
Unemployment, 292
UNESCO, 89, 280, 299-300, 316, 326, 330-331, 336, 338, 357
United Nations' Charter, 326
Unity-centred world, 12
Universal moral values, 27
Universal problems, 292
Universalisation of education, 347
UNO, 325, 329, 336-337
Unrestricted freedom, 214

Value classification, 23
Value education, 23
Value-orientation, 18, 358
Verbal commitments, 144
Vietnam War, 340
Virtual classrooms, 176
Visa rules for tourism, 325
Vocational aim, 15, 354
Vocational career, 265
Vocational education, 91, 276, 280, 300

Vocational guidance, 106, 278-279, 283, 295
Vocational interest, 282
Vocational training, 277, 280
Vocationalisation, 276-278, 280

War mongers, 135
Wasteful luxuries, 95
Water pollution, 310
Weisner, Jerome B, 345
Welfare agencies, 196, 241, 252, 377, 383
   politicisation of, 196
Welfare organisations, 49, 148, 228
White-collar crime, 243
Wisdom-centred society, 12
Woman-centred family, 12
Work culture, 283, 297
Work experience, 277-278, 282
Workaholic, 281
World drug problem, 35
World environmental crisis, 35
World Health day, 329
World Health Organisation Commission, 309
World Peace Day, 337
World wars, 200, 291, 334, 340
Would-be-teachers, 105

Xeroderma pigmentosum, 313

Yoga exercises, 69

Zeal, 281
Zero pollution, 314